EXCELLENCE IN LIBRARY SERVICES TO YOUNG ADULTS

The Nation's Top Programs

SECOND EDITION

Young Adult Library
Services Association

Mary K. Chelton
Editor

AMERICAN LIBRARY ASSOCIATION
CHICAGO AND LONDON 1997

This publication is partially funded by the Margaret Alexander Edwards Trust.

Credits
The poems on p. 26 are reprinted by permission of the New York Public Library.

The poem on p. 29 is reprinted by permission of the Richmond Public Library, Richmond, British Columbia.

The poem on p. 107 is reprinted by permission of the Mesa Public Library, Mesa, Arizona.

While extensive effort has gone into ensuring the reliability of information appearing in this book, the publisher makes no warranty, express or implied, as to the accuracy or reliability of the information, and does not assume and hereby disclaims any liability to any person for any loss or damage caused by errors or omissions in this publication.

Project editor: Louise D. Howe

Cover designer: Richmond Jones

Compositor: ALA Production Services in Linotype Melior and True Type Futuri Extra Condensed using Corel Ventura No. 4.2, and camera-ready pages output on a 600-dpi HP LaserJet 4MV

Printed on 50-pound Domtar White, a pH-neutral stock, and bound in 10-point cover stock by Braun-Brumfield, Inc.

The paper used in this publication meets the minimum requirements of American National Standard for Information Sciences—Permanence of Paper for Printed Library Materials, ANSI Z39.48-1992. ∞

Library of Congress Cataloging-in-Publication Data
Excellence in library services to young adults : the nation's top
    programs / Mary K. Chelton, editor. — 2nd ed.
        p.   cm.
      "Young Adult Library Services Association."
      Includes bibliographical references and index.
      ISBN 0-8389-3474-9 (alk. paper)
      1. Young adults' libraries—United States—Case studies.
    2. Public libraries—Services to teenagers—United States—Case
    studies.   3. High school libraries—United States—Case studies.
      I. Chelton, Mary K.   II. Young Adult Library Services Association
    Z718.5.E93   1997
    027.62'6'0973—dc21   97-16917

Copyright © 1997 by the American Library Association. All right reserved except those which may be granted by Sections 107 and 108 of the Copyright Revision Act of 1976.

Printed in the United States of America.

01 00 99 98 97   5 4 3 2 1

This book is dedicated to

Hardy Franklin, former director of the District of Columbia Public Library, without whom this project would not have been possible,

and to

two outstanding youth services librarians who died in 1996:

>Martha Brey MacCallum, coordinator of youth services, Lincoln City Libraries, Lincoln, Nebraska, whose homework center program was included in the previous edition,

and

>Mike Printz, librarian at Topeka West High School, Topeka, Kansas, whose work with young adults was an inspiration for all the librarians and kids lucky enough to come into contact with him.

The greatest compliment we can offer Ms. MacCallum and Mr. Printz is to continue their love for and work with adolescents.

MARY K. CHELTON

Contents

Acknowledgments vii

Introduction ix

THE TOP FIVE

1. Dunbar-Pulaski Middle School, Gary Community School Corporation (Indiana) 3
2. Franklin County Public Library (Florida) 5
3. Lee County Library System (Florida) 8
4. New York Public Library, Regional Library for the Blind and Physically Handicapped (New York) 11
5. New York Public Library, Chatham Square Regional Branch (New York) 14

THE BEST OF THE REST

Collaborative Efforts

6. Chicago Public Library, Woodson Regional Library (Illinois) 19
7. Hammond Public Library (Indiana) 21
8. Meriden Public Library (Connecticut) 23
9. New York Public Library (New York) 25
10. Richmond Public Library (British Columbia) 28
11. San Diego Public Library, Scripps Miramar Ranch Library Center and Scripps Ranch High School Library (California) 31

Education Support

12. Brooklyn Public Library, Main Youth Services Division (New York) 33

Information Services

13. Berkeley Public Library (California) 36
14. Cumberland County Public Library and Information Center (North Carolina) 38
15. Cuyahoga County Public Library (Ohio) 40
16. Newport Beach Public Library (California) 42
17. Toledo-Lucas County Public Library (Ohio) 43

Intergenerational

18. Clermont County Public Library (Ohio) 45

Reading Promotion

19. Allen County Public Library (Indiana) 47
20. Arlington County Public Library (Virginia) 49
21. Berkeley Public Library (California) 51
22. Berkeley Public Library (California) 53
23. Cumberland County Public Library and Information Center (North Carolina) 56
24. Dade County Public Schools (Florida) 59
25. Geneva Free Library (New York) 60
26. Leominster Public Library (Massachusetts) 63

27. Multnomah County Library (Oregon) 65
28. New York Public Library (New York) 67
29. Newport Public Library (Oregon) 69
30. Oak Park Public Library (Illinois) 71
31. Rahway Public Library (New Jersey) 73
32. San Antonio Public Library, Central Library (Texas) 75
33. Upper Arlington Public Library (Ohio) 77
34. Vashon High School Library (Washington) 79

Special Needs

35. Allen County Public Library (Indiana) 81

Staff and/or Volunteer Development

36. Brooklyn Public Library (New York) 83
37. Chicago Public Library, Children's Services (Illinois) 85
38. Massachusetts Library Association, Children's Issues Section (Massachusetts) 87
39. Pioneer Library System (New York) 89

Youth Participation

40. Chicago Public Library, Albany Park and Douglass Branches (Illinois) 91
41. Chicago Public Library, Northtown Branch (Illinois) 93
42. Chicago Public Library, Rudy Lozano Branch (Illinois) 95
43. Clearwater Public Library (Florida) 97
44. Farmington Community Library (Michigan) 100
45. Hutchinson Public Library (Kansas) 102
46. King County Library System, Burien Branch (Washington) 104
47. Mesa Public Library (Arizona) 106
48. New York Public Library, Belmont Regional Library/Enrico Fermi Cultural Center (New York) 109
49. Newport Beach Public Library (California) 111
50. Stratford Library Association (Connecticut) 113

Index 117

Acknowledgments

This book would not have been possible without the following people:

Josephine Sharif, Coordinator for Publications in the AASL/YALSA Office within ALA, who gave advice, clarified contractual obligations, ran interference when asked, answered endless queries, and remained competent and pleasant throughout a major project with a very short deadline.

Linda Waddle, Interim Co-Executive Director of the AASL/YALSA/Library Power Office, who is largely responsible for the design, formatting, and distribution of the revised application form, as well as the management of the application review process.

The YALSA Executive Committee, who reviewed seventy-eight applications to select those presented here. Members include Michael Cart, retired director of the Beverly Hills Public Library, writer and lecturer, Los Angeles, California; Pat Muller, Young Adult Supervisor, Arlington Central Library, Arlington County Department of Public Libraries, Arlington, Virginia; Pam Spencer, coordinator of Library Services, Fairfax County Public Schools, Annandale, Virginia; and Deborah Taylor, coordinator of School and Student Services, Enoch Pratt Free Library, Baltimore, Maryland.

Louise Howe, project editor, who copy edited this publication and shepherded it through publication with patience and expertise.

Jameson Watkins, lead developer for Blue Skyways (a shared information service of the Kansas State Library for the Kansas library community), who did all the preliminary electronic organizing of multiple disks and formats from winning applicants into a coherent, unified document from which the basic text for this book was edited.

Dorothy M. Broderick, who rose from her recuperation from heart surgery to help with the copy editing necessary to meet the publisher's deadline.

Introduction

Purpose

Well worthy of emulation at the state level, the Excellence Project, established by Hardy Franklin and supported by the Margaret Alexander Edwards Trust, is based on several simple ideas, the most basic of which are: (1) young adults are an important audience for library services; (2) library services for young adults are often underrepresented and deserving of more attention in professional literature; (3) library services for young adults offer some unique perspectives on matching services to particular life development stages; (4) application for recognition should be kept simple for busy practitioners; and (5) if more librarians knew about successful ideas for serving adolescents, they might be inclined to try them out in their own local settings. It would be Hardy Franklin's fondest wish that the state chapters of ALA institute state-level recognition programs based on the Excellence Project model.

Margaret Edwards' Legacy

Margaret Alexander Edwards' will stated clearly what was to be done with the proceeds from her estate by her appointed trustees and their successors:

> It is my observation that in the lives of most people, meaningful experience is rare and that without it, it is difficult to understand one's self or to establish good relationships with others. Since I believe the book supplements experience and since I have faith in young people and am concerned that they read—not only for their personal enjoyment and enrichment but so that they may equip themselves to remake society—I bequeath the bulk of my estate to further the personal reading of young adults.
>
> As most library schools and library administrators in my lifetime stressed informational services to the neglect of the promotion of reading, I should like what worldly goods I leave behind, however small in value, to be used to experiment with ways of effectively promoting the reading of young adults and of inspiring young adult librarians to realize the importance of reading and to perfect themselves as readers' advisors.
>
> Since it was at the Enoch Pratt Free Library in Baltimore that I worked with young adults for over thirty years, I should like for that library and Baltimore City to benefit from my bequest, but if other places appear to be more fruitful grounds for experimentation, the Trustees of the trust should feel free to decide on places and methods selected. . . . With these thoughts in mind, all of the rest and residue of my estate and property . . . I give, devise, and bequeath unto Ray Fry, Sara Siebert, and Anna Curry, in trust, however for the following purposes:
>
> My Trustees are hereby authorized to pay or to apply all or any part of the income and so much of the principal . . . as my Trustees . . . deem advisable for the purpose of promoting the free reading of teenagers and young adults, and the final decision in this matter is to rest with my Trustees. I suggest such projects as billboards, newspaper ads, work in the streets of underprivileged neighborhoods, possibly a reading clinic or whatever will promote reading for the enjoyment and enrichment of teenagers and young adults. I would like to see experimentation made with various approaches but I leave such decisions with the Trustees. If some project or projects seem likely to make a lasting contribution to the enrichment of youth through reading, the Trustees in their sole and absolute discretion, can invest the entire principal of the trust in such project or projects. . . .[1]

Youth Participation

Many of the fifty projects recognized in this book not only fall squarely within Edwards' framework, but actually extend it in several ways. Beyond the traditional and unique ways in which many programs included here promote reading (Vashon High School Library's candid snapshots, for example), the most important extension is the involvement of young adults in decision making, a concept called "youth participation" in library literature. Adolescents involved in youth participation activities learn about themselves and their own interests and capabilities through offering service to others and reflecting on that service under the facilitating guidance of one or more caring adults. As Joan Schine, the founder of what is now the National Helpers Network, Inc., once aptly put it,

> Young people need to learn how to make wise decisions in much the same way they learn other skills—by starting gradually, testing their strength, increasing the complexity and the urgency of the decision they are called upon to make—until they can apply those skills as thoughtful, responsible adults. In making the transition from the role of child to that of an adult, the young person needs opportunities to learn skills through practicing them. Talking about the Australian crawl is interesting; reading about buoyancy and water displacement may be informative, but the only way to learn to swim is to be in the water.[2]

Edwards would have easily recognized this philosophy because the learning gained from youth participation is a natural extension of the valuable vicarious experience found in books and stories. In this regard, however, learning is found in one's personal story. David Carr, Director of the Library and Information Studies Department of Rutgers' School of Communication, Information, and Library Studies, eloquently explains, "Libraries exist to allow us to experience an involvement with story, meaning the creation of narrative for sorting and constructing the multiple contexts of the world. . . . In order to live lives without chaos, we depend on narrative. And so the library exists to tell us stories, most often our own."[3]

Edwards' collection development policy at Enoch Pratt was based on a model of vicarious self-understanding through books and reading. The fact that the youth participation activities in the excellent programs documented here take place in libraries and involve reading-related presentations to peers and others might well have been viewed by Edwards as an ideal experiment of the type she hoped for in her will. They certainly are an extension of her belief in the importance of vicarious learning, or what is sometimes called "role rehearsal" for adult life. Edwards never lost sight of the fact that her work was intended to produce adults, not to prolong adolescence.

Youth participation can be viewed as a particular form of information provision, but in this type of library service, the "information" is not just recorded data retrieved and transmitted through a library information system, but rather, understanding and mastery of self in relation to others. This understanding is not "retrieved" for young adults by librarians; rather, youth experience it for themselves in a context provided by the library. Better understanding of themselves in relation to others is the "data" encountered in youth participation activities—a form of information that is at once personal and emotional as well as cognitive. The adolescent participant not only better understands and thinks about social bonds as a result of the library youth participation experience, but also *feels* them. This careful attention to the emotional landscape as well as to cognitive processing is a unique contribution of excellent library programs for young adults, and an intrinsic part of many programs described here.

Information Services

The second extension of Edwards' philosophy, one which might perhaps be less obvious to her, is demonstrated in those programs categorized as "Information Services." Edwards was quite unhappy with the way in which reference services began to eclipse readers' advisory services in libraries and library education, because she felt so strongly that the latter were the grounding for services for young adults. She was openly scornful of the empty retrieval of "facts" to the exclusion of understanding, which she saw coming from interaction with stories in books. How differently she might have felt had she been able to see the "reviews by teens" feature that is part of the Berkeley's Public Library's Teen Services Internet homepage, or if she had recognized that adolescents in crisis situations often need vital survival information such as that created and distributed by the Cuyahoga County Public Library, which is a far cry from the mere retrieval of "facts." Both these programs share the passionate caring for adolescents and their lives characteristic of Margaret Edwards' work.

Margaret Edwards' disdain for the empty retrieval of facts as opposed to improved knowledge and understanding, which she saw happening primarily through reading books, is disconcerting to many contemporary youth services librarians forced to cope with the ever changing ambiguities of the so-called "Information Age." However, if the problem of defining practice is reframed from Edwards' era-driven "facts-versus-books" dichotomy to how librarians can best assist young adults "to promote self-transformation through independent learning,"[4] one senses that her resistance to information work might have been softened. The information work of services to young adults is basically how to turn adolescents into lifelong learners who are able to ask questions and make knowledge, a condition that might be called a "literacy of self-designed inquiry."[5]

Young adult work is information work for life, not just for the moment. Even the most mundane school assignment request takes on new meaning and professional behavior from this conceptual vantage point.

Community Engagement

Another facet of Margaret Edwards' personal philosophy, which often spilled over into her professional work, was a passionate civic engagement. She was active in many political organizations and loved to discuss the political ramifications of government activities. Her concern about disenfranchised youth ranged from the Enoch Pratt experiment of taking a horse-drawn book wagon into Baltimore's ghetto neighborhoods to selecting and booktalking titles about civil rights long before doing so was *de rigueur* among many other librarians. She saw library service as a means of engaging youth with others, making them comfortable first within their own skin, and then gradually broadening this comfort to membership in family and community.

Unfortunately, because of demographic shifts in the population[6] and relentless scapegoating of and moralizing about adolescents by politicians and the media,[7] many communities are actively hostile to young adults, resulting in youth feelings of abandonment, boredom, and alienation, rather than engagement. Malls hire security guards to prevent individual shoplifting and stop groups of teenagers from assembling. Convenience stores do not allow minors to enter unaccompanied by adults. Museums charge entry fees and reduce hours; public libraries reduce hours and staff; public parks are closed at night, and so on. School buildings are locked up tight at 3 p.m. Curfew and anti-loitering laws are passed, with adolescents in mind.

In poorer neighborhoods—those that policy makers and those living elsewhere regard as "problem" or "deficient" communities—the nothing-for-kids-to-do issue is often exacerbated by guns, drugs, and random violence. Residents begin to see themselves as victims with needs to be met by those outside their own community. An alternative view espoused by Libraries for the Future,[8] for example, and one that is useful in implementing young adult services, focuses on assets in the community with the idea of developing these as a form of community renewal. One of the assets found in many poor communities is a branch of the public library. Viewed as a community asset, the library becomes a source of community renewal rather than a symbol of decay. As McKnight and Kretzmann point out, "Considered not only as a repository for books and periodicals, but also as the center of a neighborhood's flow of information, the library becomes a potentially critical participant in community regeneration."[9] They go on to suggest ways in which the library can be "captured" as a local institution for community building. Examples given include mobilizing young people into "Advisory Councils" that can plan youth activities, utilizing the talents of local youth as group leaders and teachers for younger members of the community and building "on strong relationships with schools by offering after-school literacy tutoring and arranging to display student artwork and other projects."[10] This is very much what Chicago Public Library's Blue Skies for Library Kids project is all about, and it is not accidental that neighborhood branch-level programs from that project such as the *Teen Parenting Course*, the *Junior Volunteers*, and the *Knight Moves* after-school chess club are included in this book.

ESCAPE!, the Friday night program offered by the Burien Branch of the King County Library System, is an ideal example of community collaboration between the public library and other agencies to mobilize community assets on behalf of young adults. New York Public's *Young Men's Conference* at the Belmont Regional Branch and Brooklyn Public Library's *Math Peer Tutoring Program* also fall into the community-building model. If the assets on which to rebuild a community are the unique untapped combination of the gifts and skills of individuals (including those of youth), the depth and extent of associational life, and the public and nonprofit institutions which make up the most visible and formal part of a community's fabric,[11] then public libraries must be part of the solution rather than part of the problem. Emulating the many programs included here will help both public and school libraries become community assets and a force for community renewal.

Staff Development

Margaret Edwards brooked no nonsense when it came to developing librarians to serve adolescents. She had high standards. The fact that she met every one of them herself was ignored by those who could not live up to them, but those who could do so have been unanimously grateful throughout their professional careers. Edwards' training shows in well-read librarians, well-read that is in what *young adults*, not librarians, find interesting; librarians who are exemplary public speakers; and librarians who understand that professional careers are best launched within a coherent institutional philosophy of service, much of which is inculcated through the example of mentors and peers. Edwards was the quintessential professional mentor; to have called her a mere "manager" would have been an insult, although she certainly was a capable one. Like Anne Carroll

Moore, she felt that her work survived through the people she mentored. Besides the promotion of reading to young adults, her greatest passion was staff development, to which many successors can attest. It is not accidental, therefore, that innovative staff development approaches for those serving young adults appear among the programs in this book.

Developing good young adult librarians forces a choice often resisted by librarians, not only among young adult librarians, but also among those hiring them; namely, whether librarians who work with young adults are primarily librarians working with a special population or youth workers in a library setting. Since good service to this age group depends so much more on personal characteristics than on technical information retrieval skills, it is often easier to ignore or resist the question than to confront the issue squarely. Hiding behind words like "maturity" and "a sense of humor," while both are arguably necessary to anyone hoping to connect with adolescents, continues to beg the question. The issue is complicated by the peculiar avoidance by many librarians of anything perceived as "social work." The comment, "I didn't become a librarian to be a social worker," is almost inevitably uttered by librarians frustrated by young adults.

Libraries have historically been more system- than user-driven, especially where adolescent users are concerned. Young adults often appear to be the proverbial "bulls in the china shop" with highly varied and unpredictable behaviors. Their interests are equally unpredictable. Adolescents do not know or often care about the unspoken "rules" of library behavior and usually arrive in noisy groups besides, wanting everything at the last minute while spending the bulk of their time studying each other. As if all that were not annoying enough, they inevitably are interested in topics that make adults nervous. Disapproval and restrictions are far more common institutional responses than joyful welcome, so a staff member who puts young adult users first, much as a good youth worker would, can be extremely disconcerting. It is not uncommon for YA staff to burn out from the energy drain of fighting to attract the kids on one hand, and keep the bureaucracy off their backs on the other. It is even harder when one's job title of "generalist" implies that everyone can be treated the same from cradle to grave, as if human development were irrelevant.

McLaughlin, Irby, and Langman studied youth-serving organizations in some of the country's poorest neighborhoods to identify characteristics in either the staff or programs that might possibly be replicated elsewhere.[12] Calling these neighborhood-based programs "urban sanctuaries" that challenge prevailing myths about the capacities, interests, and ambitions of inner-city youth, the authors try to describe the characteristics of the adults who create and sustain them. Librarians serving young adults, and those hiring them, might find the list interesting and relevant. The six youth workers, or "wizards," frame their missions around five deceptively simply beliefs. The first is a passionate commitment to young people, whom they view as resources they can help develop through engaging them in experiences that transform their lives. They do not view youth as people to be "fixed, remediated, or otherwise controlled but as young people of promise, largely ignored, wrongly perceived, and badly served by society at large." They create an atmosphere of success, a place where adolescent self-identity is affirmed through learning and growth opportunities.

The second characteristic of the youth-worker wizards is an absolute focus on youth "before organization, program, or activity." This means that they fit the program to the kids, not vice versa. The youth workers know that adolescents do not particularly agree with adult ideas about what is good for them. This focus results in "full-service" organizations that do not define responsibilities and roles solely within a narrow job description. They never forget that meeting their "basic survival concerns is integral to those adolescents' ability to acquire competencies, belonging, and hope."

The wizards described reinforce their focus with a strong sense of personal efficacy. They have a firm conviction that they can and do make a difference in the lives of young adults, and they resist nay-sayers who feel that it is too late to help teens. They feel that their job is a total commitment, on the job and off, because they have a responsibility to make a difference through their example as well as through their work.

Part of the commitment felt so strongly by these youth workers comes from an overwhelming desire to give back to youth some of what they had growing up. As one wizard, Reggie Jones, explains, he is repaying "what I owe for what I am today. . . . My personal mission is to try to help as many young people as I possibly can to come through this world and benefit from this program and go out and be productive citizens. I don't want them to be on public aid. I want them to be gainfully employed. I want them to be educated. I want them, once their feet are firmly planted on this Earth, to do what I have done, and that is to give back to their community."[13]

The final important characteristic of the six youth-work wizards is the authenticity they show to youth in their work. They feel that one-size-fits-all programming ignores adolescents' need to feel that they are pursuing activities and goals that they themselves have chosen. Feeling much the same, the wizards mesh their own talents with their youth work and serve the kids of their communities in many different ways. This characteristic is what turns many ordinary programs into extraordinary ones. As wizard Luanna Williams says, "You can't be phony. . . . These kids can see through you if you are not really genuine and really don't care about them. They can completely see through it."[14]

Good service to young adults transcends institutionally focused activities for a "special population." Library service to young adults *is* youth work in a library setting. It is a kind of service that allows libraries "to enable their users to go beyond the institution as we know it, and to go beyond themselves as they know themselves."[15] Mike Printz, a much-loved school librarian from Topeka, Kansas, compared librarians who work with young adults to the people of Chartres in a speech he gave at the 1991 ALA Annual Conference. "I've always thought about the people of Chartres. They began something they knew they would never see completed. They built for something larger than themselves. They had a vision. For . . . librarians it is the same. Most of us will never see our students grow up. But from where we are and with what we give, we serve a vision of how the world ought to be. The old woman of Chartres was a spiritual ancestor of librarians who build cathedrals to the human enterprise in our own quiet way. From us, young people learn to live—with knowledge and care."[16]

Notes

1. Margaret A. Edwards, "Will" (excerpt), in *Margaret Alexander Edwards Trust* (brochure, n.d.).
2. Joan Schine, *We Can Make a Difference: A Youth Participation Training Manual* (Mineola, N.Y.: Nassau County Youth Board, 1986), p. 9.
3. David Carr, *Why Libraries? Twenty-Five Responses.* (Rutgers LIS Student Orientation). Photocopy. (September 2, 1994), p. 2.
4. Ibid, p. 3.
5. Ibid.
6. Victor R. Fuchs and Diane M. Reklis, "America's Children: Economic Perspectives and Policy Options," *Science* 255 (January 1992) 41–45.
7. Mike A. Males, *Scapegoat Generation: America's War on Adolescents* (Monroe, Maine: Common Courage Press, 1996).
8. Libraries for the Future is a citizen advocacy group for the future of public libraries directed by Diantha Schull at 521 Fifth Avenue, Suite 1612, New York, NY 10175-1699.
9. John L. McKnight and John Kretzmann, "Mapping Community Capacity," *New Designs for Youth Development*, 10 (Winter 1992): 9–15.
10. John L. McKnight and John Kretzmann, *Building Communities from the Inside Out: A Path Toward Finding and Mobilizing a Community's Assets.* (Evanston, Ill.: Center for Urban Affairs and Polity Research/Neighborhood Innovations Network/Northwestern University, 1993), p. 196.
11. Ibid.
12. Milbrey W. McLaughlin, Merita A. Irby, and Juliet Langman. *Urban Sanctuaries: Neighborhood Organizations in the Lives and Futures of Inner-City Youth* (San Francisco: Jossey-Bass, 1994).
13. Ibid., p. 101.
14. Ibid., p. 103.
15. David Carr, *Why Libraries? Twenty-Five Responses.* p. 1.
16. Mike Printz. "A Big Fat Hen; A Couple of Ducks," *Voice of Youth Advocates* (June 1992), 85–88.

THE TOP FIVE

1.
Dunbar-Pulaski Middle School, Gary Community School Corporation

Gary, Indiana

Idea

Partners in Reading

Customers

Middle school students, grades six through eight

Community

Dunbar-Pulaski Middle School has a population of 756 adolescents in a sixth, seventh, and eighth grade configuration. Ninety-eight percent are African American. With 75 percent poverty, the D-PMS community has the highest poverty rate of the six middle schools in the district. The middle school is located on the east side of the city in a community made up mostly of homeowners. There is a sense of pride in this neighborhood. Lawns are maintained; homes are in good repair, and there is no graffiti in the neighborhood. A sizable percentage of students live in the Dorie Miller Housing Project. Another group lives in the St. John Homes, a federally subsidized housing development.

Setting

As you enter Dunbar-Pulaski, colorful posters provide a pictorial gallery of young adolescents in various aspects of the reading program. Not one photo has been defaced, and students love seeing themselves. The media center is the hub of the school. During the last five years the media center has piggybacked on various grants to afford planning time and resources to build a multi-tiered reading program. Collaborative planning is the norm for a School Improvement Team and a Literacy Committee that includes parents and students. Grade-level teams have common planning time to talk about student needs. A weekly advisor/advisee program reinforces a caring learning environment

Students attend six fifty-five-minute classes of varied course offerings. Three-fourths of the young adolescents have a reading class to reinforce skill building and a love of reading. They also participate in computer literacy activities linked to career education. The school just received the Accelerated Reader Program. Each marking period students are recognized for good citizenship, attendance, most improved scholarship, and highest achievement. A varied extracurricular program provides everything from athletics to service project emphasis.

Staff development strengthens interdisciplinary planning and reading development. For example, the "Algebra Project," a constructive approach to learning, is a new initiative supported by a community agency called The Accord at Indiana University Northwest.

Program Description

Reading is valued at Dunbar-Pulaski. Collaboration with parents, teachers, and community organizations extends the many book-sharing activities included, such as sustained silent reading each Friday from barcoded baskets of books selected by students from the media center; workshops on poetry; after-school guest appearances by writers and illustrators; monthly readings of favorite books by community role models; and the publication of *Literacy Wise*, a newsletter. Parents serve on a literacy committee, work in a school bookstore, read on Fridays, and have developed a reading T-shirt and bookmark designed to reward readers. The librarian facilitates orientations to the school and public library. "Literacy Zones," including quiet areas for lunchtime reading and a bookstore, were established, and grand openings were held.

News headlines identify Gary as a city with a high murder rate. The reading program seeks to get the young adolescents of the Dunbar-Pulaski Middle School community to read beyond the obituaries and become partners for an improving, healthy economy and culture.

Partnerships with the New Mt. Moriah Church, the neighborhood, Dunbar-Pulaski Library, businesses, alumni, the Indiana Department of Education, a funeral home, medical doctors, Indiana University Northwest, and the Altrussa Club of the Indiana Dunes energize both the school and members of the organizations. People feel good when they contribute to student improvement. Students are nudged to improve reading and writing skills not only to satisfy teachers, but also to understand the impact and power of literacy in a changing world. In order to allow the adolescents of Dunbar-Pulaski Middle School to develop their full potential as participants in the "club" of literate citizens, the adults of the community joined together to focus efforts on creating a shared vision, improving students' access to materials, and meeting the adolescent literacy needs of exploration and invention. Various literacy activities engage not only all of the school's 756 young adolescents, but also many of their brothers and sisters who are being read to and who model behavior they see.

Sixty-five staff members and thirty-seven parents and community volunteers are involved in Partners in Reading. A fifteen-member literacy team of staff, parents, and students shepherd all the activities. Last year a reading teacher chaired the committee and this year the media specialist chairs it. Eight sixth, seventh, and eighth graders served on the literacy team and helped to plan the read-ins, provided intercom messages to promote reading, helped design a program bookmark, and participated in a reading celebration. Also, they participated in all discussions regarding the program, and their point of view was important in evaluation of successes and failures. Fifteen sixth graders participated in a play to highlight favorite book characters. Their costumes were made by a teacher's aide. Several students worked in the bookstore. The entire student body participated in book selection for purchase from a Permabound collection brought to the school for students to preview. Students participated in the "Literacy Zone" grand opening luncheon program, bookstore opening, and end-of-the-year community reading celebration. The REAP #3 Post Attitude Inventory (also referred to as the "student Garfield" reading survey because it features the cartoon cat) was used to assess improvement in reading enjoyment, and during Literacy Week six students wore advertisements for books such as *Maniac Magee*, *There's a Girl in My Hammerlock*, *Hoops*, *Southern Fried Rats*, and *Roll of Thunder, Hear My Cry*. A group of students participated in Reader's Theater and in a local TV segment. Fifty students participated in after school read-ins. They wrote for the *Literacy Wise* newsletter as well as the student newspaper, and they selected books for prizes. The storytelling contest included many students who received books as rewards.

Citywide and state testing for 1996 indicate some gains, especially vocabulary gains for sixth graders of three NCEs (normal curve equivalents). The school meets minimal standards on the statewide performance-based assessment for a middle school of its size with high poverty rates. The infusion of funds helped to fill shelves in the library and in each classroom with over two thousand appealing books at various levels of readability. Staff became familiar with new adolescent literature. Reading teacher surveys report students are reading more books and the media specialist reports a 50 percent improvement in circulation. Successful reading models such as

Staff dress as book characters.

Nancy Atwell's *Reading Workshop* and Linda Reif's *Seeking Diversity* are being used.

Parental involvement beyond the PTA now includes "Parents and Staff Sharing Books," "Partners in Reading," Friday sessions over breakfast, community readers, volunteers in the bookstore, and committees; both a Parent Resource Center and an African-American Infusion section are being planned for the library.

The media specialist facilitates all these programs.

Funding

The project was funded by the Middle Grades Reading Network, directed out of the University of Evansville, for $25,000. Staff also piggybacked on a Reading Excitement and Paperbacks grant funded by the Indiana State Department of Instruction for $5,000. The latter helped to purchase hundreds of high interest paperbacks to support the Sustained Silent Reading program. Both grants helped provide staff development to support reading initiatives. A Reading Is Fundamental grant supported the distribution of free books to students.

Contact Persons

Eugenia Sacopoulos, Principal, and Anne Eldridge, Media Specialist, Dunbar-Pulaski Middle School, 920 East 19th Avenue, Gary, IN 46407. (219) 886-6581

2. Franklin County Public Library

Eastpoint, Florida

Idea

WINGS

Customers

At-risk young adults, ages ten through seventeen

Community

There are 1,038 young people in Franklin County between the ages of ten and seventeen; 860 Caucasian and 178 non-Caucasian, of whom 35 percent are in poverty. According to a 1994 *Florida Kids Count Report*, there is a teen violent death rate (ages fifteen through nineteen) of 31.3. There is a functional illiteracy rate in Franklin County of 42 percent, and the County ranks number one in teen pregnancy. The decline in the seafood industry and the rise in tourism have impacted the community badly. Consistent employment opportunities for young people are almost nonexistent. Kids repeatedly have echoed that there is "nothing to do." This community is in transition from one that for generations has gleaned its living from the local waters to one that has to find other means of support. A large number of the people will need to learn new skills. They will be in need of help to earn a GED, they will need a place to obtain information about resumes, interview techniques, other occupations, and many other things that a library does provide.

Setting

The Franklin County Public Library, now beginning its fourth year, is a member of Wilderness Coast Public Libraries, a multi-county system which includes Franklin, Wakulla, and Jefferson Counties. There is a small library branch in Eastpoint and a second in Carrabelle, both rented spaces. There is a WINGS program site at each branch. The Program Center services Apalachicola and houses the Apalachicola WINGS program, the Summer Reading Program, and the Literacy Program. From the time a donated storefront with a handful of paperbacks opened on October 1, 1992, library borrowers have grown to number 2,400. In a rural county such as this one, the library becomes more than just a place to keep information and provide access; the library necessarily becomes the community center. In January 1994 the Franklin County Public Library received the Public Library Association's Excellence in Small and/or Rural County Public Library Award for its outstanding service to the community, in particular for the WINGS program.

Program Description

Prior to WINGS, there have been no programs where youth could gather with peers and caring adults for recreation, skill enhancing activities, use of computers, art and musical programs, tutoring, counseling, and friendship. It is important to note that in this economically depressed, rural county, there is no movie theater, shopping mall, bowling alley, children's theater, science museum, or public swimming pool. WINGS has provided programs that extend in scope from tie dyeing to money management, conflict resolution to poetry, fiddling, storytelling, sewing, painting, exercise, sailing, nutrition, cooking, employment counseling, journalism, courtroom procedures, and life skills. Young adults have learned the satisfaction of contributing to their community through their participation in the Adopt-a-Shore program and have received recognition from the Keep Franklin County Beautiful Association. They have learned the dynamics of supply and demand, the effects of advertising, and the importance of a budget through their fund-raising efforts. WINGS has provided educational and cultural exposure through field trips to the Tallahassee Museum Jazz & Blues Festival, a program featuring poet laureate Dr. Maya Angelou, an introduction to reggae, a Northwest Ballet Company performance, and the multicultural "Up with People" presentation. Participants have met various authors and have had the opportunity to talk to people in varied and interesting professions such as an astronaut, an archaeologist, the owner of a circus, a musician, a journalist, and a sculptor. They have been regular participants in their own radio show "For Teens, By Teens."

WINGS participants have learned some of the functions of government in their county with tours of the animal shelter, the recycling center and landfill, the jail, and the Sheriff's Department, and are planning to spend a morning in the courthouse. A chess club was formed, causing a coach at the high school to comment that he often must pry athletes from the chess board to participate in other sports. A very significant part of the program is the availability of computers and the Internet. These are used for research, for homework assignments, printing posters for fund-raisers and other activities, and just having fun. Homework time and tutors are provided. Teachers and parents have noted the difference in study habits, class participation, and report-card grades. Many of the young people have progressed from being shy and timid to demonstrating a more self-assured attitude. There is a growing sense of pride about being a *WINGS* person.

The effect of this program is not limited to young people, but extends to their families as well. Intergenerational programs are provided. Younger and older siblings want to take part in this dynamic program. The parents stay to see what their children are doing; they ask about programs available to them including the Adult Literacy Program. Parents and other caregivers are seeing the impact the Franklin County Public Library can have on their daily lives and their future.

The completion of a youth-focused cooperative mural on a major wall in Eastpoint was highly significant for the program and the community. In its early stages, the wall had fallen victim to vicious graffiti. The community gathered and rallied and supported the children. The sheriff was called, the radio station made announcements, the County Commission was notified, people gathered and were openly upset about the fact that the *WINGS* program was doing something so positive and that anyone would attempt to disrupt the good that was being done. The young adults gathered at the wall and with small brushes reconstructed the faces and necessary parts of the mural. The vandalism did not recur, and the mural was completed magnificently. Teens are now preparing to purchase and paint waste receptacles in an effort to encourage a community cleanup. The young people, especially those who have been participants in the *WINGS* program, are the ones who are carrying the banner for a transformed community, and they will continue to be a force that will make the Franklin County Public Library a contributor in the future growth and direction of the county. Every effort is made to enroll and involve youths in this program. Coordinators work diligently with parents to try to maintain a level of involvement. A teen council has been established with a minimum of two representatives from each site. Teen council workshop and leadership training was provided with the hope that this will develop into an even stronger voice in the community.

There are 224 registered *WINGS* participants. An average of fifteen young people a day attend at each of the three locations. Results are not always measurable in terms of statistics, but if fifteen young people are in the library at some particular moment, then they are not out in the streets getting pregnant, stealing cars, fighting, doing drugs; they are getting positive reinforcement and learning life skills in a positive manner. Over two hundred books and magazines relevant to young adults have been supplied through the *WINGS* program. The R. L. Stine and Christopher Pike paperback books that are in demand are there, as well as award-winning titles and classics. In addition, the display shelves reveal in-your-face titles dealing with AIDS, sex, drugs, self-esteem, stealing, school problems, parents, dating.

There is one *WINGS* coordinator per site and one or two teen aides, and one project director working directly with *WINGS*. In addition, there are a literacy

---

WING IT!

APRIL/MAY 1996

WINGS is the teen branch of the Franklin County Public Library

The official newsletter of the Franklin Co. WINGS program

The goal of WINGS is to provide constructive and positive activities for the youths of Franklin County, and to make available all possible information, art forms and life skills training which will enhance thought processes and result in intellectual, emotional and social growth.

coordinator, three to six tutors, a library assistant, two Green Thumb workers, one grant-funded youth coordinator with an aide, two volunteer Dominican Sisters, two VISTA volunteers, and two to twelve parent volunteers.

Youth have determined the "House Rules," which are consistently addressed and updated. *WINGS* teens also participated in a community Teen Health Fair. The library has been awarded an additional five-month grant from the Florida Commission on Community Service, which will work as an enhancement to *WINGS*. The focus of this grant is environmental issues.

The *WINGS* program is evaluated semiannually and annually and a report is sent in to the Juvenile Justice Program. Coordinators keep journals and records and confidential files on all participants. Each December the School Report comes out, and issues such as truancy and their effects on the program are discussed. More notable are comments from community members and parents and the success rate of some of the participants. In addition, a *WINGS* Advisory Committee meets quarterly to discuss the program with representatives from the interagency partners, i.e., the Sheriff's Department, the Franklin County School Board, the Florida Department of Children and Families, the Apalachee Center for Human Services, the Juvenile Justice Council. Staff meetings are held regularly to discuss successes and to analyze things that are not up to par. Teens are consulted for input on a regular basis.

Funding

The *WINGS* program was funded by a Juvenile Justice Partnership Grant. The 1995–96 budget year provided for one ten-hour-per-week project director, three twenty-five-hour-per-week coordinators, three to six young adult aides for ten hours per week per site, and one interagency partner on a contractual basis for seven grant hours. Total salaries were budgeted at $38,595. Other costs included: contractual services $2,690; equipment $3,600; small equipment $1,800; field trips $2,150; materials and supplies $3,120; rent/telephone and utilities $5,940; training and seminars $270; travel/per diem $335; and audit and accounting $1,000. This year's funding was cut from $59,600 to $30,000: all but $162 is for staff salaries.

Additional funding is being provided by a challenge grant from the J. Ben Watkins Foundation ($5,000), United Way ($1,045), Knights of Columbus ($500), and a variety of fund-raisers by participants and coordinators, which range from bake sales and car washes to T-shirt sales to *WINGS* suppers.

Contact Person

Eileen Annie Ball, Franklin County Public Library, Member of Wilderness Coast Public Libraries, Eastpoint Branch & Administrative Office. Point Mall, Island Drive, P.O. Box 722, Eastpoint, FL 32328. (904) 670-8151

3.
Lee County Library System

Fort Myers, Florida

Idea

Science and Invention Connection

Customers

Middle school students, grades six through eight

Community

One of the most rapidly growing areas in the country, Lee County has an estimated population of 388,392. The population has increased 64.9 percent since 1983. Largely adult, 26.1 percent of the county is twenty-five through forty-four years old, and 25 percent are sixty-five and over. Of the total population, 91 percent are Caucasian, 7 percent African American, 4.5 percent Hispanic, and 2 percent other.

Lee County's young adult population (students in grades six through twelve) totals 27,695. They comprise 7 percent of the total population, 25,385 of whom are in public schools and 2,310 in private schools. The majority of young adults are Caucasian (73 percent). Young adults are 50 percent of the school-age population.

Setting

The Lee County Library System, established in 1964, is located in rapidly growing southwest Florida. The library system consists of a main library, a regional library, nine branch libraries, a bookmobile, and a Talking Books Library. The service area encompasses urban areas in the cities of Fort Myers and Cape Coral, rural areas in Lehigh Acres and North Fort Myers, and island populations on Pine Island and Captiva. The mission of the Lee County Library System is to "provide the facilities, staff, materials, and programs required to meet the informational, educational, cultural, rehabilitational, and recreational needs of the broadest possible spectrum of the Lee County public." The library system also seeks opportunities for partnerships that enhance access to library services.

Program Description

The *Science and Invention Connection* program was started in response to the expanding interest in science and technology in Lee County. Students needed science materials and research assistance at the public library, but often did not know the best methods for finding information and were unaware of available resources. The goal of *Science and Invention Connection* is to inspire Lee County's young people in creative, scientific thinking, as well as lifelong learning and discovery through the resources and programs of the public library. Students, teachers, parents, and community groups are connected with science and technology library resources.

The connection is made through three major activities: school visits, library programs, and collection enhancement. The project staff present outreach and in-house science programs for middle school students at public and private schools, all of which include relevant slides, experiments, booktalks, and an introduction to library services and bibliographies.

One program, *Science Is Everywhere*, motivates students to discover science through connecting science with their everyday lives. Another, *Super Science Resources*, promotes resources for science projects and research. A third program, *Invention!* promotes inventing resources. These programs have informed thousands of area young adults about science resources. The project staff consists of a Project Coordinator, Toni Vanover (Librarian I), who works on all phases of the project, and a part-time library assistant who assists with outreach visits and clerical duties. The Lee County Library System's Youth Services Programming Specialist, Marilyn Long Graham (Librarian II), wrote the grant proposal and assists with its administration. Branch staff are apprised of *Science and Invention Connection* activities through e-mail, meetings, and reference workshops. Whenever possible, a branch staff member visits schools in that service area along with the project staff. Before developing the school programs, Toni consulted with the Coordinator of Instructional and Library Materials for Lee County schools and the Lee County Science Fair Coordinator. To publicize school visits, a colorful program brochure was mailed to all public and private school principals and media specialists in Lee County. Toni also promoted the programs at Lee County school media in-service meetings.

Library services and science resources are introduced by a videotape produced in cooperation with Cypress Lake Center for the Arts, a local high school. Toni Vanover and Marilyn Long Graham wrote the script. A focus group of middle school students provided ideas for the video's content. Cypress Lake Center for the Arts students worked on all aspects of the production, including script coordination, actor selection, filming, acting, and postproduction. The video is now part of the library system's circulating collection, is used for school visits, and is available for loan to schools.

The fifty-minute *Science Is Everywhere* program consists of an introduction to library system services, a slide presentation, a book display, booktalks, and science demonstrations. The slide show features pictures of manatees, automobiles, panthers, the space shuttle, and other examples showing that science is everywhere. Slides of the library system are shown and students are told about library services. Exciting and informative science and technology books and magazines are highlighted by booktalks. For the finale, slime is made following the experiment in William Wellnitz's book *Homemade Slime & Rubber Bones*. Each student receives a *Teens! Discover Science* bibliography and a library system brochure.

Super Science Resources includes science project topics highlighted from outstanding science books such as *100 Amazing Make-It-Yourself Science Fair Projects* by Glen Vecchione and *Plant Biology Science Projects* (Best Science Projects for Young Adults series) by David R. Hershey. A slide presentation featuring actual projects and inventions by Lee County students is included. Student volunteers from the audience help demonstrate science experiments selected from library books. Students received the science resource bibliography, *Ideas for Science Projects & Inventions!* in 1995 and *Need a Science Project Idea . . . Get It at the Library!* in 1996. Teachers and media specialists received the *Super Science Resources for Science Teachers* bibliography.

Amazing Science II is based on a program developed by Sherry Hill and Bonnie Ward of the Lee County Library System staff. The program starts with demonstrations of experiments such as making slime, blowing up a balloon (with vinegar and baking soda to produce carbon dioxide), and optical illusions. Students participating in the program explore ten hands-on stations set up around the room. For example, clean a dirty penny with salt and vinegar, play with magic mud (a cornstarch and water suspension), and learn about density with a wave bottle (oil, water, and food coloring). Some of these stations are supervised by an adult staff member or volunteer.

True Tales Inventions Tell was presented during the summer of 1995. Volunteers from the audience helped the staff present skits about the history behind several popular inventions such as chocolate chip cookies, roller skates, and potato chips.

The Science Games was presented during the summer of 1996. The audience learned about the center of gravity by trying balancing challenges, arm and leg muscles in the name-that-muscle game, and the athletic abilities of various animals in the animal athletes contest.

From January 1995 through December 1996, a total of 8,580 young adults attended a science program. A total of 8,268 middle school students and 172 teachers were visited at their schools. Approximately 192 young adults attended an in-house library program presented by the project staff, and 120 young adults attended an in-house library program presented by a science expert.

Invited science experts, some paid, some volunteer, presented in-house library programs advertised for ages six and older. The programs presented were:

Paper Airplanes & Engineering: Make the Connection presented February 1995 by Julie Nemeth and Jacque Gahman, professional engineers (volunteers).

Tales Fossils Tell presented summer 1995 by Betty Gibson, geologist (seven paid programs).

The Hows and Whys of Student Science Fairs presented October 1995 by Dr. Jed Klein, science teacher (volunteer).

Invention Projects for Students of All Ages presented October 1995 by Jan Klein, teacher and creativity consultant (volunteer).

Build a Bridge presented February 1996 by Sam Marshall and Trudi Williams, professional engineers (volunteers).

Science Surprises with Author Vicki Cobb presented March 1996 by Vicki Cobb (two paid programs).

Climb Every Mountain! (volcanoes) presented summer 1996 by Betty Gibson, geologist (seven paid programs).

Science Tales with Judy Gail presented summer 1996 by Judy Gail, storyteller (three paid programs).

Total attendance was 1,205 students and 262 adults. Approximately 10 percent of the audiences were young adults. Many of the in-house programs were rated excellent or good by 96 percent of the respondents.

Teachers, media specialists, and some students were asked by project staff to complete an evaluation survey for outreach programs. The outreach program received an overall rating of excellent on 94 percent and good on 6 percent of the surveys. Many positive comments were included on the surveys, such as: "All of us can't wait to visit the library!" "The students got to see the large variety of books available to help them with science projects." "Please do this again next year!" The *Super Science Resources* program has been extremely popular. Eleven of the twelve public middle schools have been visited. Teachers and media specialists often call months in advance to schedule programs at their school. Students remember the experiment demonstrations and the project staff months after their school visits.

As the project coordinator, Toni Vanover has attended numerous science fairs and was even invited to be a middle school science fair judge. She noted that a large number of the students gave the Lee County Library System credit for research materials and assistance.

This project has definitely made an impact on the young adult community. Thousands of young adults throughout Lee County have learned about their public library system and are utilizing the library. Students and teachers praise the programs and express appreciation for what they learned. This unique project has fostered a strong link between the Lee County School System and the Lee County Library System. Branch library staff report many students visiting the library mentioning the *Science and Invention Connection* program they saw at their school. The *Science and Invention Connection* was awarded a 1995 National Association of Counties Achievement Award and the Florida Library Association's 1996 Betty Davis Miller Youth Services Award. By igniting the imagination of students, invoking an appreciation for the importance of science and technology, and promoting public library use, these programs are helping Lee County students excel in science and mathematics achievement.

Funding

The project is funded by a Library Services and Construction Act (LSCA) grant administered through the State Library of Florida. In year two, October 1994 through September 1995, this was a $68,583 project, $51,000 or 74 percent LSCA funded. Costs related to programming included salaries and benefits ($46,393), videotape production ($3,500), printing ($1,851), and paid library program presenters ($525). In year three, October 1995 through September 1996, this was a $74,002 project, $54,365 or 73 percent LSCA funded. Costs related to programming included salaries and benefits ($50,265), printing and paid presenters ($1,600), and equipment ($2,500).

Contact Persons

Toni Vanover and Marilyn Long Graham, South County Regional Library, Lee County Library System, 21100 Three Oaks Parkway, Estero, FL 33928. (941) 498-6420

4.
New York Public Library, Regional Library for the Blind and Physically Handicapped

New York, New York

Idea

Don't "Dis" Ability: Special needs outreach

Customers

Young adults with disabilities and agencies serving YA students

Community

New York City is a vast melange of 8.5 million people, 2.1 million of whom are under the age of twenty. Of the latter group, 800,000 are over the age of twelve, forming the core audience for young adult services. Racially, New Yorkers are a diverse lot, with African Americans comprising 26.4 percent of the population, Asians 7.1 percent, and Hispanics 21.6 percent. More than 15 percent are of immigrant birth, with the largest groups coming from the Dominican Republic, China, Jamaica, Colombia, and Korea. Despite the city's high cost of living, fully 40.3 percent survive on incomes of less than $25,000 per year. Of the adult population, 55 percent have a high school diploma or less, making the effort to promote literacy and reading extremely vital. New York's mosaic of challenges makes it an exciting and rewarding place to perform library services.

Setting

The Andrew Heiskell Library for the Blind and Physically Handicapped is one of the eighty-four branches of The New York Public Library system. It is also the regional library administering the National Library Service for the Blind and Physically Handicapped, the Library of Congress program that provides recorded and Braille books to patrons with disabilities that curtail their use of standard print. The library, serving the five boroughs of New York City and Long Island, is a fully accessible facility which provides a browsing collection of large-print, Braille, and recorded materials, reference and referral service, and library programs. Children's and young adult library services include class visits and special programs. Although the library is fully accessible and is located in midtown Manhattan, most service is provided via free mailing of materials to individuals, schools, and other institutions.

Program Description

A campaign, *Don't "Dis" Ability*, was created to reach out to serve New York City's young adults with disabilities and make them aware of the services of the Andrew Heiskell Library for the Blind and Physically Handicapped, and to provide a general information component to foster awareness of the rights of individuals with disabilities and other sensitivity issues. The goal was to contact all schools and agencies serving teens in New York City in order to: (1) provide information about the library's special service for students with print reading disabilities and for the schools and agencies serving them and (2) invite all classes and groups to visit the library or have the young adult librarian visit their sites.

Don't "Dis" Ability, the phrase which became the tie-in that coordinated outreach materials and activities, was born in the summer of 1994 as a catchy phrase for use in flyers and letters to schools, in hopes they would not be consigned to the "circular file." At that time the phrase "don't dis me" was newly in vogue among the library pages, and was thought to be a useful play on words in the phrase "Don't 'dis' ability" to call attention to an offer of free materials and activities to support teaching goals of assisting students with disabilities. Supervisors immediately liked the idea and enthusiastically suggested the possibilities of developing the theme in buttons, booklists, and other items. The button was designed by a team of four librarians, using the international access symbol as a focal point with the wheelchair user climbing a ramp, just about to make the grade. Delighted with the prototype button, the team continued to develop the theme in a flyer and booklist. NYPL's Offices of Young Adult Services and Services for People with Disabilities generously provided the funding for the buttons, flyers, booklists, speakers and refreshments for the subsequent events.

In fall 1994 the first flyer using the "Don't 'Dis' Ability" slogan was mailed to special education instructors and librarians at one hundred public schools known from a database of prior users. The response to this mailing was immediate and gratifying, with seventeen requests for additional applications and/or inquiries about classes verified as responses to the flyer. The increase in applications for school service and telephone inquiries shortly after this mailing also seemed related to the mailing. Respondents included several very enthusiastic teachers and one librarian, whose eagerness to avail themselves of the service and schedule classes for their students formed the nucleus of activity for the 1994–95 semester. One librarian invited staff to address several classes, including two vision resource classes, at a middle school, and later arranged for two classes to visit the library. Another teacher asked if she could bring her class for a visit every month to choose and discuss books, and also persuaded a colleague at another school to bring her students for joint programs. They brought their classes for five library visits and even developed a class skit to act out their favorite book, *How to Sink a Sub*.

In the face of such encouragement, all classes who visited the library were promised a special end-of-year party. The spring 1995 event was attended by a core "booster club" comprising one hundred students from six schools. On May 25, 1995, author Janet Bode was guest speaker at a gala event because her book *Beating the Odds* was used in classes, and her wonderful rapport with the students at the program helped make the event an unqualified success. Bode candidly spoke about her own recent experiences with chemotherapy, and her candor and genuine interest in the students truly demonstrated the theme *Don't "Dis" Ability*! At this event the *Don't "Dis" Ability* buttons and booklists were proudly presented, along with the *Books for the Teen Age, 1995* list of titles available in special media. The euphoria induced by the successful class activity and the raves about the party reinforced the feeling that the outreach program should be continued, so a full schedule of classes and activities for teenagers was established.

Fall 1995 planning included a mass mailing of an information package to every school serving teens ages twelve through eighteen in New York City. The assistant librarian had the inspiration of making origami envelopes for the buttons, and color-coordinated flyers and paper complemented the button. Five willing librarians made 250 origami envelopes, but began to flag after this effort, and the project was delegated to teenage library pages, who were so enthusiastic about their work they kept requesting more purple paper. To date, eight hundred origami envelopes have been made and distributed with the information package. The *Don't "Dis" Ability* booklist, designed to accompany the button and information flyer, is a list of books about individuals dealing with a wide variety of disabilities and includes many of the books booktalked to classes. Disability sensitivity issues are a component of class presentations, and one or two books from this list are included in each presentation. Students have responded enthusiastically to the books from this list, which seem to strike a chord with them; and they participate in discussions and like to wear the buttons, and quickly volunteer to explain what the button means. One

---

You are cordially invited to attend a

Young Adult Reception

on

Thursday, May 25, 1995, 10:30 AM - 12:30 PM

at the

Andrew Heiskell Library for the Blind and Physically Handicapped

featuring

Guest Speaker: Janet Bode

Author of *Beating the Odds: Stories of Unexpected Achievers* and *New Kids on the Block: Oral Histories of Immigrant Teens*

Books for the Teen Age 1995,
a list of titles available in special media,
will also be presented

Refreshments will be served.

The New York Public Library
The Branch Libraries

Celebrating Its Second Century

young man who is a blind quadriplegic said it best: "It means treat me right!"

Spreading the word about these services and classes became a joy, as the YA librarian was invited to address colleagues at several meetings, including those of the Staten Island young adult librarians, the Connecting Libraries and Schools Project (CLASP), the NYPL young adult training seminar, and other regional librarians' meetings. These opportunities to distribute materials and explain the scope of the services were critical in establishing a network of contacts for continuing outreach. Meanwhile, the schools that had participated in last year's programs began calling early in September to ask if they could schedule classes again, and all wanted assurance they would be invited to any events like the wonderful program with Janet Bode. Of course the teens wanted to know when the next party would be!

In the meantime, the buttons had established a cachet of their own. One of the teens, who is blind and mobility impaired, was planning a workshop on disabilities for her camp group and came to the library to research materials for her own presentation and booklist. She asked if she could have twenty-five buttons for her group, and later called to revise her request when over fifty students signed up for her workshop. Two library school students visited the library and were delighted to be offered a quantity of buttons and literature for their class presentations. The media even got the message! When the library staff's union steward wore the button to the Labor Day parade, Jerry Ruth of the Public Employee Press, D.C. 37, AFSCME, saw the button and liked it so much she did a feature article "Librarian Coins a Phrase," which appeared in the October 6, 1995, *Public Employee Press Newsletter*. The booklists and flyers with buttons were also sent to all participating regional libraries comprising the Library for the Blind and Physically Handicapped network. The booklist and button were also mentioned in the library's patron newsletter, and many requests for a button were received. A basket of buttons is kept on the information desk; library patrons love to share them with family and friends.

The 1995–96 year sped remarkably quickly, with the positive responses indicating the project was not only on the right track, but seemed to have gotten aboard a runaway train. In addition to handling a significant increase in applications for students and schools, speaking to library colleagues, and continuing to distribute the information packages at teachers conferences, the librarian scheduled twenty-five classes and held several Saturday programs. The end-of-the-school-year program was slated, and popular young adult author Todd Strasser was invited to help celebrate. On May 24, 1995, over one hundred students and their instructors crowded into the meeting room for the program. The event was again an overwhelming success.

The contacts and structure that have developed, and the goodwill that has been generated by the activities set in motion by the fluke phrase, continue. Special summer classes were attended by a group of multiply disabled students in a special Inclusion program. The students participated in the summer reading club, enjoyed a jewelry making workshop, and had a movie date with one of the library's DVS captioned videos. The YA librarian has again been asked to speak at the Young Adult specialty training seminar offered by NYPL, and has again distributed countless information packages to the vision education teachers, other librarians and special educators. Registration for library materials has doubled since the program began. She is again counting on the lure of an end-of-year speaker and party to entice an even greater number of classes to get acquainted with the range of services, materials, and events the library offers to all teens, who will never again settle for being "dissed" by barriers to using their libraries.

Funding

Printing costs	$ 650
Buttons	2,500
Origami envelopes	250
Two parties	300

Contact Person

Agnes Beck, Andrew Heiskell Library for the Blind and Physically Handicapped, The New York Public Library, 40 West 20th Street, New York, NY 10011-4211. (212) 206-5423

5. New York Public Library, Chatham Square Regional Branch

New York, New York

Idea

School-hour programs for visually impaired young adults

Customers

Special needs young adults

Community

New York City is a vast melange of 8.5 million people, 2.1 million of whom are under the age of twenty. Of the latter group, 800,000 are over the age of twelve, forming the core audience for young adult services. Racially, New Yorkers are a diverse lot, with African Americans comprising 26.4 percent of the population, Asians 7.1 percent, and Hispanics 21.6 percent. More than 15 percent are of immigrant birth, with the largest groups coming from the Dominican Republic, China, Jamaica, Colombia, and Korea. Despite the city's high cost of living, fully 40.3 percent survive on incomes of less than $25,000 per year. Of the adult population, 55 percent have a high school diploma or less, making the effort to promote literacy and reading extremely vital. New York's mosaic of challenges makes it an exciting and rewarding place to perform library services.

Setting

The Chatham Square Regional Branch, one of eighty-four branches in the New York Public Library system, is located in the heart of Manhattan's Chinatown. Dedicated to outreach and high quality community and public service, the Chatham Square branch is one of the busiest, most heavily used, and most active branches in the entire NYPL system. Young adults and children make up a majority of Chatham Square users, and strong relationships are maintained with local schools, teachers, community agencies, and political leaders. Last year, almost two hundred school visits and special programs were organized for the community's young adult population, attracting thousands of students. Additionally, the branch is a magnet for new immigrants, particularly those from China and other parts of East Asia. Many Chatham Square staff members speak at least one Chinese dialect, meaning that multilingual assistance can be offered.

Program Description

Involving young people in activities that stimulate creativity and enhance self-image is a primary objective of all young adult library programming. An additional objective is to reach out to young members of the local and greater communities who might not otherwise make an effort to take advantage of public library services. With these objectives in mind, the Chatham Square Regional Branch of the New York Public Library chose to establish, in 1994, a yearly series of school-hour programs designed especially for a specific group of young adults with special needs. Moreover, it was also a goal to design programs that might be considered a bit "out of the ordinary"—programs that would provide challenges and experiences which might not be encountered in other library or school programs. The initial target audience for such programs would be visually impaired teens.

A series of phone calls and letters determined that approximately three private and four public schools throughout New York City were working actively with visually impaired teens. All were extremely interested in participating in the proposed programs, meaning that they would be willing to bus their students from as far away as Queens and the Bronx all the way to Manhattan's Chinatown to attend the programs.

Once these contacts were made and a relationship was established with school directors and individual teachers, the task of creating programs began. Not only in terms of funding, but also for ultimate program approval, plans were discussed with NYPL's Offices of Special Services (OSS) and Young Adult Services (OYA). The enthusiastic response given and the useful ideas passed along by OSS administration were very welcome.

To launch the new series of programs, in keeping with the "out of the ordinary" objective, an introduction to dance for visually impaired young adults was planned. Exciting, entertaining, and very participatory, such a program would enhance both the body image and self-esteem of each participant. The idea came from reading an article in a local college newsletter about an exceptional student who had been an aspiring professional ballerina before a severe visual impairment made it impossible for her to continue dancing. The article stated, however, that she was now involved in teaching dance to other young people with visual impairments (as well as maintaining an almost 4.0 average in school!). While she was very interested and excited about the proposed program,

> **THE NEW YORK PUBLIC LIBRARY**
> **CHATHAM SQUARE REGIONAL LIBRARY**
> **PRESENTS**
>
> # AN INTRODUCTION TO DANCE FOR THE VISUALLY IMPAIRED
>
> GIVEN BY
> **THE NATIONAL DANCE INSTITUTE**
>
> A <u>FREE</u> HANDS-ON WORKSHOP IN DANCE AND MOVEMENT FOR TEENAGERS
> ALL ARE WELCOME
> MONDAY JANUARY 9, 1995 10:30 AM
> CHATHAM SQUARE
> REGIONAL LIBRARY
> 33 EAST BROADWAY
> NEW YORK, NEW YORK 10002
> (212) 964-6598
>
> THIS PROGRAM IS SPONSORED BY THE BRANCH LIBRARIES' OFFICE OF SERVICES FOR PERSONS WITH DISABILITIES.
> IT IS PARTIALLY SUPPORTED BY THE U.S. DEPARTMENT OF EDUCATION PROJECT FOR INITIATING RECREATIONAL PROGRAMS FOR INDIVIDUALS WITH DISABILITIES.
>
> The New York Public Library

she could not manage the time because of school and other work commitments. However, she did refer staff to Lori Klinger, a master teacher with the world-renowned young people's dance ensemble, the National Dance Institute, who agreed not only to lead the workshop for no fee, but also to bring assistants and a musician from the school. The only expense OSS was responsible for was the rental of a portable electric piano and a small honorarium for the musician.

Over fifty visually impaired young adults registered to attend the National Dance Institute's Introduction to Dance for Visually Impaired Teens! At Klinger's suggestion, a non-visually impaired eighth grade class from a local school was invited to participate in the workshop. These sighted students would act as "helpers" for the nonsighted students, with a total of more than eighty-five teenagers participating in this incredible dance experience at Chatham Square Library.

The workshop turned out to be a wonderful experience for students, teachers, presenters, and librarians alike. For over an hour, the library was filled with music, dancing feet, laughter, joy, and a brilliant sense of cooperation and accomplishment. It was a successful day, and it provided the library with a great foundation for future programs involving visually impaired teens.

In subsequent months, a variety of equally inspiring and successful programs have taken place at the Chatham Square branch, including a two-part Martial Arts Workshop led by Mr. Vinnie Thomas of the Chinese Martial Arts Institute, which provided over twenty teenage boys and girls with an introduction to kung fu and a positive self-image experience that teachers report is not available at school. Also, the nationally acclaimed music and drama group Theater by the Blind (made up of sighted and nonsighted actors and actresses) has performed twice at the library, each time involving over sixty young people in the action, as well as performing their own uplifting and hilarious theatrical skits. Happily, there has also been a return engagement by Lori Klinger and the National Dance Institute, bringing the beauty and excitement of dance to yet another group of over eighty visually impaired New York City teenagers.

In the coming months, the Chatham Square branch is hoping to expand its special needs school-hour programming and reach out to other audiences. Hearing-impaired students, for example, have benefited from a number of after-school programs that included sign language interpretation. As yet no school-hour programs have been created specifically for this audience, but this need will be a primary focus in 1996–97. Certainly, much more can be done and the Chatham Square Regional Branch of the New York Public Library will continue to seek even more innovative ways to provide these often neglected members of the community with great experiences and inspiration.

Funding

National Dance Institute	$200
Martial Arts Workshop	150
Theater by the Blind	No charge

Contact Person

Jeff Katz, Young Adult Librarian, Chatham Square Branch, The New York Public Library, 33 East Broadway, New York, NY 10002. (212) 964-6598

THE BEST OF THE REST

Collaborative Efforts

6.
Chicago Public Library, Woodson Regional Library
Chicago, Illinois

Idea
Teen parenting course

Customers
At-risk senior high students

Community
A great number of youth in the neighborhoods surrounding Woodson are young adults who do not continue their schooling beyond high school and do not use the library. Within this group, problems of gang pressures, violence, drugs, a high dropout rate, and the rise in the number of young unmarried teens having babies are of concern to the community.

Setting
Located on the South Side of Chicago, Woodson is a central gathering place for that area of the city. Built in 1976, the building is surrounded by moderate and low income housing and fronts one of the main streets of the South Side. The population is predominantly African-American (98.4 percent), and 34 percent of the population is under age nineteen. The regional library serves twenty-seven high schools.

Teen parents on the South Side of the city, especially those on Public Aid, receive little or no help in growing as responsible parents and individuals. Often neglected by their own parents, barely grown up themselves, they are likely to continue the cycle of poverty, dropping out of school because of the overwhelming task of caring for their little ones. These young parents are left with little contact with good adult role models who might assist them in their new role.

In 1995, Woodson Library became a member of the "Blue Skies for Library Kids" grant project. The purpose of the Blue Skies grant is to involve library branches with community groups for the benefit of all concerned. The Teen Parenting Project is being implemented by the librarians and team members of this grant.

Program Description
To aid teen mothers in becoming better parents, the Woodson Regional Library teamed up with the Illinois Department of Public Aid and Sinai Parenting Institute in Chicago to offer an extensive set of parenting courses. All aspects of parenting, including nutrition, discipline, child development, living on a budget, and the importance of reading and using the library to raise successful children were covered. The classes were held in the library's meeting rooms.

Carol Cannon, children's librarian at Woodson, wanted to try to meet the concerns of teenage parents through her library's Blue Skies project. She conducted a needs assessment of the community and formed a Blue Skies team consisting of local clergy, staff from Chicago State University, youth workers, and concerned citizens, all of whom desire to promote library use and better the quality of life for youth in their area. Because early literacy promotion goes hand in hand with raising thriving children, helping mothers learn the importance of reading and the library was an integral part of the courses. The library provided materials for parents and children in its Parenting Center, which also features computers, educational toys, and puppets for children. Through the courses, the girls also met caring adults, highly qualified in their fields of expertise, who become mentors and teachers.

Carol initially tried, somewhat unsuccessfully, to recruit teen mothers and fathers by advertising through traditional channels (flyers, radio, etc.). She

> **Parenting Program for TEENAGE Moms and Dads**
>
> Enroll TODAY in a 25 week program which will help you:
>
> o LEARN HOW TO BE A BETTER PARENT
>
> o LEARN HOW TO DEAL WITH ISSUES SUCH AS:
>
> disciplining your child
> building self-esteem
> proper nutrition
> toilet training
>
> o LEARN HOW TO KEEP YOUR CHILD FROM BECOMING ANOTHER STATISTIC
>
> The Chicago Public Library
> Woodson Regional Branch Library
> 9525 S. Halsted Street
> Chicago, IL 60628
>
> Classes will be taught by trained professionals of the Parenting Institute of Mount Sinai Hospital, and held in the library's first floor conference room:
>
> April 9th - September 26th
> Tuesdays and Thursdays
> 4:00 - 6:00 P.M.
>
> Call (312) 747-6915 to schedule an appointment.
>
> The Teen Parenting Program is made possible by Blue Skies for Library Kids, a grant project funded by The Chicago Community Trust through The Chicago Public Library Foundation
>
> Richard M. Daley, Mayor, City of Chicago
> Cindy Pritzker, President, Board of Directors
> Mary A. Dempsey, Commissioner
>
> The Chicago Public Library: Read, Learn, Discover!

discovered that many at-risk parents do not read the newspaper, visit the library, or think they need the help if they hear an ad on the radio. What proved to be successful was collaboration with groups who deal routinely with teen parents: hospitals and the Department of Public Aid. Mt. Sinai hospital has a fine parenting course available—the Sinai Parenting Institute. The Public Aid Young Parent Service Department has a huge pool of teen mothers who are in great need of these courses, but unable to afford them. Through a tri-agency collaboration, Woodson's Blue Skies team paid for the course tuition. Public Aid required the teen mothers to attend the sessions as part of the assistance they obtained, and the Sinai Parenting Institute provided classes that met twice a week in the evening (a fifty-hour curriculum).

Initially the program was received with some resentment and reluctance by these young women, who saw it as "punishment" they had to go through to get their Public Aid checks. However, their ending comments proved they were surprised and grateful for what they learned and saw changes for the better in their lives. During the program the adolescent mothers wrote personal journals, and their words serve as testimony to how valuable the program was in helping them become stronger, more responsible parents. Besides enhancing their own self-esteem, they worked on developing methods for dealing with their children in a loving, patient, and knowledgeable way. They also learned more about their children's emotional and physical development, and what is necessary to ensure they thrive.

The planning team has been somewhat frustrated because they have failed to enroll young men into the parenting course. However, plans are being made to find ways to interest them in participating. The Woodson Blue Skies team plans to make the parenting program an ongoing offering for teen parents, and to expand it to include other parents who are not necessarily from this at-risk group, because they have shown interest in attending. It is also hoped that mothers who have graduated from the courses will volunteer their time in future library projects. Some of the young mothers have already started to become library-using parents who bring their little ones to programs in Woodson's Children's Department.

Because Carol Cannon and her Blue Skies team believe strongly that the library is an invaluable resource for all parents, all classes for the teen parenting course were held in Woodson's meeting rooms. All the teen mothers, many of whom thought the library was an intimidating place they did not need, were required to attend a session in which they were introduced to the library and to the children's department and Parenting Center, and where they learned how crucial a parent's role as book-sharer is in contributing to the success of their children as they develop and get ready for school. Each young woman was taken through the process of getting her own library card—most of them had never had one before. Thirty-one mothers between the ages of fourteen and sixteen began the program and twenty graduated. The program proved so successful that it will be implemented again in the near future.

Funding

Woodson Regional Library is a member of the "Blue Skies for Library Kids" grant, funded by the Chicago Community Trust, through the Chicago Public Library Foundation. Money from the grant was used to pay the tuition for the parents who took the course taught by Sinai staff members. The cost for this program was $4,725.00 ($236.25 per graduating mother). As the program continues and grows, the Blue Skies team will be asking local charitable organizations to sponsor girls or young men.

Contact Person

Linda Thompson, Blue Skies for Library Kids Director, Chicago Public Library, Children's Services Department, 400 S. State Street 10-S, Chicago, IL 60605. (312) 747-4784

7.
Hammond Public Library
Hammond, Indiana

Idea

AIDS awareness and prevention

Customers

Seventh grade students

Community

The Hammond Public Library and the School City of Hammond serve an ethnically diverse, older industrial city of 84,000, adjoining Chicago, with many transient and economically disadvantaged families. Of the 13,440 students, 1,050 are seventh graders. Reported cases of AIDS are rising in northwest Indiana, especially among youth. Hammond students are diverse ethnically and come from a mix of economically disadvantaged, working class, and some affluent families. Suburban students are predominantly white, and fewer are economically disadvantaged.

Setting

Hammond Public Library is ninety-five years old and provides service through seventy staff members (approximately half part-time) in a main library, six branches, and reading centers. The library system has received ALA awards for multicultural services, international understanding, and handicapped accessibility. The school system has received wide recognition for its innovative program approaches, increased use of technology, school-based management, and business-community partnerships.

Program Description

For the past two years, centered around World AIDS Day on December 1, a collaboration of organizations and committed individuals in northwest Indiana have come together in a project to raise the awareness of Hammond seventh grade students on the human face of the AIDS crisis. With a rise in AIDS rates among young people in the area, especially young women, it is vital that public agencies collaborate in an effective educational approach. The best way to show how the program makes a difference in the lives of the young people is to quote their questions and the responses of the HIV-positive AIDS educator:

"What did your family say?"

"What did your friends say?"

"What did your co-workers say?"

And from group after group:

"Are you scared to die?"

The educator begins with the facts, listing the ways we can get AIDS. Knowing so much and yet so little, the kids are shocked to hear that a mother's milk is one way the virus is transmitted. They didn't know. They are uneasy when he asks them to call out what they like to do and their plans after high school, once they have AIDS, and then listen to his responses:

"Read."
Forget it, with a $2,000 monthly drug bill.

"Sing."
You will be too depressed.

"Swim."
How can you have the physical energy? Besides, nobody will want you to go into a public pool.

"Military."
That's out.

"College."
You will die before completing it.

"Car."
Not only can't you afford insurance and gas, you're losing the sense of feeling in your fingers and toes. You will no longer be able to drive.

"Teach."
What parents will want you to be with their kids?

There is no second chance, he tells them; you are going to die. The twelve- to fourteen-year-olds are very quiet.

At these discussions, there was a display of AIDS quilt panels provided by the NAMES Project AIDS Memorial Foundation in San Francisco. In 1994 and 1996, the panels were rented from the foundation; in 1995, Indiana panels were borrowed at no cost from a state agency. After each one-hour discussion between 125 students and the educator, staff from the participating organizations and volunteer docents walked around with the students in groups of twenty-five. They viewed the AIDS quilt panels on display, discussing what they conveyed about the lives that were lost, personal interests and accomplishments, and the impact of these lives on the family and friends left behind.

In 1995, with the expansion to include other school districts, 1,631 seventh graders were reached, as well as fifty staff members from the school system, library, and other agencies, and fifteen volunteers involved in planning and serving as docents.

Youth are extensively involved in implementing and evaluating the program. At each session, the educator asks two students to stand. Through role-playing, he shows that a single sexual encounter is at risk from previous partners, and partners further back, who did not know they were affected. Fairly quickly, still role-playing, twenty students are standing in the group of seventy-five. The risks of being sexually active are stark.

Curt Ellis, Executive Director, Aliveness Project of Northwest Indiana, an HIV prevention and service program, leading the program. He is living with HIV.

As the classes leave the program, the students are asked for immediate feedback. Almost unanimously, the program has been sobering and informative, and the seventh graders don't hesitate to say so. The school board president, superintendent, and other administrators came to the Parents' Night. Each adult who attended that night and each teacher during the two weeks of programs was given a packet of PTA and Red Cross brochures, information on local AIDS services, and a list of books and videos in the Lake County and Hammond public libraries.

After each program, teachers are also given evaluation forms. The students at one school completed a learning unit by making paper quilt squares on "Celebration of Our Lives" and held discussions.

"Many of them felt that the demonstration of how AIDS is spread from sexual contact with only one HIV-positive person was the most significant part of the program," a teacher wrote in the evaluation. One group did worksheets, saw a video, and discussed the disease more thoroughly. "My students all responded favorably to the program. They thought the program was excellent," another teacher wrote. A third noted that the reading and science teachers were incorporating units on AIDS before the program, including reading excerpts from *Ryan White: My Own Story*, by Ryan White and Ann M. Cunningham (Dial, 1991; Dutton, 1992). Ryan was an Indiana teenager whose family was hounded out of the community when he contracted AIDS. Ryan was also in the display, "A Day without Art," which was an exhibit of empty black frames; in the center of each, a caption noted a person from the arts community lost as a result of AIDS, including authors Arthur Ashe and Ryan White, and various musicians, actors, dancers, painters, etc.

"The students were touched as well as informed by the program. Do not change a thing for World AIDS Day in 1996." The speaker's impact came through in the evaluations, too. "One felt a speaker with HIV was extremely effective for seventh graders." One teacher wrote, "Please get all school systems involved." Another reported, "Many positive comments were made in later discussions and students remembered important facts." All of the evaluations showed seventh grade was the right age group. One teacher added, "Parents should be as informed."

Funding

In the first and second years, the project was funded through a variety of individual and group donations, school system support for bus transportation, and AIDS support group funding for the HIV+ discussion leader. Costs for 1995 totaled $1,443 and included suburban schools. For 1996 the cost was $2,739, which included suburban students even though the suburban school system chose not to participate that year. In 1996 the NAMES Foundation donated videos that were shown to the students in the schools and also paid for shipping the panels.

Contact Persons

Arthur S. Meyers and Margaret Evans, Hammond Public Library, 564 State Street, Hammond, IN 46320. (219) 852-2230

8.
Meriden Public Library

Meriden, Connecticut

Idea

Summer Youth Employment Program

Customers

At-risk young adults between sixteen and twenty

Community

Meriden is a mid-size city, with a population of 60,000. Ten thousand people are school-age youth, and 40 percent of this population are minority.

Setting

Meriden Public Library is centrally located in downtown Meriden, Connecticut. The library is an easily accessible public facility and serves as the information and cultural center of the city. It provides and promotes print and nonprint resources and serves as a major point of access for needed information. Six thousand people use the library's services weekly. The 52,000-square-foot facility serves its citizenry through varied programs of lending materials, answering reference questions, and presenting activities for people of all ages. It is a dynamic agency that opens an opportunity for self-development to each member of the community regardless of education, culture, age, or physical condition. The library maintains a collection of over 200,000 items. During the after-school hours, attendance by the city's youth is high. Because it is centrally located, it often serves the need of "a place to go."

Program Description

The Meriden Summer Youth Employment Program was established to provide job opportunities within the Meriden business community to local teens. This program supplements other programs that target disadvantaged youth. The city government established criteria for eligibility: teens must be between sixteen and twenty years of age and local residents, and one parent must be employed (a characteristic that would make these teens ineligible for some other programs). Local businesses who participated in the program had to guarantee that they would have the teen employed during the ten-week summer break; that they would offer on-site training; and that they would report any difficulties with the program to the library. If they met these criteria, the businesses that participated were reimbursed for 50 percent of the teen's salary for the ten-week program. Forty young adults and ten local businesses participated in this program.

The program was based on the premise that teens who are kept busy in a constructive manner will have less unsupervised time in which they might get themselves and others into trouble. It also exposes them to careers and job opportunities that they may not have considered before. The library recognizes that it is difficult for teens to find work, and for businesses to hire them when they lack job skills. This program established a central clearinghouse as the first step in job assistance and job information. The program also helped the participants develop both job skills and interpersonal skills and build relationships within the community. The program contributed to the quality of life for the entire community because it kept participating kids out of trouble. The young adults also saw first-hand the effect of government planning and the use of taxpayers' money for the good of all. Other benefits include:

1. In addition to the specific work/career related materials, participants were also presented with many appropriate young adult selections.
2. The teens received a tour of the library and were taught how to look for materials, including the use of the OPAC. They were also introduced to the idea that the library should be used throughout life to obtain information.
3. Homework assistance was provided for those who needed it.
4. Teens worked with library staff members and adults in the business community, thus developing a "mentoring" process which supported the students in their work.
5. In bringing the students to the business community, the library developed a true public/private partnership.

In addition, the library worked with the school community for the recruitment of the students; with the local Chamber of Commerce to reach the businesses; with the city government and the businesses themselves; and with local social service agencies that work with youth, in order to refer them to other programs as appropriate. All of this has had the effect of having many people look at the library in a way they had never done before. The long-term benefits of the programs will be realized in the years to come through the program participants who become responsible citizens.

Youth are not involved in the program until they are recruited, but the evaluation process includes input from both the business community and the teens as well as staff. All the businesses were very pleased with the outcome, and said they would be interested in participation in the future. They were also happy to see that city government was doing its part to help them do business in Meriden. The teen participants said the work was important to them because they were able to contribute to the cost of their education; it helped them develop good lifetime work habits. Their suggestions will be incorporated into the next program. The City of Meriden will evaluate the program through the report that the library files with them. Their pleasure with the 1995 program encouraged them to contribute more funds in 1996.

Finally, there is the benefit of the program for library staff. After-school hours with teens are no longer dreaded, but rather productive, exciting times. This program provides them with the encouraging reminder that libraries indeed change lives!

Funding

All of the funding for the program was provided through the city budget, as a small-business incentive program. During the summer of 1995, the library was presented with $10,000 to offer as reimbursements. Because of the success and the enthusiasm of that program, the 1996 program was funded at $25,000. In addition, $2,500 was set aside through a Community Development Block Grant Project to provide funding for part-time staff at the library. The program was administered by one full-time staff member with the supervision of the Director. Two part-time college students, funded through the aforementioned grant, assisted. Efforts involved identifying the businesses in the city that had work for teens; recruiting, interviewing, and training the teens; matching the teens with the particular jobs available; monitoring their progress during the summer months; processing the payments; and reporting back to city government about the success of the program.

Contact Person

Michelle L. Baker, Meriden Public Library, 105 Miller Street, Meriden, CT 06450. (203) 238-2344

Marialyce Francoeur
File clerk
Internal Medicine Associates

Heather Bellobuono
Cashier
Towne & Country Market

9.
New York Public Library

New York, New York

Idea

Poetry in the Branches

Customers

Young adults, twelve through eighteen

Community

New York City is a vast melange of 8.5 million people, 2.1 million of whom are under the age of twenty. Of the latter group, 800,000 are over the age of twelve, forming the core audience for young adult services. Racially, New Yorkers are a diverse lot, with African Americans comprising 26.4 percent of the population, Asians 7.1 percent, and Hispanics 21.6 percent. More than 15 percent are of immigrant birth, with the largest groups coming from the Dominican Republic, China, Jamaica, Colombia, and Korea. Despite the city's high cost of living, fully 40.3 percent survive on incomes of less than $25,000 per year. Of the adult population, 55 percent have a high school diploma or less, making the effort to promote literacy and reading extremely vital. New York's mosaic of challenges makes it an exciting and rewarding place to perform library services.

Setting

The New York Public Library includes, besides four research libraries, eighty-four branch libraries whose mission is to meet the educational, informational, and cultural needs of millions of New Yorkers of every age and ethnic background. For this project, one branch library from each of the boroughs served by NYPL (the Bronx, Manhattan, and Staten Island) was chosen with suggestions for sites coming from Marilee Foglesong, Coordinator for Young Adult Services.

The Allerton branch in the Bronx serves four junior and three senior high schools with approximately five thousand students. The neighborhood is very diverse ethnically—African-American and Caribbean-American, Hispanic, Cambodian, Vietnamese, Italian, Jewish, Indian, and Pakistani groups are the most widely represented—and this mix has been reflected in workshop attendees.

The 96th Street Regional Branch serves teens attending twenty-nine junior and senior high schools and four community-agency after-school programs. Teens come from a wide variety of ethnic backgrounds, and 11 percent of branch circulation comes from teens.

The New Dorp Regional Branch serves a population of 150,000 people on the South Shore of New York City's most "suburban" borough, Staten Island. The community is largely made up of white, middle-class Italian Americans and Irish Americans, along with a steadily increasing Asian and Russian population. The young adults who use the New Dorp branch and attend its programs tend to be mostly white females between the ages of twelve and sixteen.

Program Description

Poetry in the Branches is a collaborative three-year project between the New York Public Library and Poets House, a thirty-thousand-volume library, literary center, and poetry presenter located in Soho. The project was initiated by Poets House, who designed the framework of the program and secured the grant needed to make the project possible. The goal of the program is to serve young readers and writers in local communities and to develop long-term partnerships with staff in the branches. This initiative particularly seeks to broaden young adult audiences for poetry in three diverse branch library sites through poetry collection development, programming, and poetry workshops. By combining the best of each other's resources, Poets House and the New York Public Library have created a multi-layered program which has broadened audiences for poetry in local communities, the results of which will be used to create a national model for joint projects between literary centers and libraries nationwide.

Teens have said that the workshops provide a forum for discussing published contemporary poetry and for sharing and critiquing their own work; two needs which are not met in the schools they attend. The workshop leaders involve the teens in well-thought-out creative writing exercises that enable them to put into practice what they are learning. The participants find fellow teen poets who have the same depth of interest in the art and the same desire to learn techniques to improve their writing.

Seeing the fruits of their labors in print in the shape of published anthologies gives teens a final product which they can treasure and share with friends and family. Copies of the anthologies are also added to library holdings and serve as examples to other teens of what peers are accomplishing. Additionally, selections from the most recent anthologies can now be accessed on the Internet via NYPL's Teen Voices page on Teen Link <http://www.nypl.org/branch/teen/teenlink.html>.

Observing these teens in and out of the workshops, one can see the true effect that this program is

> ### The Music
>
> *The music makes me feel*
>   *like I am in a foreign land.*
> *I am away from the world.*
> *There is a girl with me,*
> *She is dancing to the music.*
> *She is wearing a long robe,*
>   *and a lot of jewelry.*
> *She tells me to follow her.*
> *I am kind of nervous but*
> *I go with her.*
> *She is trying to teach me her dance*
> *I close my eyes and when I look*
>   *she is gone.*
> *Then I am in my room,*
> *I listen carefully and I*
>   *hear the music on the radio.*
>
> *Omari Rivera*

having on these young people. They are introduced to the work of the workshop leader—each site has poetry titles by workshop leaders on hand for teens to check out—as well as to the works of new and emerging poets. Before and after workshops, teens can be observed checking out poetry from both the young adult and adult collections. The fact that participants never leave the workshops at the official finishing time, but stay on to pick the facilitator's brain, and that they have all stressed in evaluations and by word of mouth that three sessions are not enough is proof that this program is filling a deep need in these teens' lives.

The program continues to have far-reaching effects both in the branches in which the program has been placed and throughout the NYPL system. The young adult librarians involved in the project—Caroline Bartels, Patricia Burn, and Jessica Rosokoff—have all experienced heightened personal awareness of the extent to which poetry can and should be promoted to teens. YA staff are sharing enthusiasm for the art of poetry and their commitment to the promotion of reading poetry to teens with other NYPL staff in both everyday work and training activities. Staff now regularly include poetry in their booktalking repertoire with classes as well as in thematic displays mounted in library branches. Project staff were involved in selecting poetry anthologies from the Poets House Poetry Showcase, and additional funds from another grant made it possible for all young adult librarians to purchase $100 in recommended poetry titles.

Ideas for using poetry with teens are now regularly included in NYPL's in-house young adult programming newsletter, *Y.A.P.*; YA staff were recently surveyed for favorite poetry to read to teens, and the

> ### Mr. Dog (A Father Named John)
>
> I could give back
> all those sometimes that you rained onto my
>   floor
> the candy hearts you gave in boxes
> the daughter that I am
> who you chose to father sometimes
> I could give back
> all the beers you never drank
> after he had given them to you
> to give to me
> my hand is open
> & filled with the liars & the fathers
> & the sometimes that I can wrap
> in this pretty box
> & hand to you
> since we are both so giving
> I could give it back
> by calling you father—
> the most hateful word I know
> the name your hidden love deserves
> every sometimes when I can't remember you
> every stupid tomorrow & next week & call me
> that I never thought you'd
> give to me
> I'd give it with a smile
> & the red eyes
> & the ice cream that you let melt
> the ice cream that could have tasted sweet
> if you didn't mix it
> with the sometimes
> that you gave to me
>
> Dayna Crozier

list was shared communally, with suggestions for using it. All YA librarians and trainees attended a one-morning training session at Poets House in November 1995. Prior to the meeting, a tip sheet, "Tips for making poetry come alive in community libraries," was compiled by Poets House with NYPL staff help and distributed to everyone attending.

Already, the monthly reports of YA activities in NYPL branches have shown an increase in the use of poetry activities by almost every YA librarian, not just those involved in the project. Recently, Marsha Spyros and Patricia Burn from the 96th Street branch were invited to lead poetry discussion groups at Murry Bergtraum High School during National Poetry Month in April. Some librarians are beginning to include poetry discussions in summer reading clubs as well as booktalking poetry titles.

"Poetry in the Branches: The Model" was the theme of a panel discussion at the ALA Summer 1996 Conference. Lee Briccetti, Executive Director of

Poets House, and the young adult and adult librarians involved in the program worked together to tell the audience of more than one hundred conferees about the success of the program, and share anecdotes and advice to encourage others to create a similar program in their area.

Since the workshops began in May 1995, seventy-one teens have participated at Allerton, fifty-seven have attended at 96th Street Regional, and forty have participated at New Dorp Regional (New Dorp has had two workshops, the other two branches have each had three). But these numbers reflect only the actual workshop participants. There is no way to count the number of teens who have browsed through the anthologies that now circulate in all three branches, no way to count the number of teens who have sat and read the poems flashing by on the TeenTalk board at Allerton, no means to determine how many teens have accessed the poems at Teen Voices on the Internet.

Staff for this project includes the YA librarian at each site, plus the workshop leader provided by Poets House. Though initially no youth participation was used to plan the workshops, recent input by teens about workshop leaders has helped the librarians at each site work with Poets House to find the best possible leader. Teens are encouraged to evaluate the workshops, and Patricia Burn at 96th Street has created a special evaluation form for teen participants, in addition to the evaluation form created by Poets House to be filled out by both the YA librarian at each site and the workshop leader.

Quantitative and qualitative evaluation has been an integral part of this project and has been carried out on a routine basis over this past year. In addition to statistics from the evaluation forms submitted by leaders and librarians after each workshop, circulation of poetry titles in the YA collection has been charted, with figures rising significantly in each branch. In May 1995, poetry circulation at the three sites was low—Allerton, 12 titles; 96th Street, 60 titles; New Dorp, 50 titles. By May 1996, those numbers had doubled and tripled in some cases—Allerton, 74 titles; 96th Street, 117; New Dorp, 145 titles. During months in which workshops were held at the three sites, circulation of poetry titles was extremely high—Allerton, April 1996, 68 titles; 96th Street, April 1996, 124 titles; New Dorp, May 1996, 145 titles. Since few writing programs were offered at participating sites prior to the inception of *Poetry in the Branches*, it is hard to determine with numbers the impact this grant has had at the sites. But teens continue to come to the workshops—many are participants who have been to every workshop offered at each site. Submissions of poems for TeenTalk at the Allerton branch have risen significantly since June 1996 (the board became operational in April), with one to three poems submitted per week by area teens.

Funding

The project is funded by a major grant from the Lila Wallace—Reader's Digest Fund with the initial grant totaling $175,000 for three years. The first drawdown of funds was approximately $60,000, with over $50,000 of that going to the *Poetry in the Branches* project. The remainder of the drawdown went toward bringing the Poetry Publication Showcase mounted by Poets House to the ALA conference.

Contact Person

Caroline Bartels, Allerton Branch Library, The New York Public Library, 2740 Barnes Avenue, Bronx, NY 10467. (718) 881-4240

10.
Richmond Public Library

Richmond, British Columbia

Idea

Young Adult Writing Contest

Customers

Young adults, ages twelve through eighteen

Community

The municipality of Richmond has 12,442 students between the ages of twelve and eighteen enrolled in school. Canadian Census statistics do not give an age breakdown for this age range.

Setting

For over twenty years the Richmond Public Library has been providing innovative services to the community. Over one million visits were made to the library in 1995 and 106,000 residents actively use their Richmond Public Library cards out of a population base of 147,500. The library is committed to community outreach with over 30,000 people attending a variety of library programs in 1995, including 3,346 children who joined the library's Summer Reading Club. Richmond Public Library is the first public library in Canada to provide a full-service multimedia centre complete with Power Macs, Pentium computers and software packages for free use. In response to changing community needs Richmond Public Library has developed one of the best Chinese-language book collections in the Lower Mainland. Recent awards include: the British Columbia Library Association Award, for the development of a multimedia information kiosk; the Public Library Association Award, for a highly successful donation campaign for Chinese-language books; the Canadian Library Association Innovations Today Award, for the innovative use of technology; and the L. PeRCy Award from the Library Public Relations Council in New York, for the best design of an Internet website.

Program Description

The Richmond Public Library's *Young Adult Writing Contest*, now in its sixth year, has attracted 1,859 teen participants. The contest encourages young writers, promotes a good public image for teens, and provides a great opportunity for the library to establish effective partnerships in the community. The Richmond Public Library believes that programming for teens is an often neglected part of library services. Many resources are traditionally dedicated to preschoolers in public libraries. Unfortunately, teenagers have often been ignored. The *Young Adult Writing Contest* was developed to address this problem.

The contest encourages an interest in writing and reading among teenagers and provides a vehicle for self-expression. The contest confirms that young people are thoughtful and creative and wish to express their feelings and concerns about their world through the written word.

The *Young Adult Writing Contest* promotes a high level of community involvement. A partial list of the 1995 contest supporters includes: the Member of Parliament for Richmond; the mayor; city councillors; city departments; school board trustees, principals, and teachers; library board trustees, administration, and staff; and Rogers Community Cablevision.

Community businesses and community organizations sponsor cash prizes: four first-prize winners of $100; four second-prize winners of $75; four third-prize winners of $50; and four honourable prize winners of $25. Community businesses and organizations who have sponsored cash prizes or gift certificates include: Vancouver City Savings Credit Union; Richmond News; Friends of the Richmond Library; Jumpstart Scholarship Foundation; Friends of the Richmond Archives; Richmond Chinese Parents Association for Better Education; Canadian Chinese Radio; Kingstone Book (Canada) Co., Ltd.; Richmond Auto Mall; McDonald's Restaurants of Canada; Canada Safeway; India Cultural Centre of Canada; and United Library Services. These partnerships provide effective resources for improving literacy at the community level and also reflect the cultural diversity of the community.

Contest entry forms are distributed to every Richmond student between the ages of twelve and eighteen. This is achieved through a partnership with the Richmond School Board which distributes the entry forms with students' final report cards. The library also distributes contest entry forms to the private schools in Richmond. Entry forms are also available in the library over the summer months.

Individuals from the community also take part in the contest as judges. Past community judges who volunteered their time include members of the Richmond School Board, Richmond Public Library Board, Richmond Health Department, Richmond Writers' Club, Richmond Chamber of Commerce, and Richmond Community Services. In 1995 a partnership with Canada Post and the Canada Post Heritage Club was created. Canada Post has a continuing commitment to a literate Canada and previously sponsored another library initiative called "Born to Read." The money from the Canada Post sponsorship of the *Young Adult Writing Contest* was directed toward the cost of printing the publication containing the winning entries. Canada Post also absorbed the cost of mailing copies of the publication of winning entries to major public libraries across Canada and the United States. A cover letter describing the contest and its importance to the community was also included. This mailing resulted in requests from twelve library systems, in both Canada and the United States, for the contest program planning package.

The contest has also proven to be an effective vehicle for building partnerships with the Richmond School Board. Richmond teachers use the contest to encourage their students to work on writing skills and creative expression. The school board assists the library in the distribution of the contest entry flyer and each year a school board trustee takes a position as a community judge. Richmond schools with student enrollment between the ages of twelve and eighteen also receive a copy of the contest publication for their school library.

In 1994 the library contacted Rogers Community Cablevision to propose that they film the awards ceremony, which features the winners reading from their winning entries. Rogers Cablevision agreed to do this, and a half-hour program hosted by the young adult librarian was aired over their cablevision network. It is now an integral part of the *Young Adult Writing Contest* and has proved to be very popular. It has greatly raised the contest profile in the community and has reached audiences in a number of municipalities within the Lower Mainland.

The winning entries are published in a publication that is also available through the library's Internet website <http://www.rpl.richmond.bc.ca>. It is this recognition that means so much to the winners.

At the awards ceremony, the winners are invited to read from their entries and the library promotes the ceremony as part of the author reading series. The winners appreciate this public recognition of their status as Richmond's newest writers. The audience of almost two hundred people enjoy this entertaining evening. The awards ceremony is filmed by Rogers Community Cablevision and broadcast over their network. Rogers reaches the community at large including nonlibrary users and those who may not be aware of the talents and creativity of young adults.

All contest participants receive certificates from the library thanking them for entering and encouraging them to continue writing. Nancy Kwan, a winner of the 1995 contest, sent this thank you to the library:

> I wish to thank you and the members of the Richmond Public Library Board for giving me the opportunity to

---

Doing Homework

by Jamie Boak

Mind-numbing

Eyes-glazing

Neck-stiffening

Hand-cramping

Pen-emptying

Papers-filling

participate in the 5th Annual Young Writers' Contest. It was an honour to have my poem selected as the first place winner for the ages 15–18 category. I enjoyed meeting other writers and to have the chance to share in their writing. It is wonderful that people such as yourselves put in so much time to make the event a success. Thank you for making the event such a special and memorable one, and thanks for all your support. Keep up the good work!

The *Young Adult Writing Contest* requires approximately 270 staff hours. This includes planning, preparation of handouts, publicity, displays, short-listing entries, producing the *Young Adult Writing Contest* publication in paper and electronic format, and hosting the awards ceremony. Each year twelve to fourteen library staff members volunteer to be in-house judges. They read all submissions and short-list them for the community judges who determine the winners.

Youth participation in program implementation is done at the Youth Advisory Board level. Members of this organization volunteer each year to be final judges in the contest. Youth evaluation of the program has been done primarily by the contest winners, who are asked for their feedback. During the year, feedback is also obtained through patron suggestion forms and class visits. Evaluation sessions are conducted when the contest is over and involve the Deputy Chief Librarian, the Head of Youth Services, and the young adult librarian. These sessions focus on developing new initiatives to keep the contest evolving. Over the past six years refinements have included: (1) allowing teens to enter both a short story and a poem; (2) visiting Richmond schools to promote the contest; (3) including winners reading from their entries at the awards ceremony; (4) filming the awards ceremony through Rogers Community Cablevision; (5) inviting former contest winners to be judges in the current contest; (6) using graphic artists to design each year's contest flyer and poster; (7) creating an electronic database to register participants; (8) adding the winning entries to the library's website in text and RealAudio; and (9) allowing entry forms to be submitted electronically via the World Wide Web.

Funding

The material costs for the contest vary from year to year depending on the number of copies printed of the publication, the graphic artist's expenses, and author speaking fees for the Writer's Workshop held in conjunction with the contest each summer. In 1995 contest expenses totaled $3,428; they are listed below:

Graphic artist (flyer and poster design)	$ 400
Writer's Workshop (author speaking fee)	200
Publication (600 copies printed)	1,673
Flyers printed	670
Rogers Cablevision (four video copies of awards ceremony)	125
Photographer (for the awards ceremony)	160
Catering (of awards ceremony)	200

In 1995 financial assistance was received from Canada Post and the Canada Post Heritage Club who sponsored the contest to the amount of $1,300. The cost of staff time is calculated at 270 hours x an hourly rate of $23, which equals $6,210.

Contact Persons

Andrée Duval, Head of Youth Services, and Susan Henderson, Young Adult Librarian, 100 - 7700 Minoru Gate, Richmond, British Columbia V6Y 1R9, Canada. (604) 231-6411 or 6412

11.
San Diego Public Library, Scripps Miramar Ranch Library Center and Scripps Ranch High School

San Diego, California

Idea

Public library/high school collaboration: freshman English class orientations

Customers

Sixteen freshman English classes from Scripps Ranch High School

Community

According to census data provided by the San Diego Association of Governments (SANDAG), the Scripps Ranch community has a total population of 21,776, of whom 1,320 (6 percent) are ages fifteen through nineteen. The community is 9.6 percent Asian-American/other, 2 percent African-American, 6 percent Hispanic-American, and 82.3 percent Caucasian-American. The Scripps Ranch High School student population (grades 9–12) is quite diversified. Of the 1,850 students, 51.9 percent are Caucasian-American, 8.14 percent are African-American, .39 percent are American Indian, 29.76 percent are Asian/Asian-Indian/Filipino/Pacific Islander, and 10.53 percent are Hispanic/Portuguese. These figures include local residents and 125 participants in the Voluntary Ethnic Enrollment Program (VEEP). Of the 525 students participating in the freshman English class orientation program, 204 were Scripps Ranch residents, 223 were from Mira Mesa (a neighboring community), 62 were VEEP participants, and 36 were from other locations.

Setting

From October 1986 to February 1993, the Scripps Ranch community was served by a branch library in a storefront location; on March 13, 1993, the current Scripps Miramar Ranch Library Center opened: it has since consistently ranked seventh in circulation out of thirty-two branches (circulating 257,598 items in FY '96, or an average of twelve books per year for every community member).

Occupying a handsome Mission-revival style building, this versatile 21,700-square-foot branch library has a well-stocked print and nonprint collection for adults and children; the Ellen Browning Scripps Foundation Computer Laboratory, which has seven computers (Macs and PCs) and two laser printers; a large community meeting room; a variety of reading spaces, including an attractive outside courtyard; and a bookstore operated by Scripps Ranch Friends of the Library volunteers. There is strong community support for this popular branch which provides a variety of resources, including computer access to the Internet and online public-access catalogs.

Program Description

Scripps Miramar Ranch Library Center staff coordinated efforts with Scripps Ranch High School Librarian Gail Richmond to host library orientations for high school freshmen. Although the Scripps Ranch High School opened in September 1993, the computer-oriented school library media center continues to have an extremely limited book collection due to the low budget allocation ($4,500 for library materials, or $5.12 per student) and the need to spend funds on the purchase of new textbooks as student enrollment increases.

This class orientation program was designed to acquaint high school freshmen and their English instructors with the resources available through the San Diego Public Library system to complement and enhance their classroom instruction. The program evolved from the statewide reading initiative in California. Dr. Bertha Pendleton, Superintendent of the San Diego Unified School District, placed the acquisition of a library card by every district student in the fall 1995 district goals.

Responding to the goal, Scripps Ranch High School Librarian Gail Richmond and Scripps Miramar Ranch Library Center Branch Manager Nancy Assaf met and scheduled sixteen freshman English classes for libarary orientation visits, which would include the issuance of SD Public Library cards to students who needed them. Application forms were distributed to teachers, and 525 young adults, their teachers, and high school library staff participated in the program over the fall semester. Because the high school and branch library are in close proximity, students usually walked to the library for the orientation program. The orientation covered the following areas:

1. the process involved in obtaining a library card and patron responsibilities;
2. how to procure materials from other branches of the San Diego Public Library system;

3. how to utilize the dial-in service from a home computer with modem;
4. a review of library policies, including loan periods, renewals, fines, etc.;
5. descriptions and examples of different types of library material, including audiovisual resources and periodicals.

Tours encompassed the entire collection of the library and included:

1. demonstration of the online public access catalog (OPAC) with standard and keyword searching techniques;
2. demonstration of Infotrac Central 2000 (IAC) for periodical research;
3. demonstration of Magazine Collecting IAC in microfilm cartridge format for January 1983 through September 1995, utilizing a reader printer;
5. review of the reference collection, with emphasis on biographical resources and literary criticism;
6. a tour of the stacks, including the Career Center collection, young adult section, fiction and nonfiction areas, the CD-ROM computer homework center for teens, the Ellen Browning Scripps Foundation Computer Lab, and the Book Nook, operated by the Scripps Ranch Friends of the Library.

Library staff facilitated the application process so that all students were assured a current library card. Scripps Ranch High School English faculty also learned how San Diego Public Library's resources could enhance their classroom teaching, and how special loan periods could be arranged for videocassettes used in presenting special units for class work.

This project was an important outreach effort, supporting the educational goals of the nearby community high school and introducing students to a wide range of library resources that they can utilize for the rest of their lives. Another benefit, less anticipated but very important, was the mutual respect that developed between library staff and school faculty and students.

Three library staff members (Branch Manager, Youth Services Librarian, Reference Services Library Assistant) led the program and provided tours. Three library clerks processed library card applications and provided circulation services. Two library aides replaced and shelved any materials used during the course of the program.

Feedback from the pilot program helped to develop the next series of orientation programs. Evaluation of the pilot program was informal, with students indicating that they enjoyed the orientation, learned valuable information and study skills, and felt they would be more comfortable utilizing the library's facilities and materials in the future. Library staff noticed a positive change in student attitudes and library behavior after the orientations.

Members of the Scripps Ranch High School faculty reported to School Librarian Gail Richmond that they were favorably impressed with the project and enthusiastic about continuing orientations for freshman classes. In the second year of the program, formal feedback from faculty and students is being elicited.

Funding

The project was fully funded by the San Diego Public Library. For this pilot project, existing materials were used and the only expenditures incurred were staff salaries. Staff time for preparation and presentations is as follows: (1) Branch Manager (preparation, presentation, tour) thirty hours; (2) Youth Services Librarian (presentation, tour) sixteen hours; (3) Reference Services Library Assistant (presentation, tour) sixteen hours; (4) Library Clerks (application processing, circulation) ten hours; (5) Library Aides (shelving) two hours. Salaries and wages (including fringe benefits) total approximately $1,935.

Contact Person

Nancy Corbin Assaf, Branch Manager, Scripps Miramar Ranch Library Center, 10301 Scripps Lake Drive, San Diego, CA 92131. (619) 538-8158

Education Support

12.
Brooklyn Public Library, Main Youth Services Division

Brooklyn, New York

Idea

Math Peer Tutoring Center

Customers

Middle and high school students who need help with mathematics, grades seven through twelve

Community

According to *Demographic Profiles: A Portrait of New York City's Community Districts from the 1980 & 1990 Censuses of Population and Housing* (New York City Planning Commission, 1992), there are over 30,000 young adults (twelve- through eighteen-year-olds) in the neighborhood surrounding the Central Library; the vast majority of these young adults are either African-American or Afro-Caribbean. The Central Library does, however, serve the entire borough of Brooklyn; students from high schools throughout the borough come to use the building's extensive collection and reference facilities. There are 230,000 twelve- through eighteen-year-olds in the borough of Brooklyn; 29 percent of the general population is foreign born.

Setting

The Brooklyn Public Library (BPL) is a community institution serving a culturally diverse population of 2.3 million people. It is the fifth largest public library system in the United States with fifty-eight branches, a Business Library, and the Central Library.

The Central Library at Grand Army Plaza is the main reference center of the BPL system. Each year more than two million people—almost the entire population of Brooklyn—use the Central Library. On Sundays, about twelve thousand people use the building in the four hours it is open.

The Central Library houses more than three million books, tapes, periodicals, videos, and CD-ROMs. In October 1996, the library opened a twelve-terminal, state-of-the-art computer center with Internet access through the "Libraries Online" program. In addition to providing top-notch youth services, the Central Library offers patrons access to an extensive art and music collection, the morgue of the Brooklyn *Daily Eagle*, award-winning adult literacy classes, career counseling, homework help, and the comprehensive resources of the Education, Job, and Computer Center.

Program Description

The *Math Peer Tutoring Center* is an after-school drop-in program for seventh through twelfth graders at the Central Library of the Brooklyn Public Library. A 1996 spring pilot program was held in cooperation with neighboring Prospect Heights High School. Three twelfth grade students volunteered as peer tutors in mathematics one afternoon a week for the spring semester. All three students came highly recommended by their mathematics teachers; after being interviewed, they attended a one-hour orientation program and received written guidelines and a three-way agreement between the student, the school, and the library. Tutors received community service credit from the school for participating in the program.

Equipped with a variety of math textbooks and review books, as well as rulers, graph paper, and miscellaneous supplies, tutors helped middle and high school students with math homework and studying for twelve consecutive weeks. At the height

Special Event

MATH PEER TUTORING CENTER

Free one-to-one help with math for 7th-12th graders

Sponsored by Main Youth Services

Mondays, 4-5 pm
(when NYC public high schools are in session)
through June 10, 1996

Main Youth Services
Central Library
Grand Army Plaza
(718) 780-7719

Brooklyn Public Library

---

of the season, each tutor juggled five or six students an hour in a small program room off the front lobby of the Central Library. In fall 1996 the program was moved to the auditorium, a much larger space, with ten individual tables and eight tutors, four boys and four girls, tenth through twelfth graders from different high schools all over Brooklyn. The expanded program makes it possible to advertise the *Math Peer Tutoring Center* to the many middle schools, high schools, and youth centers in the neighborhood, resulting in better service to young adult patrons.

Thousands of young adults come to the Youth Services Division of the Central Library each month during the school year for homework help. While the library provides reference and circulating materials to support most academic subject areas, math is one area in which the collection and resources remain lacking. Private math tutoring can be prohibitively expensive to most students, and high school math is a subject in which most parents and librarians lack sufficient knowledge or familiarity to be of assistance. The *Math Peer Tutoring Center* gives students the opportunity to get much-needed help in a demanding academic subject area at no charge in a relaxed, welcoming atmosphere. Students learn from their peers, a situation that is beneficial to both tutor and tutee. The tutor reinforces and strengthens his or her own math skills by explaining and demonstrating, gains pride and self-confidence by helping others, and often makes new friends in the process. The tutee gets free, quality one-to-one help from a nonthreatening peer tutor in a friendly, nonjudgmental environment. Even those schools that offer math tutoring usually offer group sessions in which students must wait their turn to ask for help. At the *Math Peer Tutoring Center* all students get individual help with their questions and problems. If a tutor has trouble with a particular problem, other tutors are consulted, so that all participants get the help they need. The program also shows the young adults in the community that the library cares about their needs and is trying to help them. As of this year, all New York City high school students are required to take Sequential Mathematics I, II, and III and pass State Regents Exams at the end of each course. Students who fail to pass these three exams will not be able to graduate from high school. Particularly in the low-income, minority neighborhoods that the Central Library serves, empowering these young adults to pass math and graduate from high school is a vital service to the community.

The *Math Peer Tutoring Center* served 137 young adults in the twelve one-hour sessions offered in spring 1996. Since the fall of 1996, with an almost 300 percent increase in the number of tutors and the larger space, the library is serving many more students who need help.

Aside from the three volunteer tutors, Barbara Auerbach was the only staff member involved in the program. She conceived of the center as a pre-promotional training project and recruited, interviewed, oriented, and supervised the tutors all semester. She also served as a liaison with Prospect Heights High School and developed all the written materials connected with the program.

A survey of one hundred young adult patrons revealed that 84 percent of the students surveyed would come to a program at the library that provided free math peer tutoring for middle and high school students. The first idea for the program occurred when a part-time staff member approached Auerbach for help with her math homework. Auerbach soon guessed that there were many students in the library who could benefit from such a program. Her own peer tutoring experience at the Writing Center in college had been both gratifying and worthwhile, leading to the decision to use peer tutors at the Math Center. At the tutor orientation, the tutors suggested certain review titles geared toward the New York State Regents Exams for purchase. In addition, they decided what supplies were needed each week.

The pilot program was informally evaluated by means of program attendance, tutor feedback, feedback from the math and guidance departments at Prospect Heights High School, and the many telephone requests received and continuing to be received about the program. While there are no statistics about students' math averages before and after attending the program, the fact that the program quickly acquired so many "regulars" who came week after week offered assurance about the quality of the program. This year, however, there is a plan to survey tutors and patrons at mid-year and again in June. The program has already been replicated at the Red Hook Branch of the Brooklyn Public Library.

Funding

The program was modestly funded with a petty cash reimbursement from the Central Office. In addition, the Youth Services division purchased multiple copies of the Sequential Mathematics Regents Review books, the cost of which came out of the division's book budget. The only other expenses were for basic supplies: loose-leaf paper, graph paper, rulers, compasses, protractors, scientific calculators, pencils, erasers, and erasable pens; the total cost was under $75. Each tutor was equipped with, and responsible for, the above supplies. Ideally, the center should have a special reference collection of math books and texts as well as CD-ROMs offering math drill, review, and problem solving. SAT software might also be appropriate.

Contact Person

Barbara Auerbach, Main Youth Services Division, Brooklyn Public Library, Grand Army Plaza, Brooklyn, New York 11238. (718) 780-7719

Information Services

13.
Berkeley Public Library
Berkeley, California

Idea
Teen Services homepage
<http.//www.ci.berkeley.ca.us/bpl/teen>

Customers
Young adults, ages thirteen through eighteen

Community
The library serves a population of 104,700, just under 10 percent of which is school age (five to seventeen years old). The high school population is 10 percent Asian-American or Pacific Islander, 11 percent Latino, 39 percent African-American, and 40 percent Caucasian. There is a wide range of income levels in this university community, and about 16 percent of the community lives below the poverty line.

Setting
The Berkeley Public Library serves the city of Berkeley with a central library, four neighborhood branch libraries, and a tool lending library. Its 213 employees fill 122.45 full-time equivalent positions to serve 116,236 registered borrowers. The library is open sixty-four hours a week and experiences 1,454,350 visits annually.

Program Description
Before constructing the homepage, Teen Services staff made three decisions: (1) design the site to reflect the structure and philosophy of BPL Teen Services; (2) direct the site at teens, not professionals; and (3) focus on substantive sites.

The homepage is essentially an overview of Teen Services. It functions as a selective index to sites of interest to teenagers. It is divided into nine categories. *Programs* details offerings of BPL Teen Services. *Reviews by Teens* features local teens' analyses of books and music and includes reviews from all over the country. *Recommended for Teens* contains annotated booklists produced by Teen Services staff. *More Reading Links* points users to annotated reading lists compiled by teachers, librarians, writers, and a broad range of other educators. *Magazines* points to online 'zines, arranged in rough subject categories. *Internet Sites* guides teen users to art, music, ethnic resources, movies and TV, games, comics, science, sports, and sexuality resources on the net. *High School* features a link to the local high school and to other secondary schools on the Web. Arranged geographically, *Library Links* plugs users into other public libraries with homepages specifically designed for teenagers. *College Info* directs users to financial aid and scholarship information, and to local, national, and international colleges and universities.

The site, which was posted in April 1996, undergoes constant revision. It is seen as a logical electronic extension of the services already offered to teenagers at the Berkeley Public Library. It fits very nicely into the library's mission to provide access to information.

Site construction was labor intensive, requiring one Teen Services librarian for two months' work. Maintenance continues to be labor intensive. A Teen Services librarian spends approximately eight hours

> **Berkeley Public Library**
> ## *Teen Services*
>
> **Recommended by teens, for teens**
>
> - **Cover to Cover reviews**
>   Reviews from teens who participate in our annual reading program
> - **Book & music reviews from YAAC**
>   Written by members of BPL's teenaged advisory board - the Young Adult Advisory Committee
> - **Reviews from all over**
>   From various places around the country
>
> ---
>
> **Want to let others know what you think about a book, tape or CD?**
>
> **Send your review to kayf@netcom.com** at Berkeley Public Library Teen Services.
> **Note**: if you are using the Berkeley Public Library's Internet workstation in the library, this won't work for you. Hand in your review the old-fashioned way, in person.
>
> ---
>
> **HOME**
>
> Berkeley Public Library Teen Services pages: http://www.ci.berkeley.ca.us/bpl/teen/
> maintained by Kay Finney - kayf@netcom.com
> Last modified: *May 20, 1996*

a month evaluating the content of new sites. A student worker, who attends Berkeley High School, spends twelve to fifteen hours each month searching the net for appropriate sites, reviewing sites, deleting dead links, and revising HTML code. The student worker is a regular employee of the library, working eight to ten hours each week assisting and advising the Teen Services librarian. The home-page invites teens to send in their own book and music reviews.

Funding

The site was developed in 1996 with no extra internal or external funding. Berkeley Public Library participates in the InfoPeople project, a grant funded by the California State Library, which in 1995 paid for an Internet workstation at each of the four branch libraries. These dedicated terminals are available free of charge to BPL patrons fifty-seven hours each week. The grant also paid for a number of training sessions. Carole Leita, a nationally recognized Internet expert and reference/Internet librarian at the Berkeley Public Library, was, and continues to be, generous with assistance. Internet access at BPL is the result of cooperation, facilitated by the Internet Librarian, among Berkeley Public Library, the City of Berkeley, and the University of California at Berkeley. The files reside on the City of Berkeley server.

Contact Person

Kay Finney, Teen Services/Reference Librarian, Berkeley Public Library, South Branch, 1901 Russell Street, Berkeley, CA 94703. (510) 644-6860

14. Cumberland County Public Library and Information Center

Fayetteville, North Carolina

Idea

Inform U

Customers

High school students needing more information about different aspects of college

Community

The population of Cumberland County is 300,893. Fayetteville is the fourth largest metropolitan area in North Carolina. Cumberland County is the home of Fort Bragg and Pope Air Force Base. Fort Bragg is the largest United States Army installation in the country in terms of population with 49,986. The county is rapidly growing because more military installations are being added. The Army recently purchased 11,000 acres to expand Fort Bragg, and a $250-million medical center is currently being built. The economy is heavily dependent upon government, and the library system serves as the public library for thousands of military families.

There are 28,245 people between the ages of twelve and eighteen in Cumberland County. Of that number, 530 are American Indian, Eskimo, or Aleu, 579 are Asian or Pacific Islander, 10,504 are African-American, 1,275 are Hispanic, 14,707 are Caucasian, and 650 are other races. Twenty-eight percent of the entire Cumberland County population is under the age of eighteen. Surveys of high school students show that almost half of the seniors plan to attend college. The high school drop-out rate is 2.90. The SAT total score for Cumberland County was 815 in 1995. There are twelve middle schools, eight high schools, several private schools, a populous home school association, and plans to build new public schools due to overcrowding.

Setting

Cumberland County Public Library and Information Center is a system consisting of the Headquarters library, six branch libraries, and bookmobile service. Branch libraries are located in Fayetteville, Spring Lake, Hope Mills, and Stedman, North Carolina. Groundbreaking for a new library occurred in July 1996, and plans have been approved to build two more in the near future. The staff includes 33 professionals and 122 paraprofessionals. The system-wide collection consists of 191,721 book titles, 354,168 volumes, 1,163 periodical and newspaper subscriptions, 93,694 paperback books, 23 CD-ROM titles, 4,290 compact discs, 4,769 video recordings, and 8,608 audiotapes. A homepage is maintained at <http://www.cumberland.lib.nc.us>. Computer terminals provide access to CD-ROMs and Netscape at the Headquarters and Cliffdale locations, with a WAN in progress for other locations. Last year, 2,015,110 materials were loaned, 169,534 customers attended library programs, and 141,924 Cumberland County residents and nonresidents were library card holders.

Program Description

A program series called *Inform U* filled a gap in providing students with information about different aspects of college and college life. In 1995 and 1996, a total of 148 young adults attended *Inform U* sessions. The project was promoted to young adults at area schools and libraries.

Claire Fitzgerald, former Information Services Librarian I at the Cliffdale library, created and implemented *Inform U*. Sadly, she died tragically in April 1996 in an automobile accident. Community involvement and collaboration have been achieved by the presentation of speakers from area universities and colleges. All were volunteers and included the associate director of admissions at Methodist College, the director of admissions at Fayetteville State University, the director of financial aid at Methodist College, a professor at the University of North Carolina at Chapel Hill, the assistant director of admissions at Methodist College, and students from the Chancellor's scholarship program at Fayetteville State University.

Inform U was planned to meet an obvious need among young adults for information about college. This need was documented through an analysis of reference transactions at the Cliffdale Library and circulation statistics throughout the Cumberland County Public Library and Information Center system. Part of the success of *Inform U* relied on questions that were asked of the speakers by the young adults present. Also, the question-and-answer period of the last session, "Part 4: What's the Difference (Between High School and College)?" depended upon young adults who voiced their concerns and questions to current college students. Everyone attending was asked to complete an evaluation form.

A four-part College Series, presents...

Part 1: CHOOSING A COLLEGE

Monday, January 9th
7:30 pm at the Cliffdale Branch Library

An Admissions Counselor from Methodist College will discuss how to choose the college that is right for you.

Call 864-3800 for more information

Coming Up in February... Part 2: Getting In

Evaluations and further audience information were collected at all *Inform U* sessions. The following is a sampling of 1995 evaluation responses: *Program ratings*: great (28), all right (14), really bad (0). *Other topics of interest*: women—how to move up to the next level in a job, going back to school, career planning, scholarships and Pell grants, symposium by the director of financial aid from another college, graduate school information, anything and everything for teens, more teen programs, self-help, motivational, how to go step-by-step of entering college, ways to get a scholarship (e.g., essay), anything related to teens and careers, law, continue college programs, seeing the specific topics colleges want for college acceptance, scholarship seminars, nursing programs, specific topics on colleges, programs that correspond with curriculum. *How can the library better serve teens?* Respondents answered more programs (2), food, SAT II: Subject Test study books!!, keeping us up-to-date, have more books on SAT, ACT, and college information, junior high and senior high curriculum, access to the information superhighway, computers and software available for use, get creative in a positive manner to promote teen-directed activities, curriculum-based programs, programs similar to the already existing "Great Books Group" for adults, think you're doing fine, fine as is, Internet service would be great, study skills. Other comments included: very interesting, liked a lot, Mr. Rice informative and personable, great program, thanks for the information packet and the guidelines.

The program, repeated in 1996, has made differences in the lives of young adults because they are more prepared for the real atmosphere of college, for applying for financial aid, and for admission requirements. Most important, young adults were exposed to the library as an information place, an especially useful tip when attending college.

Funding

The project was funded by the library budget, and the only cost, besides staff hours, was advertising. Four different flyers, one for each segment of the series, were produced and distributed to high schools and local libraries. The total cost of the program was less than one hundred dollars.

Contact Person

Sheila Anderson, 300 Maiden Lane, Fayetteville, NC 28301-5000. (910) 483-7878, ext. 225

15. Cuyahoga County Public Library

Parma, Ohio

Idea

Teenage Survival Guide

Customers

Young adults, ages thirteen through eighteen, including at-risk and special needs

Community

In Cuyahoga County there are over 1.4 million people, of whom over 123,000 are young adults between the ages of twelve and eighteen. The communities within the county are fairly diverse in terms of cultural backgrounds, including 24.8 percent African Americans, 2.2 percent Hispanic Americans, and 1.3 percent Asian Americans. The average household income is just over $35,000, with only 10 percent of the total household population living below the poverty level.

Setting

Cuyahoga County Public Library (CCPL) is one of the nation's ten busiest library systems, with twenty-nine locations serving forty-seven distinct suburban

TEENAGE SURVIVAL GUIDE

Cuyahoga County Public Library.
It's more than you think.

communities in the Cleveland Metropolitan area. CCPL has staffed a separate Young Adult (YA) Services Department for more than twenty years, with professional YA librarians in every branch.

Program Description

The agenda for the Federation for Community Planning, a nonprofit planning agency in the Cleveland community, includes seven key points for children, youth, and families: (1) public/private coalitions must be formed to advocate for youth; (2) early childhood services need to be expanded; (3) services for the abused and neglected must be improved; (4) services for juvenile sex offenders must be improved; (5) runaways and homeless youth need safe shelter and crisis services; (6) overcrowded conditions in juvenile correctional facilities must be addressed; and (7) aftercare services need to be strengthened with emphasis on education and related support services.

While the library cannot address or have a direct impact on all of these, the *Teenage Survival Guide* is an important first intervention step for youth in crisis. The *Guide* is updated annually by five to ten YA staff members. In 1995–96, 6,500 *Guides* were printed and distributed through the system's branches and regionals, reaching many thousands of teenagers who either took a copy or were given information from the *Guide*. In addition, two thousand copies were sold to thirty-two community agencies and schools.

Each year the project rotates from one region of the library system to another and is coordinated by the Regional Young Adult Services Manager and the YA staff in that region. To keep the *Guide* current, each agency is contacted to verify name, address, phone number, contact person(s), services provided, costs, and whether or not services require parental consent. The staff also approaches new agencies and agencies that have been suggested by teenagers for inclusion. This process has proven to be very effective in keeping the *Guide* vital and useful.

CCPL has not formally evaluated this service, but each year additional schools, agencies, and teenagers request copies of the *Guide*. This is thought to be the only service of its kind in Cuyahoga County. It is one of the most successful services offered by Cuyahoga County Public Library's Young Adult Services Department, both in terms of usefulness and popular demand, as well as in terms of the time and money commitment made to its production. The *Guide* is now planned as an ongoing service.

Funding

The *Guide* is funded by CCPL, with materials and printing costs totaling $800. Updating the *Guide* is part of the staff's regularly assigned tasks, so no additional moneys are required to cover that cost.

Contact Person

Candace Bundy, Cuyahoga County Public Library System, Fairview Park Regional, 4449 West 213th Street, Fairview Park, OH 44126-2189. (216) 333-4700

16.
Newport Beach Public Library

Newport Beach, California

Idea

YouthNet

Customers

Young adults, grades seven through twelve

Community

The local adolescent population is 90.4 percent Caucasian, 5.2 percent Hispanic, 3.8 percent Asian and .4 percent African-American. Newport Beach is an oceanside community with a stable population of 70,098 residents (4,500 of whom are young adults enrolled in local schools) with an average household income of $61,865. Young adults between ages fourteen and twenty-four comprise 12.2 percent of the population. Over 46 percent of adults in the community have earned college degrees.

Setting

The Newport Beach City Library system was formally established in 1920. It now includes a 54,000-square-foot central library opened in 1994 and three branch libraries. The central library includes a young adult section offering paperback books and magazines specifically suited to adolescents. A system collection of over 278,000 materials has a 1.3 million annual (18 per capita) circulation. The system serves over 927,000 customers each year.

Program Description

YouthNet is a cooperative project of the Newport Beach Public Library, the Newport/Mesa Unified School District, and two private junior high schools. The project provides an intelligent modem device at the Newport Beach Central Library by which students in grades seven through twelve, as well as teachers and librarians at six local schools, can access the library's online catalog, Wide Area Network, and the Internet. Each school provides a 386 computer, modem, and dedicated telephone line.

YouthNet has made effective use of the library's technological and resource-sharing capabilities and enhanced its cooperative relationship and communication with local schools. By making it possible for junior and senior high school students to access library resources without leaving campus, it has encouraged use of the library by young adults. Instruction in use of library resources has made the library more user-friendly to students and raised students' and teachers' awareness about information accessible through the library's online catalog and Wide Area Network, as well as the Internet. Besides helping to meet the informational needs of 4,500 local students, *YouthNet* has provided a critical link for students with disabilities at all schools and students with special learning needs who attend the Alternative Education Center.

Two part-time librarians were assigned to the project. Their duties included visiting all targeted schools to provide a total of twenty-five technology and library resource orientation sessions with teachers, school librarians, and students. The library's Youth and Branch Services Manager and a full-time reference librarian, plus a representative from the Management Information Systems department, conducted five *YouthNet* Nights at the library to familiarize students with resource use in a public library setting. Student members of the library's Young Adult Advisory Council served as hosts and tour guides for their peers at these events. At least one follow-up visit was made by a librarian to each of the six schools to monitor effectiveness of the project.

Over six hundred online searches made from local schools indicate participation by significant numbers of junior and senior high school students. In addition, twenty members of the library's Young Adult Advisory Council produced posters publiciz-

YouthNet Night at the Central Library, led by student instructor Grant Gochnauer.

ing *YouthNet* Nights at the library and served as hosts and tour guides at these events. Hundreds of *YouthNet* Night teenage guests participated in instructional games at these programs.

After accessing the library from their school, students, teachers, and school librarians complete a questionnaire about satisfaction with the system. Oral surveys will also be conducted. Computer-generated statistics are being used to measure use of reference resources. Dynix-generated statistics will continue to be used to measure student use of library materials and services.

Funding

YouthNet is funded by a $40,000 Title III grant from the California State Library's Library Services and Construction Act.

Contact Person

Judy Kelley, Newport Beach Public Library, 1000 Avocado Avenue, Newport Beach, CA 92660. (714) 717-3807.

17. Toledo-Lucas County Public Library

Toledo, Ohio

Idea

Youth Connection

Customers

Young adults, ages twelve through eighteen, their parents, and other adults who work with teens

Community

Lucas County has a total of 45,484 teens between twelve and eighteen. 26,481 live within the Toledo city limits; 20,051 are above poverty level, 5,826 below.

Setting

The Toledo-Lucas County Public Library consists of a main library, eighteen branches, and two bookmobiles, as well as libraries in correctional institutions. The Lucas County area serves seven school districts and a large group of parochial schools. The area is multicultural, economically diverse, and about equally divided between urban and suburban.

Program Description

Youth Connection provides materials and programs on teen crisis topics to teens, teachers, parents, schools, and agencies in the Toledo-Lucas Public Library service area. Started in response to a "sound-off" survey that was part of the Summer Reading Program in 1994 and resulted in the establishment of an interagency adult advisory board, the program includes five sections: (1) a notebook containing volunteers information, self-help bibliographies, and names and locations of agencies serving teens housed in the YA sections of all branches and the Main Library; (2) a book collection of fiction and nonfiction on crisis topics at all reading levels; (3) a pamphlet collection of materials dealing with social problems available free at branches; (4) kits containing books, tapes, and instructional materials on fifteen topics for use by agencies, teachers, parents, and teen groups; and (5) ongoing programs using the materials at schools, libraries, and agencies.

Youth Connection materials have been used to provide programs throughout the county for teens who are not regular library users. Examples include the Mayor's Youth Summit, a Local Interagency Transition Team, four Ohio Department of Youth Services workshops for teens on probation and parole, Phillips AME Church, Springfield High School's Peace Day, the Braden United Methodist Youth Summit, an "Act on Violence" town hall meeting with WGTE Public Broadcasting in Toledo, and a YMCA "Family First" program.

The program has met the needs of young adults and adults in the county in several different ways: the enthusiastic use of the collections and attendance at programs by teens, and collaboration with agencies not traditionally paired with libraries, such as the Health Department, Alcohol and Drug Rehabilitation, local churches, Planned Parenthood, and United Way.

Attendance at programs has been over six thousand, plus those young adults in schools where teachers and guidance counselors have checked out kits monthly. The teachers particularly like the copyright-free sheets included in each kit, which can be used to make individual packets to meet particular students' needs. All books in the YC collections have circulated at least once, many used to the point of needing replacement.

Youth Connection is administered by the young adult specialist as an ongoing part of her job.

Funding

The project was originally funded through an LSCA Title I Major Urban Resource Library grant totaling $35,000, which was spent on materials and equipment. Staff time came out of the library's personnel budget and replacement materials from the regular YA budget.

Contact Person

Betsy Fried, Special Services, Toledo-Lucas County Public Library, 501 River Road, Maumee, OH 43537. (419) 259-5315

**TOLEDO-LUCAS COUNTY PUBLIC LIBRARY
ANNOUNCES
YOUTH CONNECTION
MATERIALS FOR TEENS IN CRISIS**

Youth Connection is a grant received by the Toledo-Lucas County Public Library to provide multi-media materials for teens in crisis. There are four basic sections to the grant.

• **YOUTH CONNECTION NOTEBOOK**
A notebook housed in the Young Adult Section of all branches and the Literature Department at Main Library contains information on locations where teens can go for help as well as a list of places where teens can volunteer and bibliographies of materials that can be used for self-help.

• **BOOK COLLECTION**
Each library houses a special collection of materials dealing with social problems. These are available in a variety of formats at different reading levels. The collection includes both fiction and non-fiction.

• **PAMPHLET COLLECTION**
Each library has a collection of pamphlets dealing with social problems. These can be used in the library or they can be taken by the teens for personal use.

• **YOUTH CONNECTION KITS**
Fifteen kits dealing with social problems are available for checkout by adults working with teens and pre-teens. Each kit contains videos, books, pamphlets and instructional material as well as a list of local agencies available for teens. The kits are intended for use by parents, teachers, youth group workers or any adult working with teens. They can be checked out on any adult library card. Kits may be reserved and sent to any Branch by calling Betsy Fried at 259-5389 or 259-5315. Topics include:

- SUBSTANCE ABUSE
- SEXUALITY
- TEEN PREGNANCY
- STD'S
- HEALTH AND NUTRITION
- DEATH AND LOSS
- MENTAL HEALTH
- VIOLENCE
- LIFE SKILLS
- FAMILY
- LEGAL PROBLEMS, RUNAWAYS
- CULTURAL SENSITIVITY
- EDUCATION
- RELATIONSHIPS

Intergenerational

18.
Clermont County Public Library
Batavia, Ohio

Idea

Sidekicks: Kids and Seniors Together

Customers

Children and young adults, grades four through twelve, with high school youth serving as "advisors"

Community

According to OKI Regional Council of Governments statistics compiled in 1990, Clermont County had 18,742 children between the ages of ten through seventeen, or 12 percent of the total county population of 150,187. The majority of the adolescent population is Caucasian; there are very few minority youth within the county. Recent statistics indicate that 11.9 percent of youth live below the poverty line. While the western side of the county has experienced the most population growth, parts of the more rural eastern side are rapidly growing as two east-west corridors provide access from home to work. The county is federally designated as Appalachian.

Setting

Clermont County Public Library is located in one of the fastest-growing counties in southwestern Ohio. Within this system of nine community-based branches, librarians are encouraged to develop a strong program of community outreach. Interagency cooperation has been a rewarding avenue, particularly with this program. The library won a National Achievement Citation from PLA in 1995 for this program.

Each branch has a team of two youth services librarians responsible for delivery of programs and services and selection of materials for ages birth through teens. A Youth Services Coordinator provides support and training to each team.

Program Description

Sidekicks: Kids and Seniors Together provides young people with opportunities to learn about issues of aging, to build upon innate desires to be of service, and to communicate the value of an individual's volunteer efforts. The program was jointly conceived and executed by a branch of the library and a county senior services agency in 1992. Since then, Clermont Senior Services, Inc., has worked with additional branches to recruit and train additional *Sidekicks* groups.

Specific objectives of the program are to: (1) provide training in aging awareness issues; (2) suggest opportunities for community volunteering; and (3) assist young people in implementing individual branch service projects to nursing homes and senior centers. Senior Services, Inc., provides the training, and librarians facilitate the volunteer opportunities and projects aspect.

Over the four years of this program, there have been numerous anecdotes about participants' experiences. The program has tended to attract youth who have few social and academic activities from which to earn recognition and social skills. In some instances, the librarian has become the confidante or parent figure who helps ease the load of adolescence. One graduate of the program became a library page after the program and is serious about pursuing a career in library science!

The relationships that develop between the Sidekicks and seniors are often touching, particularly when youth participants encounter the death of a newly made friend. *Sidekicks* has led to other volun-

> **Grades 4-12**
>
> **YO! KIDS COMING**
>
> July 15, 22, 29
> 2:00 - 3:30 pm
>
> **SIDEKICKS**
> KIDS & SENIORS TOGETHER
>
> - Find out what **YOU** can do to brighten the lives of our senior citizens.
> - Find out how **GOOD** it feels to give.
>
> The Sidekicks program is a series of training sessions that prepare young people for special projects with senior citizens.
>
> Registration accepted through July 15
>
> *On August 13 we will wrap up our summer SideKicks program with a barn dance for the Sidekicks and Clermont County Seniors.*
>
> **AMELIA BRANCH**
> **Clermont County Public Library**
> 58 Maple Street
> Amelia, Ohio 45102
> Phone: 752-5580
>
> *Co-sponsored by Clermont Senior Services, Inc. and Clermont County Public Library*

teer opportunities with seniors. Last summer, librarians watched with delight as seniors and Sidekicks exchanged hugs and smiles after a rousing square dance.

On average, each branch has maintained the interest of ten youth during the course of the program. Three branches participated in 1996; four in 1995. A youth services librarian at each branch location was responsible for recruiting youth and managing the group's volunteer activities. Library materials are utilized in planning activities and brief booktalks are often given to the youth. The library's publicity department prepared flyers for distribution. A Senior Services, Inc., staff member was utilized at each branch to offer the aging issues training; the branches' training schedules were staggered in order to schedule multiple sessions.

The culminating activity for *Sidekicks* is participation in a large intergenerational social event. At this event, youth are primed on their roles as hosts and hostesses. They are encouraged to mingle and converse with seniors, participate in the games that may be too physically challenging for the seniors, become dance partners, serve meals and drinks, and tell tall tales.

In the summer of 1996, an "Old-Fashioned Barn Dance" included square dancing, games, and a liars' contest. This big event required the cooperation of librarians and Senior Services, Inc., staff. Since the majority of participants in the events were seniors, the agency used their center directors and other agency staff to provide transportation and assist at the event.

The program demands youth participation in the selection of, preparation for, and implementation of a group project at the branch level. Projects have ranged from performances at senior centers by a kazoo band, assembling "memory" boxes or joke bags to be delivered with Meals on Wheels, and visits to nursing homes by Sidekicks and their pets. Groups visiting nursing homes are prepared for the range of disabilities that will be encountered.

Evaluations by former staff, youth, and senior participants are available to librarians who have not yet participated in the program. The library and Senior Services, Inc., have engaged in informal evaluation of the previous year's program during planning meetings.

The initial group continued activities throughout the school year, meeting regularly at their library branch, and several youth continued with the program for a couple of years. Subsequent groups have met only in the summer and have attracted new members each time.

Funding

Staff time, craft supplies, refreshments for meetings, publicity flyers, and mileage to centers or nursing homes for individual *Sidekicks* projects compose the expenses for the library. Expenses for the big event have been funded by a grant from the Greater Cincinnati Foundation. The grant has been received each year since the inception of the program.

Cost per branch: Service Specialist (paraprofessional) salary, 26 hours (twice weekly meetings, craft preparation, individual project, big event participation) x $11.25 hourly rate = $292.50. Refreshments, $15 (these are thrifty people). Craft supplies $25. Mileage to project site, 30 miles (to cover two cars) x $.24 = $7.20. Publicity flyers (paste-up, printing/cutting, duplicating, paper) $30.

Total estimated project cost per branch: $369.70

Contact Person

Jody Risacher, Clermont County Public Library, 326 Broadway Street, Batavia, OH 45103. (513) 732-2736

Reading Promotion

19.
Allen County Public Library
Fort Wayne, Indiana

Idea
Enter . . . the Reading Zone

Customers
Students in grades six through twelve

Community
According to the 1990 census, 35,188 young people ages twelve through eighteen reside in Allen County. The county's young adults live in rural areas where there is a significant population of Amish and Old Order Mennonite, in small towns, and in the city of Fort Wayne. Approximately 10 percent are African-American. The majority of young adults are enrolled in the county's four public school systems, the largest being the city system. However, the Catholic, Lutheran, and Christian school systems are very active, and the number of families who homeschool is growing rapidly. The graduation rate for the county is in the 81 to 85 percent range, though not all schools report that data.

Setting
The Allen County Public Library, located in northeast Indiana, serves a population of 319,000. The main library and thirteen branches house a collection of over two million books, newspapers, CDs, musical scores, recorded books, and more. The library is a government document depository, has the second largest genealogy collection in the country, and houses the local cable television public and governmental access channel studios. ACPL has a separate young adult department that has been in operation for over twenty years. Circulation of all library materials for 1996 was over 4,000,000.

Program Description
The Young Adult Summer Reading Program, *Enter . . . the Reading Zone*, was designed to promote the pleasures of reading, to bring teens into the library, and to introduce them to all the library has to offer. Research conducted by Jack Humphrey (1992) for the Middle Grades Reading Network in 460 of Indiana's secondary schools and published by the Indiana Youth Institute found that access to current and appropriate books is vital to increasing reading proficiency and voluntary reading and that cooperative programming between school and public libraries must occur if young people are to be well served. An assessment done by Langer for the Educational Testing Service in 1990 showed that interest in books decreases as students advance through school and that teens who have more access to books have higher reading proficiencies than those who have had less access. Reading proficiency is linked not only to school success but also to job performance, community involvement, and self-esteem.

Enter . . . the Reading Zone, the Allen County Public Library's 1996 Young Adult Summer Reading Program, invited teens to read in a variety of subject areas. Reading cards in six subject areas, Funny Bone Zone, Imaginary Zone, Action Zone, People Zone, Chilling Zone, and Your Own Zone, guided teens in reading selections. The incentive for completing the first card was a T-shirt with the *Enter . . . the Reading Zone* logo. This shirt was the ticket for free admission to programs at the Zoo, Science Central, Diamond Jim's Water Park, and a Ft. Wayne Wizards baseball game. Incentives for completing additional cards were paperback books. Participants were encouraged to complete as many cards as they wanted. Each agency held a drawing at the end of the program and the winner chose a party for six at Diamond Jim's Water Park or the

ULTRAZONE, a laser tag experience. Because the library is committed to serving those teens who are unable to access the library for reasons of incarceration, institutionalization, or lack of transportation, the program was taken to ACPL's Teen Agency Program (T.A.P.) facilities.

During the program, which ran from June 1 through July 31, 2,455 young adults read 34,290 books. Programs were attended by 1,310 teens and their families. All library youth services staff members were involved in school visits and in conducting the program.

The success of the program is measured primarily by the number of teens participating in the reading activities, but another measure analyzed is the retention rate, or how long teens stayed in the program.

Three-Year Comparison of Program Statistics

	1994	1995	1996
Participants	1,127	1,884	2,455
Cards completed	2,394	6,216	6,896
Books read	11,970	31,080	34,290
Retention			
1st card	1,127	1,884	2,455
2nd card	790	1,310	1,406
3rd card	NA	917	952
4th card	431	630	661
5th card+	46*	1,034	1,425
Agency participation	NA	30	36

*1994 ended with 5th card

Ten young adults from participating agencies attended the Wizards Baseball game and visited Science Central.

Funding

Since 1994, the program has been partially funded by the Foellinger Foundation as part of their Summer Youth Initiative. The library must provide 34 percent of the total grant amount approved by the Foundation, either in-kind or as a cash contribution. The amount approved for 1996 was $51,467. The library's required contribution was $17,467; its actual contribution was $21,807. Foellinger's contribution was $34,000. Some of this grant was used to hire additional employees during April and May to cover for the regular employees who were making school visits.

The number of staff involved included: twenty regular staff members, four twenty-hour employees during April and May, twelve full-time summer employees to assist with programs, one Youth Services Coordinator, and one full-time summer assistant for the Coordinator.

In addition to the obvious expenditures for books, T-shirts, admissions, printing, and staff, ads were purchased in all school newspapers during May.

Contact Person

Sharon Harvey, Youth Services Coordinator, Allen County Public Library, 900 Webster Street, P.O. Box 2270, Fort Wayne, IN 46802. (219) 424-7241, ext. 2401

20.
Arlington County Public Library

Arlington, Virginia

Idea

Teen Advisory Board

Customers

Primarily middle school students, but also some high school

Community

School district figures for Arlington show an ethnic breakdown of 10 percent Asian, 18 percent African-American, 30 percent Hispanic, and 42 percent Caucasian, with over fifty-five native languages spoken. Recent significant immigration has been from Eastern Europe and Eastern Africa (Somalia and Ethiopia). Economic levels span a very wide range in Arlington, from extremely wealthy to extremely poor, all within a very small area of only 19.5 square miles.

Setting

Arlington County Public Library serves an extremely diverse urban community of 175,000, just across the Potomac River from Washington D.C. The library system consists of one central library and six full service branches. It is a department of county government. There are YA specialists assigned to each branch (some part-time), and a YA staff of four at the central library. The young adult collection has always been considered a recreational reading collection; books for curriculum support are also included in the collection. The middle school population numbers just over four thousand students. There are five public middle schools and one alternative secondary school program. The library is moving from a NOTIS online system to CARL. School libraries are in the process of going online and will share the database, with school and public library records displaying on the OPACs.

Program Description

The *Teen Advisory Board (TAB)* began in Arlington in 1990 with a pilot program at one Arlington County middle school. *TAB* was designed to be an after-school reading and reviewing group with books supplied by the Arlington Public Library. Staff believed that in order for *TAB* to be successful, the group had to meet at the schools so participation would not be limited only to those who had transportation. This also allowed the public library to partner with school library media specialists who were an important link in promoting and facilitating the group meetings, as well as providing assistance to members between meetings.

The *Teen Advisory Board* has now grown to eight groups: one in each of Arlington's five middle schools, one in a parochial school, a high school group, and a HILT group (High Intensity Language Training). A Spanish-language group is planned for next year. *TAB* not only means "Talking About Books" but also "Teens Are Beneficial." *TAB* advisors in each school (usually the school librarian) work closely as a team with YA library staff to promote and conduct *TAB* meetings in each location. Each group has flexibility to meet at the time and frequency that works for it as a local option. Therefore, some groups meet every two weeks, some every three weeks, and some monthly. Times of the meetings also vary from before school, during lunch, to after school. The high school group meets monthly at the central library in the evening with pizza. The year 1996 was special because four high school seniors, who had begun with the first *TAB* group in 1990, graduated. They were each presented with copies of Benet's *Reader's Encyclopedia*, a gift from the local Borders bookstore.

Books for *TAB* are selected from the nominations lists of the Young Adult Library Service Association's Best Books for Young Adults (BBYA) committee and also by staff. Four copies of each title are ordered. The larger groups each get their own copies and the smaller groups share copies. The books are purchased specifically for the *TAB* groups with money from the Friends of the Library. Review copies are also requested from publishers who have, on occasion, sent

Teen Advisory Board members meet at the Swanson Middle School.

a positive response. Books are kept on a cart or shelf in the school media centers, so that students have access to them between meetings. In addition to regular meetings, there have also been special events such as an Australian storyteller, author visits, and an All-*TAB* day, which brings together all the *TAB* groups at the central library for a day of discussion, fun, and voting on favorite books. One of the most memorable events was a field trip to Philadelphia in 1995 at the invitation of the BBYA Committee. Arlington *TAB* members, along with students from other schools, critically discussed BBYA nominations and provided their input directly to the BBYA committee.

TAB is important on many levels. *TAB* allows students to have a voice in reviewing and recommending books. They develop the ability to read and review critically and to recommend books to others. Students use an evaluation form similar to one developed at Enoch Pratt Free Library in Baltimore several years ago. The cards are used by the library when making purchasing decisions, and staff are looking into compiling these into a readers' advisory database.

The *TAB* Favorites lists are a way of reaching a wide audience. Copies are available in the libraries and at the schools (with each *TAB* group's list represented on a distinct, bold color of paper). The lists are extremely useful when students, parents, or teachers come to the library looking for something to read. It's a real bonus to be able to say "Here are some recommendations from kids at your school." *TAB* favorite books are also marked with a gold seal so that they are easy to identify.

For staff, *TAB* provides the opportunity for first-hand knowledge of the reading tastes and interests of young adults. It is invaluable for maintaining currency with YA literature, kids' likes and dislikes, and for keeping the collection interesting and responsive.

TAB also promotes both reading and the public library as a positive force in the lives of young people. *TAB* has been featured in *VOYA*, in local papers, and in the Arlington Library *Bulletin*. *TAB* students have become involved in the library and in the community, forming the nucleus for a successful volunteer program this summer, providing other departments with staff for paid positions, and even testifying at county board meetings on behalf of the library. Two recent Young Adult Services student clerical aides were recruited from *TAB*. In August 1995, a member of the YA staff teamed with one of the school *TAB* advisors to present the Arlington *TAB* program to a Library of Virginia–sponsored seminar on school–public library cooperation.

TAB attendance at all meetings (including high school *TAB*) totaled 2,230 during October through May of the 1995–96 school year, compared with first-year attendance of 425 in 1990. There are currently ten staff members and six school advisors involved in *TAB*. Reading specialists and English teachers frequently attend. A library school intern from Catholic University recently led an eighth grade group at one of the middle schools.

Youth participate indirectly in planning and implementation through an annual evaluation of *TAB*. Their suggestions and input are used to plan for the following year. Youth input was solicited for the evaluation card, which is being redesigned. The success of *TAB* has led to the integration of young people into many aspects of the library, as advocates, volunteers, employees, and as writers of reviews and articles for library newsletters. In the future *TAB* members will be recruited for focus-group sessions relating to YA programs and services.

The story of *TAB*'s success is borne out by the statistics: The project grew from one group with twenty-five regular readers in 1990, to eight groups with almost two hundred regular readers last year. Average meeting attendance for 1995–96 ranged from a high of forty-eight at Jefferson, to a low of twelve at Williamsburg, with the three largest groups averaging thirty-five or more per meeting, and the smaller groups averaging about sixteen per meeting. Circulation statistics for the middle school *TAB* groups correspond strongly to the meeting attendance, with over 2,000 circulations for the same year and total meeting attendance of 2098. Young adult circulation statistics have increased annually with each expansion of the *TAB* program; staff attribute this in part to the heavy use of the *TAB* Favorites lists as a readers' advisory tool.

Funding

Staff began by using advance copies, publishers' gifts, and new books from the library collection. After two years, when the program expanded to all of the middle schools, $2,000 to $2,400 was budgeted for *TAB* from the YA budget, on the assumption that many of the titles would be added to the permanent collection. The Friends of the Library were asked for assistance. For the past two years the Friends have contributed $2,000 to $2,400, which has been used to purchase books for *TAB*. Books from the previous year are traded between groups to augment the *TAB* collections. The Friends also provide funding for refreshments, pizza parties at the end of the year, and special events (such as $600 in funding for the bus to Philadelphia in 1995). Total nonbook support averages $500 annually. For the library system, *TAB* uses 180 hours of staff time at an average of $17 per hour, equaling $3,060, from October to May.

Contact Persons

Pat Muller and Margaret Brown, Arlington County Department of Public Libraries, Central Library, 1015 N. Quincy Street, Arlington, VA 22201. (703) 358-5951

21.
Berkeley Public Library
Berkeley, California

Idea
Cover to Cover

Customers
Young adults, twelve through eighteen

Community
The city of Berkeley is ethnically and economically diverse and this is reflected in the teen population. Sixteen percent of Berkeleyans live below the poverty level. The city has one public high school and a majority of Berkeley residents ages fourteen to eighteen attend it. However, both the public high school and the public library are utilized by teenagers from surrounding communities as well. The local adolescent population is 40 percent Caucasian, 39 percent African-American, 10 percent Asian-American or Pacific Islander, 11 percent Latino, and includes teens from homes in which the primary language is other than English: Spanish, Vietnamese, Chinese dialects, and languages from India and Africa are spoken by teen library users and potential users.

Setting
Berkeley Public Library serves an ethnically and economically diverse urban population of 104,700 through a central library and four neighborhood branches. Open sixty-four hours a week, the library employs 213, filling 122.45 full-time equivalent positions. Each site has a Teen Services librarian and a teenage student worker on staff. Teen Services' staff invite formal input from fourteen- through eighteen-year-olds through monthly Young Adult Advisory Committee meetings. Additional programming and collection development input comes from circulation statistics, written suggestions, and discussions with teens at numerous service points throughout the library. Teen Services sponsors three to five systemwide informational or recreational single-session programs a year, in addition to several ongoing programs, some of which are site-specific.

Program Description
Cover to Cover, originally designed in 1991 by Berkeley Public Library's Young Adult Advisory

Cover to Cover players watch a short story performed by professional actors during the 1996 end of summer party.

Committee as a summer reading activity for twelve- through eighteen-year-olds, has become a year-round series of annual events. From June through August, teenagers read and write brief reviews of books each selects individually. A party in late August brings together all who have participated. From September to December, an art contest invites entries from which the cover illustration for the collected *Cover to Cover* reviews is selected.

Teens may register for the summer program at any point during its nine-week run and do not need to complete the reading and writing segment in order to attend the party. In 1996, forty-four attended the party. An autumn art contest to design the cover for the annual collection of reviews submitted during the summer invites the participation of teens looking for artistic outlet and recognition. The contest is publicized through high school art classes as well as at the library. Fifty-three submissions were received during the 1996 art contest. The annual publication of the review is distributed widely to both individuals and organizations, reaching an audience composed of (1) teens who participated the previous summer, (2) teens who would like to participate in the coming summer, (3) library staff, (4) teens' families, and (5) teachers who are in search of information about what teens like to read and what critical remarks they have to make about their reading.

Each year's version of the summer reading and writing component of *Cover to Cover* has been unique in its details as the program incorporates annual recommendations made by the Young Adult Advisory Committee. In 1996 these teen advisors suggested that, in addition to awarding prizes at the summer's end party, weekly drawings at each library location be included. To that end, contests ran simultaneously with the basic program.

The fall art contest component of *Cover to Cover* invites a different interest group's participation, although there are, of course, teens who immerse themselves in both the summer and autumn activities. One requirement of the art contest is that the entrant have a Berkeley Public Library card (available to any resident in the state of California), ensuring that each participating teen will actually have visited the library and had an opportunity to discover the variety of services it has to offer beyond the immediate contest.

All prizes awarded to *Cover to Cover* participants are donated by community businesses or agencies. A generous cinema chain provides movie passes, each good for a recipient plus one companion. Professional theaters and a radio station provide tickets to upcoming productions, and the local university's athletics department provides passes to games. Local independent bookstores provide books, including comics. An electronics store has provided one big-ticket item (usually a portable compact disc player) each year, which becomes the grand prize won by lottery at the August party. Staff time, at the rate of about fifteen hours each year, is required to garner specific and appropriate donations, but most of the prizes are donated by businesses which both the library and the teens patronize habitually, making the process of soliciting prizes a natural part of the library's day-to-day good community/merchant relations.

Each Teen Services librarian selects those reviews that merit publication from those submitted at the individual library site. The Teen Services Coordinator recruits two high school volunteers to transfer these cumulated reviews from individually rendered handwritten work into a tidy booklet, using library word-processing equipment. The physical production of the booklet is done in-house, from photocopying through stapling, in the course of a week-long, post-schoolday work party in which the library's five student workers (high school employees whose duties include outreach as well as clerical tasks) all participate.

Those who registered for *Cover to Cover* during the previous summer, whether they submitted reviews or not, receive a copy of the booklet. Free copies are available at each library site and others are added to the library's reference collection to be used in readers' advisory work. Because the booklet appears in March, it stimulates interest in the upcoming repetition of the program, while giving Teen Services staff planning time to respond to suggestions made by teens to improve, or simply make interesting alterations in, the next annual *Cover to Cover* program.

The ethnic and socioeconomic class composition of *Cover to Cover* participants reflects the general adolescent population of Berkeley, with one exception: the percentage of Asian/Pacific Islander participants is about twice that of African-American participants in the summer portion of the program. The art contest seems to attract African-American teens in numbers reflecting their proportion of the general teen population. Given the broad spectrum of teens that *Cover to Cover* reaches with annual consistency, this program stands as unique among those provided by the library. Teens tend to register for the summer segment of the program each year subsequent to their initial involvement with it. In 1995, there were more first-time art contest entrants than repeaters. In both 1995 and 1996, publicity for *Cover to Cover* included the invitation to teens to read and write in their preferred language. While this has brought in only a few reviews in languages other than English, teens enrolled in English as a Second Language curricula have responded to the "open-language" policy by participating in all components of the program. For these teens, *Cover to Cover* usually has been their first recreational use of the public library.

Besides those teens who participate directly by reading and reviewing, contributing art work, or attending the annual party, hundreds of teens and adults derive value from the published reviews. Teachers from local schools, students of education, and visitors to the library ask for and compliment the usefulness of these annual collections. The 1995 collection went through a print run of 300 and was mounted on Berkeley Public Library's Teen Services Homepage <http://www.ci.berkeley.ca.us/bpl/teen/>, giving it an even wider potential audience.

Cover to Cover evolves to suit teens already active in the library while broadening the library's appeal to teens discovering libraries and reading perhaps for the first time. The published *Cover to Cover* collection provides teens, library staff, teachers, and families with a popular and credible reader's advisor. The appearance of the publication in the spring reminds teens that the new *Cover to Cover* season is once again on the horizon.

Funding

The initial spring planning and preparation phase consumes a total of twenty librarian hours, distributed among five Teen Services professionals. The mechanics of running the program require an average of one staff hour a week at each location during the summer. The art contest requires negligible staff time, beyond initial production and dissemination of publicity, which amounts to less than five hours annually. Judging the entries is undertaken by the library's art and music librarians and any student workers who did not contribute entries. Production of the annual booklet is labor intensive, but requires a maximum of ten librarian hours. Utilizing high school volunteers for much of the production process also provides more teens with the opportunity to be involved in the library. Entertainment and some food at the summer party, as well as incidental costs like preparing photographs for photocopying, cost $450 annually, paid by the Friends of the Library. A system Teen Services materials budget of $18,000 buys books, magazines, and music for all sites. Funds for teen programming are provided by the Friends of the Library, in an annual amount of $1,400 for the system.

Contact Person

Francisca Goldsmith, Berkeley Public Library, Teen Services, 2090 Kittredge Street, Berkeley, CA 94704. (510) 649-3926

22. Berkeley Public Library

Berkeley, California

Idea

Teen Playreaders

Customers

Senior high students

Community

The library serves a population of 104,700, just under 10 percent of whom are school age (five to seventeen years old). The high school population is 10 percent Asian-American or Pacific Islander, 11 percent Latino, 39 percent African-American, and 40 percent Caucasian. There is a wide range of income levels in this university community, and about 16 percent of the community lives below the poverty line.

Setting

The Berkeley Public Library serves the city of Berkeley with a central library, four neighborhood branch libraries, and a tool lending library. Its 213 employees fill 122.45 full-time equivalent positions to serve 116,236 registered borrowers. The library is open sixty-four hours a week and experiences 1,454,350 visits annually.

Program Description

The *Teen Playreaders* program began in 1990 as a way to encourage teens who were interested in drama, but perhaps timid about getting involved in a production, to try their hand at exploring some of the theater literature without the pressure of performing for an audience. Teens aged thirteen through eighteen meet weekly to read plays aloud, changing parts frequently. The teens never know when they will be called upon to read or what part they will be reading. The play is usually unfamiliar to them as well, so each teen is on an equal footing.

The plays read are selected by the teens from offerings presented by individual Playreaders or the Teen Librarian. Playwrights have included Shakespeare, Christopher Durang, Neil Simon, and Tom Stoppard. Although originally intended as a reading-only group, the *Playreaders* have naturally evolved into enthusiastic, committed actors, who put on three to five productions a year, ranging from traditional classics to multilingual poetry readings to outdoor celebrations of *Winnie the Pooh* for children.

The *Teen Playreaders* program targets teens aged thirteen through eighteen who have an interest in drama. In a nonthreatening, relaxed setting (no audience, no teachers), teens read plays aloud, changing parts frequently. The program develops reading skills and self-confidence, while introducing the teens to the wealth of theater literature. The program is advertised through library flyers (which are also distributed at the local schools), through periodic newspaper articles and listings, and most importantly, by word of mouth.

Teens who have participated in the program often show extraordinary growth, from shy introverts to confident actors. Their experiences in *Playreaders*

> Join in
>
> Join in the fun
>
> Join in the fun Join in the fun Join in the fun
>
> ## The Teen Playreaders present
> ## a do-it-yourself performance
>
> Join in the fun Join in the fun Join in the fun
>
> ### *Philip Glass Buys a Loaf of Bread*
>
> Saturday, September 10
> 2 pm
> on the lawn at North Branch
>   Berkeley Public Library
>   Hopkins at The Alameda
>
> All ages All ages For all ages All ages All ages
>
> Bring whatever seating accommodations you take to the beach
>
> Free For all ages Join in the fun Free For all ages
>
> For all ages Join in the fun Free
>
> 644-6850 for information
>
> To request a sign language interpreter for this event, call (510)644-6095 (voice) or (510)540-1240 (TDD); at least five working days' notice will ensure availability.
> Wheelchair accessible

help them scholastically as well, making them feel more comfortable speaking in front of a group and making oral presentations. Based on their positive experiences in *Playreaders*, many have gone on to audition for and take part in school drama productions. As a natural progression, the *Playreaders* have become an active live theater group, selecting, planning, and producing as many as five programs a year. There are still some members who prefer the more relaxed "readings" to the exciting but conspicuous productions, and so the program maintains a balance between reading and performing.

The benefit to the teens involved is immediate and obvious—but the program also provides a chance for the library to take an active role in welcoming them, their friends, and family. By showcasing the talents and interests of the teens, the library also gives other members of the community a chance to see them in a role other than the common stereotype of noisy disruptive patrons: as talented, hardworking actors.

The program requires a minimal amount of preparation and expense. The selected play must be photocopied, with sufficient copies for all readers, and the play must be reviewed by the group leader in advance, to note the number of characters, good places to switch parts, significant roles, etc. For actual productions, minimal props and thrift-store costumes keep the costs to a minimum. The teens have also learned to be resourceful and economical in constructing their own costumes and props. The Teen Librarian promotes, organizes, and leads the weekly one-hour meetings. Other staff members assist with production details, such as videotaping and still photography, but no other staff members or volunteers are assigned to this program.

Though the composition of the group changes as the participants grow up and out of the teen years, the group is diverse enough in age range to keep a nice balance between old and new members. Originally recruited from five thirteen-year-old girls who worked at the library as Student Friends, helping with the children's summer reading game, the group has grown steadily over the last six years, and now consists of twenty-five young men and women. Performances draw large crowds (often eighty to one hundred attendees) of not just friends and family, but interested library patrons who now regularly inquire about the teens' next performance.

The teens that comprise the current group of *Playreaders* are a most diverse group. With an almost equal male/female ratio, they are residents of Berkeley and three neighboring cities, range in age from thirteen through eighteen, and include two college freshmen. Nearly half the members are homeschoolers, who seem especially to appreciate this chance to make new friends outside their immediate circle. The public and private school students have learned a lot about homeschooling from their fellow actors, and strong friendships have grown between the two groups.

Performances have included:

Readings of Eleanor Coerr's book *Sadako and the Thousand Paper Cranes*, followed by the folding of 1,000 origami cranes by the *Playreaders* and the audience. This program is presented on Peace Day, August 6, to commemorate the bombings of Hiroshima and Nagasaki, and always draws a multiethnic, multigenerational crowd. It is inspiring to see seniors and teens working together assisting younger children to reach their goal.

A multilingual poetry reading to celebrate National Poetry Month. The teens read/performed poems of their own choosing, from such diverse poets as

Rilke and A. A. Milne. One highlight was Allen Ginsberg's "America" with saxophone embellishments. A park ranger and poetry lover who attended was so impressed with the teens that he invited them to participate in another poetry reading sponsored by Poet Laureate Robert Hass, celebrating the environment. The teens received ribbons and had their photos taken with Hass.

A performance piece of the David Ives' play *Philip Glass Buys a Loaf of Bread*. Following the style of a sing-it-yourself Messiah, the audience was divided into four sections and led by the teens in chanting phrases such as "loaf of bread" in Glassian rhythms. Cacophony and silliness reigned as the audience of adults and teens followed the teens' "choral" directions in chanting their nonsense phrases.

A traditional staging of Dickens' *A Christmas Carol* was set in 1930s America, with Scrooge as a gun-wielding gangster and the Cratchits as a Depression-era family.

As the teens gain experience and confidence in performing, their roles in the *Playreaders* grow also. The group tries for at least one student-directed production per year, and responsibilities for sets, costumes, organization, and publicity are assigned to teens who are interested in taking on these duties. The *Playreaders*' latest project, an outdoor celebration of A. A. Milne called "Pooh Day," was conceived by the teens themselves. It included a play, a sing-along, a mini-poetry reading, a Bouncing race, a "Hoppity" contest, and booths where young children made masks and puppets and sampled Pooh and Tigger's favorite foods. This program drew a capacity crowd of nearly five hundred Pooh fans of all ages, from infants to seniors.

The *Playreaders* program also offers teens a chance to develop their writing skills. One production was composed entirely of original poetry, penned by Playreaders and students from the neighboring junior high school English classes. The teens have also adapted prose and poetry to dialogue for performance, and several Playreaders have written their own plays.

One surprising aspect of the program's growth has been its multigenerational appeal. Younger children view the teens with awe and admiration, and the teens respond by creating programs designed especially for the young, such as "Pooh Day," *Sadako*, and an outdoor interactive circus of Alice in Wonderland. The younger children often come up and ask when they can join the *Playreaders* group, and this too is a valuable recruitment tool for future members. Performances of the classics often draw seniors, who appreciate seeing teens exploring, enjoying, and sharing theater more familiar to an older audience. The program benefits not only the teens who take part in it, but the community at large. While providing high-quality entertainment for all ages, the program spotlights an often underserved population of library users.

The *Teen Playreaders* meet at a branch that unfortunately has neither a meeting room nor a stage of any sort, and the teens have been resourceful and inventive about doing serious theater work in a most untheatrical setting. But their productions are always alternated with the easygoing, relaxed "readings" that started the program in the first place: a chance for teens interested in drama to get their feet wet without the pressure of creating the perfect performance.

Funding

The regular library budget, which provides for a Teen/Reference Librarian at each location, supports this program.

Contact Person

Debbie Carton, Teen/Reference Librarian, Berkeley Public Library, North Branch, 1170 The Alameda, Berkeley, CA 94707. (510) 644-6851

23. Cumberland County Public Library and Information Center

Fayetteville, North Carolina

Idea

Teen Read

Customers

Sixth graders through recent high school graduates

Community

The population of Cumberland County is 300,893. Fayetteville is the fourth largest metropolitan area in North Carolina. Cumberland County is the home of Fort Bragg and Pope Air Force Base. Fort Bragg is the largest United States Army installation in the country in terms of population, with 49,986 soldiers. The county is rapidly growing because more military facilities are being added. The Army recently purchased 11,000 acres to expand Fort Bragg and a $250-million medical center is currently being built. The economy is heavily dependent upon the government, and the library system serves as the public library for thousands of military families.

According to 1990 census information, there are 28,245 people between the ages of twelve and eighteen in Cumberland County. Of that number, 530 are American Indian, Eskimo, or Aleu, 579 are Asian or Pacific Islander, 10,504 are African-American, 1,275 are Hispanic, 14,707 are Caucasian, and 650 are other races. Twenty-eight percent of the entire Cumberland County population is under the age of eighteen. Surveys of high school students show that almost half of the seniors plan to attend college. The high school dropout rate is 2.90. The SAT total average score for Cumberland County was 815 in 1995. There are twelve middle schools, eight high schools, several private schools, a populous homeschool association, and plans to build new public schools due to overcrowding.

Setting

Cumberland County Public Library and Information Center is a system consisting of the Headquarters library, six branch libraries, and bookmobile service. Branch libraries are located in Fayetteville, Spring Lake, Hope Mills, and Stedman, North Carolina. Groundbreaking for a new library occurred in July 1996, and plans have been approved to build two more in the near future. The staff includes 33 professionals and 122 paraprofessionals. The system-wide collection consists of 191,721 book titles, 354,168 volumes, 1,163 periodical and newspaper subscriptions, 93,694 paperback books, 23 CD-ROM titles, 4,290 compact discs, 4,769 video recordings, and 8,608 audiotapes. A homepage is maintained at <www://cumberland.lib.nc.us>. Computer terminals provide access to CD-ROMs and Netscape at the Headquarters and Cliffdale locations, with a WAN in process for other locations. Last year, 2,015,110 materials were loaned, 169,534 customers attended library programs, and 141,924 Cumberland County residents and nonresidents were library card holders.

Program Description

Teen Read is a self-paced, genre-related summer reading program in which participants read one book from each of seven different genres (adventure, horror, mystery, sports, science fiction/fantasy, romance, and reader's choice). After completing the children's summer reading program in fifth grade, adolescents in Cumberland County were without a summer reading program. *Teen Read* was created in order to supply a means for youth to satiate their interest in reading during adolescence and directly resulted from an outcry by early adolescents who desired a summer reading program. Bookmarks assist participants in finding a book for a specific genre; those who do not enjoy fiction, or are not allowed to read fiction for moral reasons, may choose nonfiction in Dewey areas corresponding to the genres. After reading, each participant completes a review form asking for the title, author, and why they liked or disliked the book. When the form is returned, a sticker is given for the *Teen Read* card in order to keep track of reading progress. After earning two stickers, readers are given a squeeze bottle, and after three more they are given a frisbee. When turning in cards with all seven stickers, they choose a free book. Titles purchased were chosen from lists produced by YALSA. The grand prizes, drawn randomly, were mall gift certificates. Movies were shown at four libraries each week, and titles related to the next week's genre were booktalked at the movies.

The lives of young adults and the community have changed since the implementation of *Teen Read*. Young adults are ecstatic because the library has shown that it is concerned with serving all ages. They become more familiar with reading and writing by joining *Teen Read*. The community has also been altered as a direct result of *Teen Read*. More young adults are spending time in the library and appreciating reading as a pleasurable pastime during the summer months. They enjoy commenting about what they have read in a written format. Instead of reacting negatively as a result of boredom in their community, they have been participating in *Teen Read*. Area businesses are so impressed with *Teen Read* and its results that they are contacting library personnel and asking to donate prizes and coupons. Educators in the area have also been positive about the program, knowing that students are profiting by reading and writing during the summer months. A stronger connection between schools and the public library system has been created.

The program is especially important because it is tailored to young adults and is self-paced and available for avid readers as well as those who have difficulty reading. The program is practical for those taking vacations who may not be in the area all summer. Also, since Cumberland County has a transient population, participants are allowed to join *Teen Read* any time during the summer. Many young adults have stated that they enjoy being able to choose a book instead of being told which book to read. Unlike school, where many young adults view reading as a chore, *Teen Read* allows participants to have fun and choose according to their interests. Many have commented that reading books in different genres has made them more well-rounded and more likely to read a variety of books.

Teen Read was promoted to all schools and organizations or agencies directly involved with people aged twelve through eighteen via posters, flyers, library tours, and booktalks. *Teen Read* was also advertised in the library's Calendar of Events and throughout the library system, and in military libraries on Fort Bragg. Postcards about the program were

---

Teen Read

How do we join?

Teen Read is a summer reading club program for students entering the sixth grade through recent high school graduates. Any student in this age group can register at any Cumberland County Public Library location beginning June 1.

About Teen Read

Our summer reading program for teens is self-paced and genre related. Each week Headquarters Library, Bordeaux Branch Library, Cliffdale Branch Library, and Hope Mills Branch Library will show a movie from a certain genre. Admission to the film is to have read a book from that genre or its corresponding nonfiction area. To show that you have met the requirement, fill out a questionnaire for the book you have read and return it to any Cumberland County Public Library to receive a sticker. The questionnaires are available at any Cumberland County Public Library location.

At the end of the program, all participants with a completed reading card (card with all seven stickers) are eligible to enter a drawing for prizes. If a member does not complete the required genre for a particular week, they are not permitted entrance to the movie. However, they are still eligible for the grand prize drawing as long as the genre is completed and all requirements are met before August 15.

	Genre	**Movie**
June 9–15	Horror / 001's, 133's	*Dr. Jekyll and Mr. Hyde*
June 16–22	Romance / 800's	*A Midsummer Night's Dream*
June 23–29	Adventure / 900's	*Treasure Island*
June 30–July 6	Mystery / 364's	*From Russia With Love*
July 7–13	Science Fiction / Fantasy / 500's	*The Seventh Voyage of Sinbad*
July 14–20	Sports / 700's	*National Velvet*
July 21–27	Reader's Choice	(To Be Announced)

All movies are shown at 3:00 p.m. at the following locations:

Mondays, Bordeaux Branch Library   Wednesdays, Cliffdale Branch Library

Tuesdays, Headquarters Library   Thursdays, Hope Mills Branch Library
(closed July 4, movie rescheduled for July 5)

mailed to people who registered for *Teen Read* '95 and those who had attended other young adult programs. Throughout the library system, 1,573 young adults registered and a total of 2,363 books were read. Sheila Anderson, Student Liaison Librarian, and Claire Fitzgerald, former Information Services Librarian I, implemented *Teen Read* beginning in 1995 with suggestions from the library's Teen Council. Sadly, Claire Fitzgerald died tragically in an automobile accident in April 1996, leaving all major *Teen Read* duties to Sheila Anderson. In some way, all staff members have been involved with *Teen Read*. Librarians answered questions and provided books, pages were responsible for shelving materials by genre instead of by author, and custodial staff cleaned up popcorn spills after movies. Community relations staff produced printed materials, circulation workers were bombarded with customers wanting to check out material, branch library staff showed movies, and bookmobile staff encouraged participation. Five young adult volunteers helped with showing movies and preparing refreshments, acting at the *Teen Read* grand finale during a mystery program, and changing book displays.

Youth were utilized in planning *Teen Read* in two ways: their evaluations from *Teen Read* '95, the first YA summer reading program, and suggestions from members of the Teen Library Council were helpful about ways to improve *Teen Read* in 1996. Their suggestions resulted in changing the length of *Teen Read* from seven weeks to ten weeks in 1996, movies were added to three additional library locations, and mall gift certificates were given out instead of purchasing a grand prize for one winner.

Participation in *Teen Read* grew from 709 young adults in 1995 to 1,349 in 1996. Evaluation questionnaires were distributed at all locations approximately two weeks before the end of *Teen Read*; these asked not only for comments on the program but also suggestions for other kinds of programs. Questions included what was liked best (reading), what should be changed (nothing), what prizes should be offered next year (same), and whether they would rejoin the program next year (yes). Further increases in participation are expected in the future. In 1997, the genres multicultural, historical fiction, humor, and inspirational will be added. Young adults will be required to read five books rather than seven and will be able to choose among the ten genres rather than having to read one book from each.

Funding

Teen Read was funded by the library budget, donations from Friends of the Library groups, and the Cumberland Community Foundation. Local businesses also donated coupons and prizes that were distributed along with the squeeze bottles and at the movies. The following is the budget, not including staff hours and cost of staff per hour:

Library budget	
Squeeze bottles	$1,450
Frisbees	590
Registration cards	500
Bookmarks	400
Postcards	300
Stickers	100
Review forms	50
Posters	25
Flyers	25
Subtotal	$3,540
Cumberland Community Foundation, Inc.	
Books	500
Friends of the Cumberland County Public Library and Information Center	
Refreshments and gift certificates	150
Cliffdale Friends of the Library	
Refreshments, pizza party, gift certificates	200
Grand total	$4,390

Contact Person

Sheila Anderson, Cumberland County Public Library and Information Center, 300 Maiden Lane, Fayetteville, NC 28301-5000. (910) 483-7878, ext. 225

24.
Dade County Public Schools
Miami, Florida

Idea

Earn a Buck, Buy a Book

Customers

Incarcerated young adults in the Dade County Juvenile Detention Center

Community

Students come from a multitude of ethnic, cultural, racial, and educational backgrounds. Many have had little opportunity to venture far outside their respective neighborhoods. Some, like one young man from Vietnam, have only faint memories of the distant shores they left as young children.

Setting

The Juvenile Justice Center School (JJCS) is a Dade County Florida Public School located in the Dade Juvenile Detention Center. The Detention Center houses accused and delinquent adolescents up to the age of eighteen. Young people are detained at the facility pending disposition of their case(s) or for a short period of time while awaiting judicial placement in a program. The population, averaging over two hundred detainees, changes daily. The JJCS provides a short-term, basic educational program which focuses on improving self-concept through academics and counseling. Although constrained by the transient nature of its population, the school attempts to provide meaningful multilevel, cooperative instruction in the areas of math, reading, social skills, social studies, career exploration, horticulture, business, and computer education.

Program Description

Imagine yourself earning "Book Bucks" (BBs) for class work well done and spending your "money" in the school library for any current magazine, comic, designated paperback, or journal you love to read. That is exactly what students at the Juvenile Justice Center School do every month. The school media specialist crams four large boxes with donated magazines and stripped paperbacks that would otherwise be shredded by the distributor and brings them to the detention facility. Students "buy" the magazines and books after earning scrip for outstanding classroom work or as a reward for good behavior. The key to the program's success is the 100 percent cooperation between teachers issuing the BBs, the distributor, and the media specialist. Students save their "Book Bucks," often keeping them rolled tightly in their socks! When class work is completed, they ask for a library pass and "purchase" reading materials at face value. Rewards and reading combine to make this program a success!

In early 1993, two studies addressing the basic elements of a quality education were published. The Colorado Department of Education's study, *The Impact of School Library Media Centers on Academic Achievement*, concluded that "students at schools with better funded media centers tend to achieve higher average test scores, whether their schools and communities are rich or poor and whether adults in the community are well or poorly educated." Research presented by Stephen Krashen in his book, *The Power of Reading*, is equally encouraging. Krashen finds that open access to media centers results in more voluntary reading by students and voluntary reading is the best predictor of reading comprehension, vocabulary growth, improved spelling and grammar, and writing effectiveness. The *Earn a Buck, Buy a Book* program makes a difference because everyone has access to current reading materials he feels were personally selected for him. The enthusiasm and eagerness to read are evidenced by how fast the news travels when the magazines arrive. There are literally scores of eager readers lined up to browse through the latest supply. Krashen's study is certainly applicable here! Another aspect of the program is illustrative of other lessons being taught. To keep the students "straight," the issuing teachers sign their names in ink and write out the value of the scrip in numerals and words. This way "counterfeiting" is kept to a minimum and students learn that they have to save their money and spend within their budgets. Book Bucks are also nontransferable and students may pay for reading materials with their reward money only.

Over the years, the *Earn a Buck, Buy a Book* program has reached literally thousands of readers. Since the media specialist averages bringing in over a thousand pieces of reading materials every month, that is over twelve thousand additional items in the hands of readers each year. The entire teaching staff, which numbers twenty-five including Exceptional Student Education teachers, is involved in the Book Buck process. Teachers are notified about one week ahead of trips to the distributor so they can begin issuing BBs to students. They have the latitude to determine the face value of the scrip. Students detained for months at a time often save any leftover

BBs in their "sock banks." A student once showed up with over $30 in saved money to spend. He left a very satisfied customer after figuring his purchases and even calculating the sales tax.

Students are not formally involved in the planning or implementation of the program because of security constraints. Informal interest surveys have determined what they and the staff like to read, including rap, sports, and car magazines, comics, and word-search puzzles. Judging by the popularity of the magazines and how fast they disappear, the students would unanimously evaluate it "two thumbs up." There is no formal statistical information about the success of the *Earn a Buck, Buy a Book* program. Because of the transient nature of the population and the limited follow-up once students leave the facility, it is impossible to provide hard data on its academic impact. However, if Krashen's study is correct, then the voluntary reading that is promoted by the *Earn a Buck, Buy a Book* program at the Juvenile Justice Center School is improving the reading skills of the entire population served.

Funding

All reading materials are donated by Anderson News of Miami, Florida. Judy Maynard, the warehouse manager at Anderson, has been a staunch ally and liaison since the inception of the program. Select JJCS staff are allowed to "shop" the Anderson News warehouse to obtain magazines for the program.

Contact Person

Deborah Samuels, Juvenile Justice Center School, 3300 NW 27 Avenue, Miami, FL 33142. (305) 638-5054

25.
Geneva Free Library

Geneva, New York

Idea

Rebound and Read

Customers

At-risk youth entering grades four through nine

Community

The 1990 census showed 775 youth between the ages of ten and fourteen living in Geneva. The number is probably higher at this time, since middle school populations are up over previous years. In the Geneva City School District, out of a total student population of 2393, 76.8 percent are Caucasian, 14.1 percent African-American, and 7.5 percent Hispanic. Reduced-price or free lunches are served to 46 percent of the student population. A local parochial school serves 285 additional students in grades K–8. According to *Kids Count 1995 Data Book* from the New York State Division of Youth, Geneva City is considered an economically distressed area. Much of the county's subsidized and public housing is concentrated in Geneva.

Setting

The Geneva Free Library is chartered to serve the city and town of Geneva, an area with a population of 17,110. Geneva is a small city with a diverse population: both a research- and college-oriented community, relatively prosperous, and a community with a sizable population that is either minority or economically disadvantaged. The library also serves as the central library for the four-county Pioneer Library System, a mix of rural, suburban, and small-town libraries in upstate New York. The library employs four librarians, nineteen paraprofessionals, and other staff, providing circulation, ILL, children's, reference, and young adult services to its patrons.

Program Description

Rebound and Read is a free one-week basketball and reading camp offered to the youth of the Geneva area by the Geneva Free Library. The goal of the program is to promote reading as an enjoyable activity to youth who do not view reading positively. Young adolescents entering grades six through nine attend the afternoon session from one to four p.m. and are coached by a paid staff of eight, made up of both experienced teachers and college-age youth. The campers begin and end their session with basketball skills, drills, and scrimmages. Each day the campers spend at least one hour in the library, reading and being read to, participating in library and reading-oriented activities.

The library is the sole organization in Geneva that promotes reading during the summer, except in a summer school or remedial situation. The library offers summer reading programs to preschoolers through young adults, but traditionally, good readers or children with a high degree of parental involvement have made up the bulk of participants. Sports camps are offered by the YMCA and the local colleges, but all involve a fee, some quite substantial. Little League baseball is available, but only the more skilled youth participate beyond June and this also involves a fee. The no-fee city recreation programs have traditionally been geared to younger children. *Rebound and Read* is the only program in the city that does not charge a fee and has successfully involved middle-school-aged young adults in an educational program in the summer.

Fifty-five young people entering grades six through nine attended in 1996. The program involved eight paid coaches, one library assistant, and one paid gym coordinator in direct contact with the campers. The basketball portion of the program was coordinated by Brian Streeter, head men's basketball coach at Hobart College, who volunteered his time. A retired teacher volunteered to work with students in the library. More volunteers were involved in previous years and more volunteer involvement is expected in the future.

Although no youth are actively involved in the planning and execution of the program, the staff receives daily evaluation through the use of reading logs. Participants report on their experience each day in these logs. They are asked to write at least one sentence each on the basketball and library portions of their camp day. Monitoring these comments has helped pinpoint both successful and unsuccessful elements of the program and make adjustments (i.e., "more girls' books") and incorporate ideas for next year ("more library activities like the clue hunt which took us all through the library").

The library tracks a variety of statistics, as well as anecdotal information, to evaluate the program. *Rebound and Read* does reach a different population than traditional library programs. Fifty-five young adults were involved in the library's summer reading program, and a similar number attended *Rebound and Read*. Only five participants attended both programs. *Rebound and Read* participants probably dislike reading more than regular library users, although there is no survey showing the level of interest in reading by regular library patrons. A survey of *Rebound and Read* participants, however, shows that, while approximately 20 percent of the participants like to read and do reading-related activities, 20 percent strongly dislike reading, and about 60 percent are indifferent to it.

Rebound and Read is a program that makes a strong effort to reach young adults who don't traditionally use the library in the summer. This includes but is not limited to economically disadvantaged and minority youngsters. This program succeeds on a higher level than any other current library program in Geneva. Minority participation approaches 35 percent. Income level is tracked by eligibility for the reduced/free school lunch program; 38 percent of the participants report themselves as being eligible. Yet participation in *Rebound and Read* carries no stigma; young people from all economic levels in the community participate freely. The association of the local college with the basketball program adds a cachet to the program as being a quality program for all.

Parents are pleased with both the pro-reading and drug awareness messages of the program. An anti-substance-abuse message began in the year the program was fully funded by the county Stop-DWI organization and has continued to be intentionally incorporated into one of the daily sessions. "It's good to keep drug and alcohol issues before the kids, especially in a sports (not school) setting." "He is less than excited about the reading part—I'm thrilled with it." "Can you sign us up for next year?" were among parent comments.

One of the best informal measures of the worth of the program is the number of kids who come back, year after year. "I've been in *Rebound and Read* each year you've had it. It just keeps getting better and better. This is my last year. Next year I'll be too old. I'm going to miss it." "The best things about *Rebound and Read* are the games, my wonderful coach," said one happy participant.

Funding

Rebound and Read was funded in its initial year, 1993, with an LSCA grant. Currently, local funding supports the program.

These figures are for both sessions, serving 122 young people entering grades four through nine.

Local private foundation	$3,500
James P. Gordon Trust	2,000
Geneva Center of Concern	750
Ontario County Stop DWI	1,500
Geneva Free Library (in kind), library assistant, 150 hours:	1,050

Expenditures

Personnel costs	3,000
Transportation	600
Gym rental	60
Basketballs	600
T-shirts (kids, volunteers, staff, PR)	900
Reading materials	2,490
Paper, copying, film, etc.	200

Contact Person

Barbara H. Garman, Geneva Free Library, 244 Main Street, Geneva, NY 14456-2370. (315) 789-5303

26.
Leominster Public Library
Leominster, Massachusetts

Idea
REACT young adult book discussion group

Customers
Young adults, grades seven through twelve

Community
According to 1990 U.S. Census figures for Leominster, teens make up approximately 7 percent of the city's population of 38,000. School department figures show 2,356 students enrolled as of October 1995. The Leominster High School and Center for Technical Education's 1995 graduating class saw 76 percent of its members pursuing higher education. For years, Leominster was known as the "Pioneer Plastic City," and the name reflected its primarily blue-collar, middle-class workforce engaged in plastics manufacturing and related industries. In recent years, Leominster is promoting its image of "The Birthplace of Johnny Appleseed," signifying a cultural shift of sorts toward an increased role as a "bedroom community" of suburban Boston. There is a large Hispanic community in Leominster and increasing numbers of Asian immigrants. The library's downtown location in an ethnically diverse neighborhood is reflected in frequent use by minority teens. The mayor has recently appointed a Youth Commission as well as a committee to investigate the possibility of a "youth center" facility in Leominster.

Setting
The Leominster Public Library is a full-service library located in the city's downtown area. The library's Young Adult Center, or YAC, was created in 1978 with a $20,500 LSCA grant and is designed to support recreational and informational reading needs of teenagers in grades seven through twelve, corresponding roughly to ages twelve through eighteen. The Center's collection is comprised of fiction and nonfiction in both hardcover and paperback formats, some reference resources, magazines, pamphlets, and audiocassettes. Until 1991, a full complement of programs for teens augmented the Center's collection. In 1991, severe library budget cuts (28 percent) reduced the YA Services Coordinator's position to twenty hours per week, eliminating all programs and drastically reducing the Center's hours of operation to three afternoons per week.

Program Description
re act (re akt) vi. to respond to a stimulus

One Wednesday evening each month throughout the school year, in the Leominster Public Library's Young Adult Center, the stimulus is books. The "reactors" are teens in grades seven through twelve, and the *REACT* book discussion group exposes them to the best in current young adult fiction and nonfiction, expanding their experiences and interests and giving them a forum for ideas. In addition to consuming mass quantities of junk food, *REACT* members are responsible for reading one book each month which forms the basis for discussion at the following meeting. The only criteria for membership are a passion for books, a willingness to discuss them, and an open, inquiring mind. *REACT* members annually recognize the power and artistry of the group's favorite discussion book by presenting the *REACTORS'* Quest Award to the author. Rodman Philbrick's *Freak the Mighty* took top honors in 1996.

REACT's importance and its impact on Leominster's young adults can be ascribed to three very potent ideas. First of all, in this age of dizzying technological advancement, there are still *readers* who love *books*. Like Mark Twain's famous cable commenting that "The reports of my death are greatly exaggerated," the book is alive and well in libraries across the country. Young adult authors are producing some astonishing literature, and groups like *REACT* expose readers to novels that, in the words of one member, "I probably wouldn't have picked up on my own."

Secondly, *REACT* gives young adults a voice, a forum for ideas and a place to express their opinions. It is a program in which their peers and their librarians will take time to really listen to what they have to say. This is an intoxicating and powerful ingredient of groups like *REACT*, especially in an age where it seems teens get less and less of what they really crave from adults: time and attention.

And last but not least, this is a program for the kids Mary K. Chelton called "the best and the brightest," in a *VOYA* editorial "We Don't Want You—We Want Your (Dumb) Friends!" (October 1994), which serves as a reminder that all too often, librarians are focusing incredible energies on attracting nonlibrary users, to the exclusion and detriment of the articulate, well-read, future-directed teens we already have in our libraries.

REACT is unapologetically designed for avid, capable, and highly motivated readers. The YA collection includes Pascal and Stine and Pike, Nine Inch Nails and Coolio and *The Macarena*, *WWF* and

Word Up! and *Thrasher* magazines. But while *Beavis and Butthead* comics are trying to entice the nonusers through the door, *REACT* is the program for the kids who've already discovered that reading "doesn't suck."

In September of 1995, thirty young adults were registered for *REACT*. The average attendance for last year was twenty-two. As of September 1996, twenty-eight young adults were signed up. The program is planned and implemented by the Young Adult Services Coordinator. Young adults are regularly consulted about discussion book suggestions and *REACT*-related activities. Their preferences determine the meeting refreshments "menu" and their comments obviously steer each month's discussion.

The most recent project is designing a *REACT* T-shirt for group members. Members would like to meet with another area book discussion group and perhaps combine the visit with a field trip to Boston. Participants were also treated to a visit recently by local author Robert Cormier after reading *We All Fall Down*; the group hopes to read a fantasy and meet with author R. A. Salvatore, another Leominster resident, during this school year.

Young adult input is solely responsible for the annual *REACTORS'* Quest Award, given to the author of the discussion book most enjoyed by members and determined annually by popular vote. The teens take this responsibility very seriously, as evidenced in their ballot comments. These ballots, along with a certificate and an official *REACT* T-shirt, are sent to the author of the winning book. Past recipients include Dean Koontz, Orson Scott Card, Mildred Ames, and this year's winner, Rodman Philbrick.

Funding

Planning, preparation, and execution

    One staff person @ $16/hr.
        for 5 hours a month = $80

    Cost for ten meetings per fiscal year $ 800

Refreshments

    Seven regular meetings
        @ $30 each = $180

    Three special meetings (pizza parties
        in Sept/Dec/June) @ $50 each = $150

    Cost for ten meetings per fiscal year   330[1]

Books

    Six paperback copies at an average
        cost of $3 each = $18

    Cost for ten meetings per fiscal year   180[2]

    Total cost $1,310

---

1. This cost is paid for by the Friends of the Library, 30 West Street, Leominster, MA 01453.

2. Prior to devastating budget cuts in 1991, the library bought multiple copies of REACT books, which were also used in the school booktalking program. When the program resumed in 1995, booktalking did not, and the library's reduced YA materials budget could no longer absorb the cost of providing books for participants. In addition, the program began attracting larger numbers of teens. REACT members now purchase copies of each month's discussion book at the library discount price. The library is committed to buying a number of copies each month to ensure that teens who cannot afford to purchase books can still participate in REACT. No teen is ever turned away because he or she cannot buy the book. The YA Services Coordinator is investigating grant funding as well.

Contact Person

Diane M. Sanabria, Young Adult Services Coordinator, Leominster Public Library, 30 West Street, Leominster, MA 01453. (508) 534-7522

REACTIONS...The Giver

"Why, if you learned to ride a bike at 5 or 6 or 7 did you have to wait until you were 9 years old to get one? There is no room for individuality."

"I thought it was great but I wished it was longer."

"I was uncomfortable with the ambiguous ending."

"Parts of it made me SO angry!"

"You have NO choices!"

"If it came over the speaker that you had to 'release' your son, you'd do it. You see how blind obedience is an obstacle to family and love."

"They are prostitutes: simply going through the motions and living on the surface."

"Their safety is an illusion."

"ELSEWHERE is Heaven."

27. Multnomah County Library

Portland, Oregon

Idea

Science Fiction/Fantasy Day

Customers

Young adults, twelve through eighteen, especially senior high students

Community

Since Multnomah County covers such a large and diverse area, the adolescent population ranges from inner-city urban youth to suburban youth to some rural youth in the outlying areas. The city of Portland covers about two-thirds of the county and twelve out of the fourteen library branches are within the city boundaries. Fifteen percent of the county residents earn less than $10,000 a year, with some neighborhoods having 24 percent in that category and some neighborhoods having 8 percent in that category. Six percent of the county residents earn more than $75,000, with some neighborhoods having 16 percent in that category and some having 1.5 percent in that category.

Seven percent of residents are African-American, with individual neighborhoods ranging from 35 percent to 1 percent in that ethnic group. Five percent are Asian-American, with a range of 2 to 7 percent in individual neighborhoods. There are also some neighborhoods with a high percentage of immigrants from Russia, Romania, and other eastern European countries.

There are twenty high schools, twenty-eight middle schools, and three middle/high schools in the county for a total of fifty-one secondary schools. There are also a number of small alternative schools, which are not included in this total.

Setting

Multnomah County Library is a county-wide library system with a central, downtown library and fourteen branches. It is the largest public library in Oregon and serves a county population of 620,000. Roughly 80 percent (495,000) of those county residents live in the city of Portland, the largest city in the state of Oregon. Multnomah County Library has a reciprocal borrowing agreement with the surrounding counties so that the entire metropolitan area is able to borrow library materials free of charge. The library's total budget for 1996–97 is $24 million.

Program Description

The *Science Fiction/Fantasy Day* program is offered at one of the large library branches every year to year and a half. Most of the science fiction and fantasy groups around the Portland area, such as the Portland Science Fiction Society and the National Fantasy Fan Club, have display tables with visually enticing displays of books, memorabilia, posters, and stand-up figures. Three major events are planned including a Filk (a type of folk music with words taken from fantasy stories or books) performance, a talk by a well-known Northwest science fiction or fantasy author, and a medieval weapons demonstration by the Society for Creative Anachronism. Western Oregon Wargamers, the largest gaming group in Portland, sets up a 3-D fantasy game, similar to *Dungeons and Dragons*, that is ongoing for anyone to join in. The program runs from one to five in the afternoon and takes over the entire library. Many of the groups, such as the Star Trek clubs, come in costume.

There is a sizable group of high school students, particularly males, who are avid readers of science fiction and fantasy books, sometimes to the exclusion of all other activities. These are the students who love this program. They are surrounded by people who love the things they love. Often they are able to join groups that have interests similar to theirs. Even for high school students who do not fit into this category, there is the attraction of the fantasy games, the medieval weapons demonstration, and the author talk. Another important benefit for the library is the opportunity to work with the science fiction community and bring them in contact with the up-and-coming members of the science fiction world.

The number of people who attend the *Science Fiction/Fantasy Day* programs has ranged from sixty to three hundred. A high turnout is expected at the next program, to be held at the brand new mid-county regional library, an area with a high proportion of young adults. Some new science fiction groups are waiting to participate in the program.

The program requires two to three staff members dedicated to coordinating the event and two to three pages to move furniture around. All of the participants in the program (except sometimes the author) are volunteers. These include: two musicians playing Filk music; three or four members of the Society for Creative Anachronism putting on a weapons demonstration; three members of the Western Oregon Wargamers demonstrating and playing one of their fantasy games; two to three members of the Portland Science Fiction Society staffing a table; four to six members of a USS Star Ship (a "Star Trek ship") in full costume; two members of the Oregon Dark Shadows society in full costume; three members of the Klingon Assault group (another Star Trek group) in full costume; two members of the Mercedes Lackey fan club; two members of the National Fantasy Fan Club; and more. Some of the *Science Fiction/Fantasy Day* programs have had gaming clubs made up of local high school students. They set up a table with their fantasy game and had as many people participating as the Western Oregon Wargamers.

Since attendance figures vary from program to program, staff is always evaluating why one *Science Fiction/Fantasy Day* brought in three hundred people and one sixty people. The two main factors seem to be time of year—the program does better in the spring or fall than it does in the summer—and the draw of the guest author. One of the most popular authors was Timothy Zahn, who spoke at the time he was publishing his Star Trek books.

Funding

The program is funded through the library's regular operating budget. The main costs are staff time during the program and the production of flyers sent to the branch libraries, middle and high schools, and community centers. Sometimes the guest author has been paid, but not always (this has ranged from $150 to $250). Staff time during the program, including setup and cleanup but not preparation time (which at this point is YA Specialist time only), comes to approximately $138.50 (this includes two librarians to coordinate the program and two pages to set up and take away furniture). Flyers are produced by the library's public relations department. The cost of producing flyers is approximately $59.24 to $68.29 for staff time and $9.05 for materials.

Contact Person

Naomi Angier, Young Adult Specialist, Multnomah County Library, 205 NE Russell Street, Portland, OR 97212. (503) 248-5412. E-mail: <naomia@nethost.multnomah.lib.or.us>

A Klingon challenges a medieval warrior from the Society for Creative Anachronism.

28.
New York Public Library

New York, New York

Idea

Booklists for young adults

Customers

Young adults, twelve through eighteen, librarians, and teachers

Community

New York City is a vast melange of 8.5 million people, 2.1 million of whom are under the age of twenty. Of the latter group, 800,000 are over the age of twelve, forming the core audience for young adult services. Racially, New Yorkers are a diverse lot, with African Americans comprising 26.4 percent of the population, Asians 7.1 percent, and Hispanics 21.6 percent. More than 15 percent are of immigrant birth, with the largest groups coming from the Dominican Republic, China, Jamaica, Colombia, and Korea. Despite the city's high cost of living, fully 40.3 percent survive on incomes of less than $25,000 per year. Of the adult population, 55 percent have a high school diploma or less, making the effort to promote literacy and reading extremely vital. New York's mosaic of challenges makes it an exciting and rewarding place to perform library services.

Setting

The New York Public Library includes, besides four research libraries, eighty-four branch libraries whose mission is to meet the educational, informational and cultural needs of millions of New Yorkers of every age and ethnic background.

Program Description

The development of booklists in varied formats is an outgrowth of professional young adult work at the New York Public Library. Goals are simple: to promote reading for information and pleasure and to introduce teenagers to the best books on a variety of subjects. Each YA librarian participates in a book committee where books read are discussed and recommendations for purchase and specific book list consideration are made. The librarians, through their work in the branch libraries, bring their expertise and knowledge of needs and interests teenagers currently have to these discussions. The lists are given free of charge to teenagers in the branches and are promoted by NYPL's YA librarians through visits to classes in schools, neighborhood agencies, and classes who visit their local library. Booktalks are given by the librarians on specific titles on the list to generate interest.

Books for the Teen Age was first published in 1929 for young adults ages twelve through eighteen and continues to be published annually. Each January a small group of senior staff look at the recommended choices by librarians from the branch libraries to make final selections for the next edition. Because teenagers vary so much in their interests and reading abilities, the list reflects this variety. Approximately 65 percent of the list are books written for adults, but with appeal for teens; the other 35 percent are books written specifically for the young adult market. There are over one thousand titles on the list and approximately one-third are changed each year. Grouped into seventy subject areas, with brief annotations, the titles in each edition hopefully entice young people to seek out included titles and read them. The structure of the list, however, is not engraved in stone. It is fluid, adaptable, and changes with the mercurial teens for whom it is intended. For example, recent additions have been the topics Vietnam Remembered, AIDS, Horror, The Universe, Being Gay, and Never Again: The Holocaust.

For over twenty years, the cover for *Books for the Teen Age* has been designed by a New York City high school student. The cover art competition offers an opportunity to showcase teen talent, and gives the list a contemporary look that will appeal to other teens. There is a first prize awarded and two runners-up. Selected entries are on display at the Nathan Straus Young Adult Center for a month. 1996 marked a turning point in the format of *Books for the Teen Age*. Graphic designers Craig Lowy and Ruth Peyser of Somersault Design worked with the Office of Young Adult Services to create a "magazine of books." The 1996 cover is a composite of past cover art by young adults. The 1997 cover will again feature a singular artwork created by a teenager.

Each year when the list is published, a very special publication reception is held. All the authors who have a new book on the list are invited and recognized for their work. The prizewinning students are honored as well as their art teachers and their school librarians. It is a day that brings together teenagers, librarians (school and public), authors, parents, and representatives from the publishing world to celebrate books, reading, and libraries. In 1996 over five hundred attended! For the duration of the following month, the new titles are on exhibit at the Nathan Straus Young Adult Center for display and examination.

In 1996, 16,500 copies of *Books for the Teen Age* were printed at a cost of $16,400. A special edition of *Books for the Teen Age* is available in a large-print format listing titles available in recorded or Braille formats. The titles are available in special media to all participants in the Library of Congress National Library Service for the Blind and Physically Handicapped program.

That young people find other NYPL YA publications as appealing as *Books for the Teen Age* is also gratifying to staff. Recent publications include:

Summer Reading Lists. The annual *Summer Reading Lists* are bookmarks prepared in collaboration with the Brooklyn Public Library, the Queens Public Library, and the New York City Board of Education. The bookmarks, available in English and Spanish, feature authors of books for young adults and nonfiction titles in young adult collections. Available in all neighborhood libraries, they were distributed to seventh and eighth grade students in targeted school districts. In 1996 the Library printed 155,000 copies supported with funds from the Connecting Libraries and Schools Project (CLASP) at a cost of $8,400. This year marked the premiere of the *Summer Reading Lists* as a link of the NYPL homepage for teenagers, Teen Link.

Teen Link: Good Books. March 1996 marked the premiere of the NYPL homepage for teenagers <http://www.nypl.org/branch/teen/teenlink.html>. The site—which includes links for homework help, college and career information, sports sites, fun and games, the arts, E-Zines, teen homepages, and TV/movie links—prominently features highly recommended books.

Good Books is a monthly feature prepared by the Office of Young Adult Services. Book covers are featured along with an intriguing annotation.

Oasis: Libros en Español Para Jovenes. Oasis is the third edition of *Books in Spanish for Teenagers.* The list is bilingual and includes ninety books featuring biographies, teen romance, adventure, sports, health, and poetry. Compiled by a committee of Young Adult Librarians, 5,000 copies were printed in-house for distribution to teenagers in neighborhood libraries.

Access Ability: Resources for and about People with Disabilities. This series of booklists contains selected titles for and about people with disabilities of all ages. The YA titles in the series, *Materials for and about People with Disabilities: For and about Young Adults*, is a recommended list of twenty-eight books selected by young adult librarians. This collaborative publication was initiated by the NYPL Office of Services for Persons with Disabilities. Seventy-five hundred copies at a cost of $20,000 were designed and printed with a grant from the United States Department of Education Project for Initiating Recreational Programs for Individuals with Disabilities. The Library Public Relations Council honored *Access Ability* with the L. PeRCy Award. The booklist was chosen over eighty-five other choices from libraries around the country and recognized with First Prize for Outstanding Achievement in Library Public Relations Promotion in the category of Materials/Book List.

Celebrating the Dream II. Over 250 books featuring African Americans and others of African descent are featured in this booklet updated approximately every five years. *Celebrating the Dream II* is distributed to teenagers at all New York Public Library branches. The primary selectors were young adult librarians. Seventeen thousand copies were printed at a cost of $10,500 supported in part with funds from CLASP. A reprinting of fourteen thousand copies was done at a cost of $12,000.

Illustration by Brian Pinkney.

Risky Times. Young people instantly recognize that red ribbons symbolize the fight against HIV and AIDS. Sixteen fiction and nonfiction titles are featured on this list designed by graphic artist Matthew Gilbert. Twenty-five thousand copies were printed at a cost of $6,000. Selected by young adult librarians, this publication was co-sponsored by the NYPL Office of Services for Persons with Disabilities and supported with a grant from the United States Department of Education Project for Initiating Recreational Programs for Individuals with Disabilities. *Risky*

Times is the recipient of the 1996 Pied Piper Award from the New York Library Association. This award recognizes exemplary library publications for youth.

Global Beat. Global Beat is a list of multicultural books for teenagers. Selected by young adult librarians, these 250+ titles are available in young adult collections throughout NYPL. Supported with funds from the DeWitt Wallace–Reader's Digest/Connecting Libraries and Schools Project, *Global Beat's* print run was 16,000 at a cost of $11,000.

Funding

Interspersed under Program Description.

Contact Person

Marilee Foglesong, Coordinator, Office of Young Adult Services, The New York Public Library, 455 Fifth Avenue, New York, NY 10016. (212) 340-0907

29.
Newport Public Library
Newport, Oregon

Idea

Books Are the Key

Customers

Young adults incarcerated at the Lincoln County Juvenile Detention Facility

Community

The city of Newport has a young adult population, ages ten to nineteen, of 1,065 (1990 census). In 1995 the Lincoln County Juvenile Detention Facility saw 153 individuals incarcerated for juvenile crime (Lincoln County Juvenile Department 1995 Annual Report).

Setting

Newport Public Library is a medium-sized (for Oregon) municipal library serving a population of 12,592 people. The full-time-equivalent staff of nine manages a collection of 50,000 items and a yearly circulation of 200,000. In FY 1995–96, the Youth Services Coordinator was responsible for providing and/or supervising 342 programs for Newport's children and families. Newport Public Library is a member of the Coastal Resource Sharing Network, a consortium of nine public and school libraries sharing an online catalog system.

Program Description

Books Are the Key is a program that provides weekly library service to the Lincoln County Juvenile Department Detention Facility located in Newport, Oregon. Newport Public Library's Youth Services Coordinator visits the incarcerated young adults for approximately one hour per week. She spends this time determining what types of materials they want to read, what their reading levels are, booktalking, and, if time allows and the young adults are cooperative, reading aloud or telling age-appropriate stories. The librarian then returns to the library, selects materials (which must be in paperback as per regulations) and delivers them to the detention facility. The

Scene inside Juvenile Detention Facility. Rebecca Cohen, *Books Are the Key* program provider, is at center facing camera.

detention facility also houses a small permanent collection that NPL maintains as budget allows.

Newport Public Library's mission is to foster appreciation for reading and learning. Because most of these incarcerated young adults have not experienced much success in school, many of them have never developed an appreciation of reading, much less read a book for pleasure. They often don't think of books as a source of enjoyment, only as work—or even torture. *Books Are the Key* changes that thinking by introducing them to the pleasures of reading.

The young adults incarcerated at the Lincoln County facility have few recreational options available to them. They may watch one hour of staff-selected television programming in the evening, they may play handball (if they haven't misbehaved) in the fifteen-by-twenty-foot caged outdoor space, or they may read. Prior to *Books Are the Key*, the only books available were paperback novels that the staff donated, most of which were hand-me-down children's titles such as *The Lion, the Witch, and the Wardrobe* (quality literature but not very appealing to these unhappy teenagers). *Books Are the Key* is providing these young adults an opportunity to get what they really want (per facility policies, which include no nude pictures, no cartoons depicting drug use) in the way of reading material. The program provider booktalks hot new young adult titles, conducts interviews to ascertain what they want to read and what their reading level is, and reads aloud for whatever part of the hour is left.

Reading aloud is a vital part of the program. The materials are chosen with this audience in mind and then read in an entertaining fashion. The facility staff does not censor what is read, although the provider is especially careful with selection. The read-aloud sometimes leads to one of the young adults reading aloud. It always means that the book will be kept and read by at least one of the youths. When the program first began in 1994, the only books being requested were by Stephen King and R. L. Stine. Booktalking and reading aloud have introduced these young adults to John Steinbeck, J. R. R. Tolkien, Alice Walker, Chris Crutcher, Edgar Allan Poe, and numerous other authors.

According to facility staff, this program has contributed to overall improvement in behavior at the facility and has resulted in an increased interest in books and reading. A number of the young adults have come into the library upon release and gotten library cards. This program has changed the way some of these young adults look at books, libraries, and hopefully, life, for the better.

This program has reached 648 young adults since its inception during the summer of 1994. One Newport Library staff member is involved in this program. Volunteers are not allowed in the detention facility. The nature of the program's location and audience preclude youth participation other than their direct input to the program provider on the day of service. The same factors contribute to the difficulty in evaluating the program. A survey is being constructed for the youth involved which will be available for use in early 1997.

Within these restrictions, *Books Are the Key* is evaluated using three different criteria: (1) number of young adults contacted (91 in 1994, 222 in 1995, 313 up to 9/15/96); (2) number of items checked out on the facility account (174 in 1994, 392 in 1995, 485 to date in 1996); (3) survey responses to be obtained from incarcerated young adults when the anticipated evaluation tool is administered.

Funding

Books Are the Key is funded entirely from Newport Library's budget. The cost for this program is $647.36 per year. That figure represents forty-eight hours per year of the Youth Services Coordinator's time at the current rate of $13.07 per hour.

Contact Person

Rebecca Cohen, Newport Public Library, 35 NW Nye Street, Newport, OR 97365. (541) 265-3109

30.
Oak Park Public Library

Oak Park, Illinois

Idea

Young Adult After-hours Coffeehouse

Customers

Young adults, twelve through eighteen

Community

Oak Park, Illinois, a western suburb of Chicago, is a thriving community with a population of 53,648. The Oak Park Public Library strives to reflect the unique heritage, rich history, and continuing growth of the community. The young adult department of the Oak Park Public Library serves two public junior high schools with a total enrollment of 1,076 and one public high school with an enrollment of 2,747. The department also provides service for students in six private schools. The young adults of Oak Park represent a rich variety of racial and ethnic backgrounds with 63.2 percent Caucasian, 28.6 percent African American, 4.2 percent Asian and Pacific Islanders, 3.6 percent Hispanic, 0.4 percent Native American.

Setting

The Oak Park Public Library has a staff of 105 employees and consists of three locations—the main library and the Maze and Dole branch libraries. The library, a member of the Suburban Library System, has over 41,000 registered borrowers, and total annual circulation is approximately 600,000. The collection consists of around 220,000 volumes. The library is well supported by the community both financially and by the approximately two thousand volunteer hours contributed last year. The library also receives outstanding coverage in the local papers. The Oak Park Public Library has made a strong commitment to serving young adults in the community, as is evidenced by the existence of a full-time young adult librarian position.

Program Description

The lights are dim in the meeting room of the Oak Park Public Library. Teens sit at round coffeehouse tables and even on pillows on the floor, slowly sipping coffee and eating refreshments, anxiously awaiting the start of the Friday night program. The atmosphere is that of a 1960s beatnik coffeehouse. The program begins with an "open-mike" segment, consisting of participants reading poetry, reciting passages from plays, or even performing music. Next, there's a feature performance by a real live local poet or musical group. Next, participants read selections from *The Spiffy TACloid*, the Teen Administrative Council's writing journal. Then, it's time for the poetry slam, where aspiring poets square off in an individual or team competition. Dig it, man. . . .

The Teen Administrative Council (the library's teen advisory board) and the YA librarian initially established the *Young Adult After-hours Coffeehouse* program in conjunction with the beat generation theme of the summer reading program. The coffeehouses are held after library hours from 7:00 to 9:30 on the third Friday night of the month. It was the dream of the Teen Administrative Council to create a coffeehouse for teens, and the after-hours element was added in response to the common complaint from local teens that there was nothing for them to do on Friday nights. As a device to promote reading, poetry reading was added to capitalize on the heightened interest in poetry across the country.

There has been a lot of community support for the program from local teachers and a volunteer who has offered her time to help with the coffeehouses, as well as several articles appearing in the local papers. Also, the Cook County Sheriff Youth Services Division will feature the coffeehouse in a new program highlighting successful youth programming in Cook County, Illinois. The coffeehouse has also served as a model for similar programs at other area libraries.

Participation in the *Young Adult After-hours Coffeehouses* continues to increase. The program got off to a slow start, competing with a Chicago Bulls playoff game (who knew?) for the first coffeehouse, which had an attendance of twelve. The numbers have dramatically increased, however, and attendance now averages between 75 and 100.

The coffeehouses are staffed by the YA librarian, a library security officer (because the program is held after hours), and a community volunteer.

The Teen Administrative Council (TAC) has been instrumental in the planning, implementation, and evaluation of the *Young Adult After-hours Coffeehouses*. They provided the foundation for the original concept, and are continually recruiting participants for the coffeehouses. At weekly TAC meetings, they make it a point to brainstorm on new ideas for improving the coffeehouses. Staff have been relying on the following to evaluate the *Young Adult After-hours Coffeehouses*: evaluation forms, which are handed out at the end of every coffeehouse; rising attendance at the coffeehouse; and feedback from local teens.

Funding

The project was initially funded as a part of the young adult summer reading program budget. However, because of the success of the program and support from the community and the library, the library has received a $1,500 gift from the Friends of the Oak Park Public Library to extend the coffeehouses through the school year. The cost of the coffeehouses has been mainly staff time, as local Oak Park establishments have been very generous in donating refreshments. Funds donated by the Friends have been used to bring in local poets, and there are plans to possibly use some of this money to hold a poetry workshop in conjunction with the coffeehouses.

Contact Person

Jill Bambenek, Oak Park Public Library, 834 Lake Street, Oak Park, IL 60301. (708) 383-8200

Coffeehouse

...the only people for me are the mad ones, the ones who are mad to live, mad to talk, mad to be saved, desirous of everything at the same time, the ones who never yawn or say a commonplace thing, but burn, burn like fabulous Roman candles exploding like spiders across the stars and in the middle you see the blue centerlight pop and everyone goes "Awww!"

Jack Kerouac

WHAT CAN YOU DO AT THE LIBRARY AFTER HOURS? EAT TREATS, READ POETRY, AND PLAY MUSIC.

JOIN OUR BEAT SCENE AT THE AFTER-HOURS LIBRARY COFFEEHOUSE! OPEN TO ANYONE GRADE SEVEN AND OLDER!

September 20, 7pm to 9pm
Oak Park Public Library
834 Lake Street
Need more info?
Contact Jill Bambenek, at 383-8200

31. Rahway Public Library

Rahway, New Jersey

Idea

Rahway Teen Roarin' Readers

Customers

Target audience is young adults, ages eleven through eighteen, or grades six through twelve; however, the primary audience reached is ages eleven through fifteen, or grades six through ten.

Community

The Rahway Public Library serves a population of 25,325; of this 10 percent are of the age group ten through eighteen (25 percent of them African-American). Rahway is a multi-ethnic community, with 19,092 Caucasian (75 percent), African-American 5,119 (20 percent), 606 Asian/Pacific Islander (2.4 percent), and other 508 (2 percent). This includes a total of 2,018 Hispanics (7.9 percent).

Students attend the usual mix of schools—public, Roman Catholic, Christian, and private, as well as a few homeschoolers. For Rahway Intermediate School students (grades six through eight) there is a choice of six "schools." These include the *Honors Academy*; *RIDES* (Rahway Institute of Developmental Environmental Studies), emphasizing hands-on projects and activities in a cooperative learning environment in the study of ecological sciences; *Math, Science, Technology*, with an emphasis on the impact of science, math, and technology on our world; *Dual Language* (Spanish); *Microsociety, Inc.*, in which students run businesses, cultural institutions, and courts and legislatures; and *Communicative Arts* for students interested in media and journalism. The high school offers the Carl Sagan program, which emphasizes science and technology, and an honors program for each grade, in addition to the CLEP program.

Setting

The library statistics for calendar year 1995 are:

Total volumes	84,477
AV materials	1,724
People with cards	8,971
Circulation	119,188
Information requests	13,757
Public visits	135,737
Hours open	60/week

Program Description

The Rahway Public Library's *Rahway Teen Roarin' Readers* (better known as the Triple R's), begun over ten years ago with the initial purpose of providing reading incentives and basic programming for teens, has a different theme each year to promote summer reading and participation in programs, workshops, and trips. The workshops and programs emphasize learning for fun including career orientation and hobby development. These have included skateboarding, hot air balloons, cooking, good grooming, crafts, museum visits, canoeing, sailing, and game nights. In the last two years the program has achieved a balance of educational, cultural, and recreational programs with the inclusion of well-chosen trips and workshops.

More advanced crafts and workshops match the abilities and interests of this age group (for example, all phases of photography, including developing; cake decorating; tie-dyeing and waxing T-shirts; theater crafts and performance; mask sculpturing; and sculptures from recyclables). The photography workshop, conducted by a community volunteer, afforded an opportunity to take black-and-white pictures, watch a video on photo development, and then actually use the chemical processes to develop their pictures. In 1995 and 1996, theater workshops were included, with a guest from Creative Theater, from whom teens learned basic theater skills; in 1996, teens did a play for themselves, *Murder in the Mall*, and created scenery, but improvised their parts with imagination instead of using a written script.

Initially, when trips were suggested as an addition to the program, the staff were concerned about taking thirty teens outside Rahway on a library-sponsored trip. Overall though, the trips have proven to be successful and of high interest to teens, even including the learning aspects of the places visited. Most of the teens have been cooperative, respectful, and pleasant. Although there have been occasional behavior problems, these have been gracefully resolved. Each year, places are chosen for visits based loosely on the theme for the summer. In 1995, the theme was "Ticket to Adventure" (and the emphasis was on science and technology); participants traveled to the New Jersey State Aquarium, including a behind-the-scenes tour, to Seton Hall University to explore the Internet, computer graphics, and the University Library CD-ROMs; to the Franklin Institute in Philadelphia, with many hands-on opportunities and their planetarium; and to the Hackensack Environment Center for a canoe trip through the Meadowlands with a guide who explained the development and ecological importance of these lands.

The theme for 1996 was "Land, Sea and Air," traveling to South Street Seaport Museum (where teens had the opportunity to raise the sail and to learn other aspects of early sailing life) and the Intrepid Museum (a World War II ship), and taking the Clearwater sloop sail, an environmental educational program on the Hudson River (the teens fished with nets, hoisted the sails, steered the boat, visited crew quarters, and learned seamanship). Howell Living Farm, an actual working turn-of-the-century farm, was also included, where students did some farm chores, as well as taking a hay ride and exploring the farm. Finally, for the closing party, the top thirty readers went to Medieval Times. One exciting program scheduled was a skateboarding extravaganza with a skateboarding group and bands, where teens were also allowed to skateboard. The programs had over three hundred people attending, and some of the ramps constructed by the library's maintenance staff were purchased by a local skate shop afterwards.

Participating young adults used various levels of library skills during the "Murder in the Library," or "Book Trail" programs. Teens had to use the card catalog and CD-ROMs, following a trail to the different collections within the adult department. Other scavenger hunts, during which factual information had to be found, were based on "Where in the World Is Carmen Sandiego?" In summary, the emphasis during the last two summers has been fewer workshops but better selected to meet the expectations, interests, and needs of teens, in addition to education-based trips.

Young adults are contacted in three different ways: (1) the librarian goes to the intermediate school to talk about the Triple R programs being offered; (2) teens are asked to keep reading logs, which assist the reference staff in providing readers' advisory services, as well as in learning reading interests and developing those interests; (3) rapport is built, particularly on trips. At events held outside the library, conversation flows relatively easily. Roughly 190 teens were reached in seven programs, and 110 on four trips. Though there is significant overlap, there are many teens who are reached only through the programs or the keeping of the reading log. The 110 active readers read over 2,100 books and many received bonus points for reading a variety of genres. The level of participation and reading for 1995 and 1996 was approximately the same.

During previous summers, young adults designed gameboards based on the summer themes such as Music Quest, where "This Is Your Life" (success in the world of music) or "Music World Tour" games were designed and played by teens. In addition, there were life-size checkers and variations of book bingo which were also created by teens. In the summer of 1995, the option for students entering sixth grade to join the Triple R's was added because of the change in the public school structure to a middle school rather than a junior high. An additional reason was that some younger adolescents felt that the programs offered by the children's department were no longer of interest to them, and they and their parents felt they were mature enough to participate in the Triple R's. In 1995 field trips were offered for the first time, because of increased support by Merck & Co., Inc. In addition to new teens joining the program each year, many teens have participated for three and five years, with a few even wanting to join after graduating from high school. The Triple R's has become a family affair as siblings and relatives continue with the program.

As part of the final party, teens evaluated the programs, orally relating what they liked and did not like, what they wanted next year, and possible ideas for programs for the school year. A year-round program and teen advisory board are in the planning stages. The staff will also evaluate this year's program's strengths and weaknesses as a basis to plan for next summer.

Funding

Excluding salaries, paper, arts and crafts supplies, and incidentals, the trips and programs were funded with a grant from Merck & Co., Inc. of Rahway ($3,500 in 1996), plus a small amount from the library's budget. As far as staff time, the library assistant spends ten to twelve hours per week of a sixteen-hour-per-week schedule ($7.03/per hour) in the summer, as well as planning and preparation time prior to the program, especially this year when the librarian was on four-fifths leave. The librarian spends about twenty-four out of thirty-five hours per week ($40,900 annually) during the summer on the program. In addition, parent volunteers accompany staff and YAs on the trips as chaperones. A semi-professional photographer also volunteered to join all the trips as a chaperone and attend some of the programs; this added a dimension which the teens enjoyed, as well as helping to document the program.

The budget breakdown includes:

South Street Seaport museum and Intrepid Museum	$ 654
Howell Living Farm	310
Clearwater Sloop sail	1,185
Medieval Times	1,085
Hot-air balloon	500
Craft materials	185
Paper and display board	76
Video blanks	20
Total	$4,015

Contact Persons

Carol Marlowe and Pamela Watkins, Coordinators, Rahway Public Library, 1175 St. Georges Avenue, Rahway, New Jersey 07065. (908) 388-0761

32.
San Antonio Public Library, Central Library

San Antonio, Texas

Idea

Enchilada Players

Customers

Young adults in junior and senior high school and children

Community

San Antonio is the ninth largest city in the United States (the third largest city in Texas) with a total population of 998,905 people. The ethnic breakdown of the city is 71.1 percent Caucasian, 7.1 percent African-American, and 49.8 percent Hispanic. San Antonio has a high percentage of teenagers: nearly 15 percent of the population is thirteen through eighteen years old. The median family income is low, at $23,584 per family. About 53 percent of the high school students in Bexar County are economically disadvantaged.

Setting

The San Antonio Central Library is a new facility serving the inner-city downtown area. Since the building opened in May of 1995 an increase in young adult patronage has been noted. The *Enchilada Players* took their name from the library's distinctive enchilada red color.

Program Description

The *Enchilada Players* is a readers' theater group made up of fifteen young adults. This summer they produced original adaptations of Native American, Mexican, Cuban, and classic American folktales by creating puppets, props, and sets, and writing songs to tell their stories. These bilingual adaptations were presented to children as part of the Central Library's summer reading program. Four original programs were performed three times each during July 1996 with attendance often exceeding one hundred children per performance.

For children, young adults are the coolest things around and, while they may be hesitant to listen to adults expounding upon the virtues of books and reading, they will emulate young adults when the message is "books are cool." The *Enchilada Players* afforded children the opportunity to see young adults reading, enjoying, and creating with books. While the players performed original adaptations of folktales, they ended each program by telling their audience that "the ideas for this program came from these books."

The San Antonio community has problems with gangs and graffiti; consequently young adults are often mentioned in a negative context. The *Enchilada Players* provided an opportunity for the participants to become positive role models for children. Young adult participants were cognizant of their status as role models and eagerly took time to speak with children after the performances. Producing adaptations of multicultural folktales helped foster pride in the young adults' Hispanic heritage and additionally gave them a chance to explore folklore from various cultures. The result was a wonderfully fresh and often irreverent take on classic tales ranging from the "Bossy Gallito" to "Little Red Low-Riding Hood."

Fifteen young adults participated in the *Enchilada Players*. Some of them used their talents as writers, set designers, puppet makers, and song writers, while the more outgoing members of the group served as actors or storytellers. The young adult participants had total creative control over their productions. They selected the stories to adapt, wrote the adaptations, and created or selected the puppets, props, and sets. The young adults themselves evaluated the success of the performance based on attendance and audience response. After each performance they got together and talked about what would make the next presentation more successful. The program was evaluated based upon attendance, audience reaction, and circulation of program display books. A comparison of previous year's statistics was not possible as this was the *Enchilada Players'* premiere year.

One staff member was involved in assisting with the *Enchilada Players'* productions.

Funding

Materials and craft supplies were provided by the library's children's department. The young adult participants used what was on hand and improvised the other things they needed. Staff hours: one staff member spent approximately twenty-six hours (at roughly $10 per hour) working with the young adults in an advisory capacity.

Contact Person

Jennifer Ellard, San Antonio Public Library, 600 Soledad Street, San Antonio, TX 78205. (210) 207-2681

33.
Upper Arlington Public Library

Upper Arlington, Ohio

Idea

An Afternoon of Medieval Revels

Customers

Young adults, ages twelve through eighteen

Community

The Upper Arlington Public Library System serves a city population of approximately 34,000; the overall county population is approximately one million. The community of Upper Arlington has approximately 1,700 middle school students and 2,000 high school students. Ninety-five percent of the high school students go on to attend college after graduation. Students come from highly academic backgrounds and offer a variety of interests and talents to the community. Over 59 percent of the Upper Arlington community has completed at least sixteen years of education.

Setting

The Upper Arlington Public Library is a medium-sized municipal public library system located in a suburb of Columbus, Ohio, one of seven district libraries in Franklin County. A portion of the Library and Local Government Support Fund, which is collected and disbursed at the county level, is received by UAPL; therefore, by law, the library must serve all county residents on an equal basis to those in the city. UAPL has over 61,000 active cardholders and had a 1995 circulation of over 1.4 million. The UAPL system is comprised of a main facility, geographically located in the center of the community, and two branches.

Program Description

From 2 to 4 p.m. on July 17, 1996, the Young Adult/Youth Services Department of the Upper Arlington Public Library was transported back in time to the age of kings, jesters, minstrels and knights. Over one hundred young adults gathered to partake in *An Afternoon of Medieval Revels*. This program was designed not only to entertain, but to encourage participants to experience life in a medieval kingdom. Period refreshments, crafts, and activities were presented, as well as information on how social class impacted on quality and style of life. Volunteers helped in the development and operation of this event. The program was designed to be the midsummer celebration for the Young Adult Book Club, as well as to inspire creativity and enthusiasm in those teens who took part.

In September 1994, Ohio State University contacted the Upper Arlington Public Library to request programming support for its library event: "The Many Realms of King Arthur" (an ALA traveling exhibit). In November 1994, in conjunction with the university's program, a day of crafts and entertainment specific to the Middle Ages was designed, with a booktalk called "Searching for the Real King Arthur." Subsequently, staff members were asked by two middle schools and the local high school to repeat the programs in those facilities. This led to more interaction with young adults who were eager to exchange their ideas and interest in that time period. After speaking with many of the library's teen volunteers, staff decided that the interest level in this subject area was high enough to support a future summer reading club theme. In the fall of 1995, the 1996 summer program theme, "Join the Quest for Summer Reading" was selected.

An Afternoon of Medieval Revels was designed as a midsummer celebration for young adults in Upper Arlington and the surrounding communities. In particular, it was to be directed toward those enrolled in the Young Adult Summer Reading Club (grades six and up), although no one would be excluded and all would be encouraged to attend. The event would be a day of fun, while allowing the teens to experience a taste of life in the Middle Ages. To this end, all of the crafts, activities, and refreshments were designed to be as authentic as possible, and planners also tried to address the questions students had raised in prior activities on lifestyles, etc., relating to the period. To make this as appealing an activity as possible, library staff relied on conversations with teenage patrons, as well as teen volunteers, to help design the program.

As plans progressed, the library benefited from a cooperative program with one of the local middle schools: students are driven to the library during the school day to perform volunteer services. In anticipation of the coming event, those teens were asked to design decorations for the department reflecting the theme of the Middle Ages. Over one hundred students participated, designing and creating heraldic shields and flags which were hung along the walls and from the ceiling in the library's central seating area. Students were able to come in and view their handicrafts, giving them a vested interest in the program.

A staff committee was formed, meeting once to "brainstorm," and later to finalize plans for publicity, crafts, food, and entertainment. Posters, news releases, and public service announcements were sent out approximately two weeks before the event. Iron-on decals (designed by library staff and created on library computers and printers) were distributed to staff members and volunteers who would be helping with the program. About a week before the event, craft materials were purchased, entertainers confirmed, and final details reviewed. At last the day arrived. The Young Adult/Youth Services Department was transformed into "The Royal Kingdom of the Public Library of Upper Arlington." Six staff members and nineteen "volunteens" assisted on the day of the program. Young adults demonstrated how to juggle, draw heraldry pogs, make laurel wreaths, play chess and checkers, and write in calligraphy. They braided hair. They sold pretzels and "the Queen's jewels." They dished up "pease" porridge, almond cardamom cakes, and "canel" cucumbers, all made (and donated) by staff members. They sampled buttermilk and "wine" (grape juice). Several volunteers even wore period costumes. The young adults were well versed in their "royal duties." They explained what different classes ate and the significance of the crafts and games.

Upon entering the Royal Kingdom, participants were given "medieval" money to spend on food and entertainment. Professional minstrels played period music. A storyteller offered verbal illustrations of the times and shared her jester puppets. A wandering juggler demonstrated his craft and taught interested teens how to juggle. A major attraction was a thirteen-year-old Ohio resident who is a nationally ranked archer. He shared his talent by demonstrating his expertise in the art of medieval archery. He wore a period costume and used a Turkish-style bow. This outdoor demonstration added another dimension to the entertainment.

One hundred nine young adults attended the event, making the day a resounding success. Staff wandered through the crowd getting feedback to confirm that the teens were as excited as they were about the event. Local newspapers provided print coverage, and one network television station was so interested in the program that they sent a camera crew to cover the event, then featured it on the 6:00 p.m. news.

As a first-time event, this program was an introductory activity for young adults in connection with the summer reading club. Statistics for the YA Summer Reading Club confirm the success of the program, showing a 20 percent increase in YA reading club participation this year.

The *Medieval Revels* program seemed to answer a need in the community for entertainment that is fun as well as educational. This was evidenced by the enthusiasm for the 1994 medieval programs and the continued interest in this subject exhibited by young adult patrons. An invitation to participate was extended to students in grades five and up, to tap their high interest in the library and to help them identify it as an integral part of their lives. Through the success of this and similar events, many of the fifth graders are eager to take part in the library's teen volunteer program, which begins once students have completed grade five. This program attracted many teens who were not library users and gave library staff the opportunity to introduce themselves and to invite them to sample a little of what they could enjoy by visiting more often. Also, seeing the teen volunteers involved in the activity emphasized the fact that the program was for and about teens.

Student volunteers enthusiastically offered their hands and ideas to help this program develop, come alive, and ultimately result in an unqualified success. As they left the *Revels*, many of the participants asked what would be done next year to have "this much fun again."

Funding

The Friends of the Upper Arlington Public Library provided the money to purchase the games and some of the craft supplies. This included: markers $8, games $12, transparent paper for "stained glass" $8, combs for braiding hair $2, "Queen's jewels" $6, pipe cleaners for laurel wreaths $4, and food $20. The Friends also paid for the musicians, the Amalia Consort, $75, and for the storyteller, Cathie Browning, $30. The juggler and archery demonstration were free. The library's public service department was able to obtain the ribbons, flowers, pogs, and additional food needed through donations from local retailers. Phone calls were made to local craft and fabric stores, resulting in eager participation by community merchants. The six staff members involved in the program spent a total of 50 hours working on the project at an average hourly rate of $12, for a total cost of $600.

Contact Person

Betty Sheridan, Upper Arlington Public Library, 2800 Tremont Road, Upper Arlington, Ohio 43221. (614) 486-9621

34.
Vashon High School Library

Vashon, Washington

Idea

Every picture sells a story

Customers

Senior high school students

Community

Vashon is an island, semi-rural, but smack in the path of urban flight. When Seattle hippies went "back to the land," many came to Vashon and settled among the working class population. Their counterculture influence on the schools remains strong today, with advocacy for the arts, environmental studies, and alternative programs. The newest "new" students also arrive mostly from Seattle, but their parents aren't looking as much for freedom as for safety. Crime and gangs threaten Seattle students; Vashon's unique combination of low crime and still-available low rents is just a ferry ride away. As a result, the student body is quite diverse economically—there are students who live in waterfront estates and students who live in backwoods cabins. All rub elbows at Vashon High School, but what makes the community unique is that *everybody rides the ferries.* Ferries link Vashon to the mainland and big-city culture; to most of the students, however, the green and white boats represent a parental plot of isolation. Vashon students yearn to connect; it's palpable. They're a librarian's dream.

Setting

The Vashon High School Library, though loved by staff, is the original seventies fashion victim. Conceived as the central axis of a school-without-walls (remember *Summerhill*?), it inevitably got walled in. The library is still circular, though, and still has avocado bookshelves, while serving 527 students with a full-time librarian and a full-time aide. The avocado card catalog was ditched two years ago as VHS became the first of the district's three schools to automate circulation, acquisitions, and readers' advisory services. Staff keeps busy doing what school librarians do: teaching library skills, ordering books, troubleshooting hardware, promising to weed the bloated collection, and so on. Most of all, though, the library strives to be a friendly place where good books fly off those (avocado) shelves.

Program Description

Every picture tells a story, and in the Vashon High School Library personalized pictures are used to involve students in reading and to promote reading to their peers. The idea is simple, low-tech, and low-cost. Bulletin boards feature color photocopied cutouts (enlarged from photos) of student life with Vashon's own students as the willing subjects. They pose with cars, pets, and teammates. They masquerade as rock stars, shooting stars, and, once a year, as Santa's elves. Then they select books for related reading displays and bibliographies. The response, as evidenced by circulation gains, "bodies-in-the-library" count, and positive feedback, outstrips every other reading promotion tried. In the VHS library, the pictures sell the stories.

At the heart of much so-called adolescent angst exists a paradox. The need to be unique, especially on artsy Vashon, duels with the need to belong. Many students have known each other since babyhood; they have attended anti-bridge meetings together. Newcomers really struggle. Librarians know that good books can help—that various studies link pleasure reading to academic success—but not if students view the library as one more "exclusive" albeit "nerdy" club and avoid it. If their picture is on the bulletin board, though, they *always* come to see it. They bring their friends. Their friends pose, too. Often, they notice the book display and leave with a book.

The librarian got clued in to the power of pictures after a stint as yearbook advisor. The first year, the yearbook committee followed Columbia journalism standards to the letter and the book bombed. To students, a "good yearbook" is one with lots of pictures, particularly pictures of one's own self and friends. Next year, camera in hand, and vowing to include *everyone* in at least one candid, the librarian ventured far beyond the library: to the local "party" beach; to the "4X sinkhole" (where students "hang out" in their four-wheel-drive sports utility vehicles); to the edge of the wrestling mat; and beyond. The yearbooks sold out.

Chosen topics for the monthly bulletin boards are fun and inclusive. Astrological signs, rock stars, "road" scholars, and tattooed teachers have been featured. In most cases, the librarian snaps the pictures but sometimes, as with a "pets" board, students bring in their own photos. One holiday board, "Season's Readings," in which students dress as Santa and elves, proved so popular that it has become a tradition. Willing subjects are easy to find through bulletin notices, teacher input, or travel to the classrooms when appropriate. The goal is that every VHS student will pose before graduation.

Not everyone who poses can recommend a book for others to read on the topic at hand; many times at least half the choices are those of the librarian. Annotations from the library book review file are printed out and clipped to the book jackets. Checkout rates are encouraging.

In a school the size of VHS, it is not unrealistic to involve large numbers of students in such a project; the project can also be a vehicle for faculty and even community involvement. The coaches, for instance, are pleased when pictures of their players and featured sports books are posted. The "Read Everywhere" bulletin board, part of an ALA photo contest, won national recognition for an art teacher and one of her students. Possibly, the most unlikely alliance forged has been with the automotive teacher, who seldom came to the library until "Road Scholar" featured all his kids. He has since donated a computer, and he has posed with a Harley "tattoo" for the latest back-to-school effort. At least three-fourths of the faculty participate in these yearly displays; the all-time favorite bulletin board featured the faculty as they looked in their own high school days. One teacher brought in a photo of herself with Elvis—the young and gorgeous Elvis!

Reading promotions and fundraising were started several years ago because a series of budget freezes left no money for pleasure reading materials. Circulation dropped. With the promotions and "brownie fund" book purchases, the circulation started to rise again. During the librarian's maternity leave in the 1988–89 school year, her replacement did no promotion or fund-raising work, and the statistics plunged again. Since her return, and the resumption of these activities, circulation has increased by 38 percent despite only small increases in enrollment. This project has an impact and the students know it. They are aware of the efforts made to promote reading; in the last few years, students have donated books and even a bit of money to the cause. They come in to see the librarian with requests for books and some even bring book reviews. They make suggestions for bulletin board and book display themes. They help with costumes and lights for "Airband," a lip-sync rock-and-roll extravaganza. They even sneaked a candid of the librarian selling brownies into last year's yearbook.

Funding

Each display costs about $50, which covers three rolls of film, developing for the film, and color photocopy enlargement for about thirty pictures. The library sponsors two fund-raising projects: two parent volunteers bake for the weekly library bake sale, and faculty members perform in "Airband." Together, these projects raise about $1,200 annually for the library, of which a total of about $400 goes for the bulletin boards and the rest goes for the purchase of student-requested books and magazines. At first, these fund-raisers were a means to an end; now they are promotions in their own right. Two years ago, VHS students at a leadership conference made a poster listing all the good things about VHS. Right up there with the senior prom and girls' basketball were "Airband," the library's rocky road brownies, and the book-promotion bulletin boards.

Contact Person

Peggy Nelson Kallsen
Vashon High School Library
20120 Vashon Highway SW
Vashon, WA 98070
(206) 463-9171, ext. 12

Elvis and friend, from the "We Loved High School" board.

Special Needs

35.
Allen County Public Library
Fort Wayne, Indiana

Idea
Teen Agency Program (T.A.P.)

Customers
At-risk young adult residents/clients at six local youth agencies: (1) Wood Youth Center, the county-operated maximum security corrections facility for male and female juvenile offenders; (2) Allen County Youth Services, the county-operated temporary residential facility for dependent, neglected, abused, or pre-delinquent youth; (3) Cooper Teen Center, operated by Juvenile Probation, a community-based teen center focusing on prevention of delinquency; (4) Crossroads–Fort Wayne Children's Home, a community-based residential treatment and educational facility for mildly emotionally disturbed adolescents; (5) Fort Wayne Juvenile Residential Facility, operated by the Indiana Department of Corrections, a minimum-security center for juvenile offenders; and (6) Northeast Indiana Juvenile Treatment Facility, a state-operated, locked facility for treatment and education of males mandated there by the court system.

Community
Approximately 35,188 people, or 12 percent of Allen County residents, are twelve through eighteen years old. About 88 percent are Caucasian, 10 percent African-American. Close to 8 percent of Allen County's young adults live below the poverty level.

Setting
Allen County Public Library began one hundred years ago as a small, rural library in northeast Indiana. It has since exploded into one of the largest public library collections in the country. Through thirteen branches and a main library, 319,000 residents have access to more than two million books, electronic resources such as InfoTrac online and the Internet, newspapers, magazines, CD-ROMs, and more. The agency within ACPL that developed and maintains T.A.P. is Young Adults' Services. YAS has been a separate department within the main library since 1952. It is currently housed in a 4,450-square-foot room with a dedicated staff of seven and 25,000+ collection of print, media, and electronic resources, all devoted specifically to young adults. For a more complete description of the materials and services in Young Adults' Services, visit the ACPL YA website: <http://www.acpl.lib.us.in/Young_Adults/yashp.html>.

Program Description
T.A.P. evolved out of a commitment to reach young adults, persons of middle and high school age, who cannot come to the library. The primary goal of *T.A.P.* is to serve youth the library would not ordinarily reach by working with local agencies serving "high-risk" teens. In reaching these kids, the library hopes to improve literacy skills, cognitive development, and appreciation for reading by providing appealing, attractive paperbacks and magazines. These materials are specially selected for the clients at each *T.A.P.* agency and are delivered and maintained monthly by a librarian from ACPL's young adults' department. While these materials are the property of ACPL, they are kept at the *T.A.P.* agency until they are no longer of use to the teens there. In addition to materials, special programs, such as booktalking and the annual Young Adult Summer Reading Program, are taken to *T.A.P.* agencies.

According to those in the Allen County juvenile justice field over the past five years, the juvenile justice population has risen 10 to 12 percent each year. And while some are currently being reached through "diversion" programs, estimates are that 25 percent or more of the young adult population would choose not to get into trouble if they had an attractive program readily accessible to them. However, facilities are old and inexcusably cramped. Staff are stretched thin everywhere, and many kids fall through some very large cracks.

With *T.A.P.*, ACPL does its part to become part of the community "safety net" by bringing ideas, inspiration, and respite, in the form of books, magazines, and staff, to those kids most in need and least able to come to the library.

Evaluations and behavioral indicators point to a strong, positive effect. For example, *T.A.P.* kids in a focus group session at one agency said that having books and magazines from the library "uses up some of our time," "[is] better to do than just watch TV," "improves the imagination and lets you take your mind away from being here," and "keeps your skills up, so you don't fall behind." *T.A.P.* agency evaluations indicate positive effects, as noted on surveys of staff: "It gives them something to do to help pass time." "It has increased their desire to read and their reading levels." "Books and magazines are interesting to the students, so in turn they read more." "Having reading materials on hand keeps their reading skills polished on a year-round basis, not just during the school year."

When librarians visit, they are often mobbed by kids shouting "Hey, the library lady's here! What magazines you got?" The smile on the face may not be "hard" evaluation data, but it is data of the best kind. Kids, some who would not have called themselves "readers" before, enthusiastically seek out books. For example, after one booktalk last March, the booktalking librarian was literally knocked off balance by the rush of kids stampeding for the books and magazines. This was an audience teachers would have classified as nonreaders when they were on the "outside."

Informal feedback sessions after special events (such as booktalking sessions) and combination circulation and book evaluation sheets provide additional information for staff, in addition to circulation/use figures. Because of the physical setup in these facilities, it is impossible to get accurate circulation counts. Since *T.A.P.* began in 1995, materials have been used at least three thousand times. However, this number is seriously flawed: it underrepresents actual circulation. The "true" number, as estimated by staff and residents of facilities, would be three to five times that. Booktalks have been attended by 468 *T.A.P.* teens. Librarians and *T.A.P.* staff observe stampedes to the new materials each month. Miscellaneous observations: One librarian reported feeling puzzled that she could *never* find any magazines (not under beds, on bookcases, near the sofas; *nowhere*) until she noticed the walls: pictures of teen idols (from *T.A.P.* magazines) decorated every otherwise dreary bedroom. This was at the shelter for neglected, abused kids . . . where the familiar faces from teen magazines meant comfort and safety to otherwise alone, scared teens. Approximately six thousand young adults are reached annually by *T.A.P.*

Funding

In order to make service to six *T.A.P.* agencies possible, ACPL added one twenty-hour-per-week Librarian I position to the Young Adults' Services Department: annual average cost is approximately $10,053. To provide for the processing of *T.A.P.* materials, the library added five hours per week of clerk time: approximate annual cost is $1,900. A total of seven staff members are involved—six librarians (one is half-time) and one half-time clerk.

The paperback book budget for the *T.A.P.* program has been increased each year *T.A.P.* has been in existence. The book budgets have been: $1,550 (FY 1994 for 1995 "opening day" collections), $3,000 (1995) and $4,500 (1996). Magazine subscriptions for each *T.A.P.* agency have proven extremely popular. The magazine budget for *T.A.P.* has consistently held at approximately $1,400. The totals indicate that ACPL has an ongoing annual out-of-pocket resource commitment of approximately $17,853.

Contact Person

Stella Baker, Manager, Young Adults' Services, Allen County Public Library, 900 Webster Street, Fort Wayne, IN 46801. (219) 424-7241, ext. 2248

Staff and/or Volunteer Development

36.
Brooklyn Public Library
Brooklyn, New York

Idea
Book Buddies

Customers
Students entering seventh grade through tenth grade

Community
Brooklyn is the largest of the five boroughs of New York City with a population of 2,300,664. The total population of adolescents between the ages of twelve and eighteen is approximately 230,000, or 10 percent of the total population. Brooklyn's adolescent population is as culturally diverse as the entire community. Brooklyn is increasingly a borough of immigrants; 29 percent of the population is foreign-born and includes large numbers of Asians, Latinos, Caribbean-born people, Russians, and other European-born people. More than ninety languages are spoken in the borough. The adolescent population varies from neighborhood to neighborhood and each area reflects its own culture or cultures and is served by its own neighborhood public library branch.

Setting
The Brooklyn Public Library is a community institution serving a culturally diverse population of 2.3 million people. It is the fifth largest public library system in the United States with 58 branches, a Business Library, and the Central Library. The Central Library at Grand Army Plaza is the main reference center of the Brooklyn Public Library system. Each year more than two million people—almost the entire population of Brooklyn—use the Central Library. The branches reflect the diversity of the communities they serve and offer a variety of programs, services, and materials tailored to reflect the neighborhoods in which they are located. Brooklyn Public Library's circulation of materials went over the ten million mark this past year. Almost 26,000 programs were presented during the past year at the Central and branch libraries with a total attendance of 543,000.

Program Description
Book Buddies is a program which has as its major aim the integration of young adults into the library and the library's summer reading program. The Book Buddies work in the branches and the Central Library for a minimum of one month. They work with younger children from three to ten years of age and assist the librarians in arts and crafts, informal read-aloud programs, film or video programs, toys and games, summer reading program, book discussions, and as teen advisors. Book Buddies are members of the library's summer reading program who have the added benefit of receiving valuable work experience which can later be included on their resumes.

Book Buddies was initiated in an attempt to bring young adults into the library and to involve them in the library's summer reading program. Young adults no longer consider themselves children, yet are still not considered "adult" by the adult population. It was important to get them involved in the summer reading program while taking these factors into consideration. This program was designed to fulfill some of the special needs of young adults: the needs to participate as a responsible member of society, to gain experience in decision making, to

BE A BOOK BUDDY THIS SUMMER.

If you are entering the 7th - 12th grade next fall and would like to work with children - become a Book Buddy this summer.

Book Buddies will be trained to read to children and to help out at library programs.

You can sign up at your local library to be a Book Buddy from June 1 to June 16. Have fun and make a difference - Be a Book Buddy.

BROOKLYN PUBLIC LIBRARY

Brooklyn Public Library MEGA READER 95

interact with adults who have an interest in them and their concerns, and to try out new roles without having to commit themselves irrevocably ("Characteristics of the Age Group," in YALSA's *Youth Participation in Libraries: A Training Manual*, 1991).

The number of young adults participating in the program has remained relatively constant over the two years that it has been in existence. An average of five young adults worked at each branch and the Central Library each year, with a total of 278 young adults taking part in 1995 and 274 in 1996. A specific goal of providing a close mentoring relationship between the librarian and *Book Buddies* required a low ratio of Book Buddies to mentors. There were approximately twenty librarians involved in training and preparation for the program, and fifty-six librarians who worked directly with the *Book Buddies* at the branch level.

Young adults were heavily involved with the planning of summer activities for children in each branch. Each Buddy worked with his or her mentor to implement summer reading program activities and was involved in choosing titles to read aloud, reading aloud to young children, choosing crafts, preparing materials for crafts programs, helping children during crafts programs, helping children sign up for the summer reading program and enter the books read in their reading records, showing films or videos to children, and designing and conducting the summer reading program celebrations at the end of the summer reading program. The mentor in each branch was trained to be receptive and to solicit ideas from his or her Buddies. Buddies were provided with an opportunity to provide written feedback about the program at the end of the summer.

The *Book Buddies* program has been evaluated using both quantitative and qualitative measures. The program has operated at capacity levels for the two years that it has been in existence (278 Book Buddies in 1995 and 274 Book Buddies in 1996). To examine the quality of *Book Buddies*, surveys were given to summer reading program participants and their parents. Focus groups comprising staff who acted as mentors to the Book Buddies were conducted annually at an evaluation meeting for the entire summer reading program. In addition to formal evaluations, anecdotal information was collected and included such information as the fact that there were waiting lists of Book Buddy hopefuls at some branches this spring.

Funding

The funding for this program comes from moneys allocated for the library's summer reading program. The funding for the summer reading program is allocated from library and corporate funds. No additional staffing was required for the operation of this program. The figures below represent the cost for the 1996 Book Buddies (274 young adults).

Book Buddy T-shirts	$1,972.80
Incentives	449.36
Certificates	60.00
Total cost	$2,482.16
Cost per Book Buddy	$9.06

Contact Person

Ellen Loughran, Public Service Support Office, Brooklyn Public Library, Grand Army Plaza, Brooklyn, NY 11238. (718) 780-7779

37.
Chicago Public Library, Children's Services
Chicago, Illinois

Idea

Junior Volunteers for the Summer Reading Game

Customers

Young adults, ages twelve through eighteen

Community

Chicago's population includes 2,731,743 (1994 estimate), of whom approximately 235,988 are ages fourteen through nineteen (1990 census). In the public secondary schools, the student population can be broken down this way: 54.5 percent African American, 31.3 percent Latino, 10.8 percent Caucasian, 3.2 percent Asian/Pacific Islander, and .2 percent Native American. Seventy-nine percent of these students come from homes classified as low income.

Setting

The Chicago Public Library is one of the largest in the nation with a central library building downtown, two regional sites, and 78 branches of various sizes scattered throughout the city. The library's holdings number 6,576,898, which breaks down to 2.4 volumes per capita, and a circulation of 2.6 per capita also. About 25 percent of library circulation comes from young adults.

Each year the children's services division conducts a citywide Summer Reading Game with a central theme. The theme for 1995 was "Visionquest" in conjunction with the Art Institute of Chicago, and the theme for 1996 was "The Great Book Feast." Participation for 1996 was 16,946, and 249,812 books were read. In addition to book checkouts, librarians also offered craft, entertainment, and educational programs for their young patrons.

Program Description

After receiving training from librarians and other coaches, young adults volunteered their time and talents to help out at various branches for the Summer Reading Game as Junior Volunteers. They aided librarians in record keeping, listening to book reports, staging programs, preparing materials for craft projects, and various other tasks. Their assistance makes it possible for the Summer Reading Game to accommodate large numbers of kids and contributes to smoothly and efficiently run programs.

Many of the Chicago Public Library branches host large groups of young readers each summer and show great desire and enthusiasm to help these patrons. However, volunteer assistance is needed to handle the increased number of summer participants and activities in a satisfactory manner. There is also a concern that the Summer Reading Game tends to appeal chiefly to young elementary school children, with fewer activities aimed toward older children. Therefore, a number of branch libraries initiated *Junior Volunteer* groups for young teens who were able to be active participants in the Summer Reading Game by assisting with its implementation for the younger children. A major emphasis of the *Junior Volunteers* project was to train young adults to be effective helpers. In 1995 the game was offered in conjunction with the Art Institute, and volunteers were actually trained at the Art Institute by education staff members so that they would be knowledgeable about art objects featured in the game.

The Central Office of Children's Services oversaw all branches using volunteers, to create unity and consistency in the way volunteers were treated and utilized. At the various branches, many of the Junior Volunteers developed into close-knit groups. In all branches the availability of the volunteers was

Junior Volunteers, Chicago Public Library

crucial to the children's librarians who relied upon their help to implement activities for the younger children. Also, the Junior Volunteers were given active, often creative, and age-appropriate ways to participate in the Summer Reading Game. Their assistance was of tangible value to the librarians in dealing with all the extra summer activity: in 1995 Junior Volunteers donated 20,464 hours of service in the Summer Reading Game, and in 1996 their contribution was 25,898 hours. Participants in *Junior Volunteers* were overwhelmingly female.

The Children's Services Department devised guidelines on how to use volunteers, and prospective volunteers went through an interview process. Upon acceptance, the librarians trained them in how to talk with parents and kids, how to fill out forms, how to act on the job, and other matters. Their hours were recorded on time sheets, both for data-keeping purposes and to indicate that their job was being taken seriously by the library. The volunteers undertook whatever tasks were within their abilities. Some were involved extensively in the program. For example, those at the Northtown branch put on puppet shows and made up games for children to play at the final party. Many volunteers helped young patrons locate books to read, shelved books, and decorated the children's area of the library. The local branch children's library staff was responsible for overseeing their Junior Volunteers. This was accomplished within the framework of their Summer Reading Game plans and duties. Participation by volunteers has been growing each year of the program. In 1995, 492 young adults served as Junior Volunteers, and in 1996, 684 youths, at 74 branches, were involved.

The Junior Volunteers have been very enthusiastic in response to their participation within their own libraries. "I want to be a volunteer for next summer again. Sign me up today!" "I've waited three years to be old enough—I liked it so much!" and "the little kids are so cute—it makes me want to be a librarian!" were just some of the responses the volunteers gave at the end of the summer. In many cases the young adults continued to volunteer in their branches after the summer was over. Young adults who work one hundred hours as a volunteer can automatically be considered, at age sixteen, for paid page positions in the Chicago Public Library; this is a nice incentive for many volunteers. The project has been such a success that it is to be part of the summer plans for the Chicago Children's Services Department in years to come.

Funding

This program did not involve large extra expenses above and beyond what was already budgeted for the library-wide Summer Reading Game. Special volunteer T-shirts, at a cost of $3,000, were donated through a grant from the Friends of the Chicago Public Library. Final "thank-you" pizza parties and certificates were funded by the local branches through their individual resources.

Contact Person

Bernadette Nowakowski, Chicago Public Library Children's Services, 400 S. State Street, 10-S, Chicago, IL 60605. (312) 747-4780.

38.
Massachusetts Library Association, Children's Issues Section

Massachusetts

Idea

Clueless in the Stacks: the YA LIVE Show

Customers

All Massachusetts librarians who provide service to young adults, including YA librarians, children's librarians serving YAs, and reference librarians, as well as directors and administrators responsible for library policy and allocation of resources

Community

According to the 1990 U.S. Census, Massachusetts has a youth population ages ten through seventeen of approximately 562,000. Librarians attending the program came from all over the state and serve a variety of young adult populations. YAs in Massachusetts live in a variety of settings, from small towns in rural western Massachusetts to large urban centers like Springfield, Worcester, and Boston, from mid-size suburban cities to resort towns on Cape Cod.

Setting

The Children's Issues Section (CIS) of the Massachusetts Library Association (MLA) was established in 1988. As an advocate for quality library service to children and young adults statewide, CIS establishes, promotes, and continually reviews documents such as *Standards for Public Library Service to Children in Massachusetts*; articulates and addresses the concerns of children's and young adult librarians; informs librarians through continuing education programs and brochures about emerging trends and issues in youth services; collaborates with other child service institutions and agencies to promote youth services through programs like the "Hand in Hand" conference, jointly sponsored with the Massachusetts School Library Media Association. In response to librarians statewide, CIS appointed a YA Standards Committee in the fall of 1995 to begin work on a document describing the philosophy and principles underlying good library service to young adults and defining essential characteristics of such service. CIS hopes to publish the YA standards document in the spring of 1997.

Program Description

In the fall of 1995, executive board members of the Massachusetts Library Association Children's Issues Section began the brainstorming process for CIS-sponsored programs at MLA's 1996 Annual Conference. Board members felt strongly that a program should be offered addressing ethics and current issues in young adult services. As the board's YA representative, Diane Sanabria began developing a program incorporating role-playing, teen involvement, and humor in a discussion of young adults and libraries. *Clueless in the Stacks: The YA LIVE Show* debuted on April 29, 1996, advertised in the conference brochure as follows:

> Does your library own audiocassettes or CDs with parental advisory labels on them? If a teenager wanted a copy of *The Satanic Bible*, would you request it through interlibrary loan? For a lively debate on these and other topics join Leominster YA Librarian Diane Sanabria, members of the MLA CIS Board, Leominster Librarian Gary Kendall, and some REAL LIVE teenagers as they tackle ethics and issues in young adult services in a "talk show" format.

The *YA LIVE Show* was designed to make *all* librarians attending the program really think about how teens are treated in our public libraries. More often than not, consciously or subconsciously, there *is* a "double standard" where young adults are concerned. How many librarians would dare interrupt a table full of seniors loudly discussing the day's events—or the neighbors chatting at the circulation desk—and tell them to be quiet!? Yet the group of young adults fresh off the bus and excitedly rehashing the school day is reprimanded the minute they walk through the door! Librarians would not dream of refusing to stock paperback romances or buy the latest offering from Howard Stern for adult patrons—and yet dismiss YA horror series and popular YA magazines as junk or marginal purchases. And who among the profession would risk a mutiny among parents of preschoolers by not staffing the children's room all the hours the adult department is open? Yet it is acceptable to staff the YA department part-time or shift service responsibilities to already overburdened children's or reference librarians.

The goal of the *YA LIVE Show* was to raise these issues, provoking thought and stimulating discussion of the following issues: young adult access to library collections and services; attitudes and behavior towards young adults, especially in relation to other patron groups and in terms of the developmental tasks of adolescence; popular materials and space for young adults within the library; issues of confidentiality and privacy; selection and censorship issues; and administrative and financial support for YA services.

Was the *YA LIVE Show* important? Yes. The humorous approach and the opinions and insights of the *real live* teenagers were instrumental in driving home the point that services for young adults will not improve in quantity or quality unless librarians stop treating young adults as second-class citizens, and start remembering that today's teens are tomorrow's taxpayers.

Will the program make a difference in the lives of young adults in Massachusetts communities? That remains to be seen. Hopefully, librarians across the state left with the words of Rebecca and Tim and Blayr echoing in their heads: "Respect. That's what we want and need most from you." And hopefully, these librarians will begin—or continue—to cultivate Pat Jones' "YAttitude" in their libraries and their communities.

Over seventy-five librarians made up the "standing-room- only" crowd for the program; there is no telling how many young adults they will impact positively in their libraries. Presenting the *YA LIVE Show* involved the time and talents of eight adults (six CIS Executive Board members, one Leominster Library staff person, one Leominster Library volunteer) and six young adults (Leominster Library teen volunteers).

Participation by young adults contributed greatly to the success of the *YA LIVE Show*. Board members may have outlined the issues tackled by the program, but the young adults involved supplied inspiration and actual lines for Diane Sanabria's script. The presence of Tim, Rebecca, Katie, Erin, Shauna, and Blayr imbued the *YA LIVE Show* with authenticity and honesty and clearly illustrated the cardinal rule of successful YA service: involve the young adults themselves!

Comments written by attendees evaluating the program were submitted to MLA's Conference Committee. *Clueless in the Stacks: The YA LIVE Show* was also videotaped and CIS plans to have copies made for each regional library system in the state. The tapes will be particularly useful as discussion starters (a weakness of the program was insufficient time for breakouts to further explore the issues raised); an information sheet to guide discussions is now being developed. A reprise of the program was held at the Massachusetts Library Trustees and Friends Conference in November 1996.

Funding

The program was produced at no cost except for staff time spent in planning, preparation, and execution. Cost of a pizza luncheon prior to the program for young adult volunteers was donated by Diane Sanabria, and the Massachusetts Library Association offered luncheon free to program presenters.

The bulk of planning and preparation (e.g., script development) was done by CIS YA Representative Diane Sanabria on a volunteer basis, with the remainder accomplished at regular CIS board meetings. Board member Catherine Zilber developed the "commercial breaks" in approximately two hours. Diane Sanabria and Leominster Librarian "show host" Gary Kendall worked with teen volunteers for two hours prior to the program. There were no rehearsals or dry runs for this program and all those involved were responsible for familiarizing themselves with the script on their own time.

Contact Person

Diane M. Sanabria, Leominster Public Library, 30 West Street, Leominster, MA 01453. (508) 534-7522

39.
Pioneer Library System

Canandaigua, New York

Idea

Young adult services for generalists

Customers

Generalists charged with serving the needs of library patrons of all ages

Community

In New York State, there are 5.1 million young people, from birth through age eighteen. Of the nearly 300,000 people in Pioneer's service area, children and young adults ages seventeen years and under make up about 17 percent of that group, or 50,100 people.

Setting

The Pioneer Library System serves four rural counties that surround metropolitan Rochester, N.Y. The service area is a three-hour drive from border to border. The forty-one public libraries in Livingston, Ontario, Wayne, and Wyoming Counties had nearly one million people walk through their doors in 1995. Of the 2.3 million items they borrowed, 42 percent were children's and young adult materials.

Only 51 percent of Pioneer libraries have a youth services specialist, and only three of those staff are specifically designated to serve young adults. Most of the twenty-five specialists are responsible for ages eighteen and under, and only eight of them (32 percent) have a master's degree in library science. For all intents and purposes, 49 percent of our libraries are termed "one-person" libraries, where the library director or manager must handle programs and services for all age levels.

Program Description

In 1994, the system's Youth Services Coordinator developed a grant proposal for LSCA funding to offer a statewide leadership conference for sixty-five young adult specialists who had a minimum of three years' experience in school or public libraries. The purpose of the conference was to strengthen training and leadership skills and to encourage the specialists' continued service to young adults. The conference offered an in-depth exploration of adolescent psychology and development as they affect library services and facilities. A primary goal was to develop a training curriculum for a three-hour workshop that would be used to train generalists. Subsequently, twenty-six specialists facilitated nine regional workshops, "YA 101: Young Adult Services for Generalists," from May through September 1995, reaching 432 generalists who were able to acquire the skills and knowledge to provide more effective library services to YA patrons.

A continuation of the grant was received for 1996. Two more "YA 101" courses were offered, as well as a series of "200" courses that covered marketing and outreach services for young adults, Internet resources for and about young adults, and library programming for adolescents. An additional 565 individuals were trained in 1996. A statewide institute on evaluation methods was held in September, highlighting various survey techniques, output measures, and portfolios as methods to provide compelling evidence of the effectiveness of library programs and services.

Four model sites received the assistance of an experienced young adult librarian to assist library staff in redesigning or establishing the young adult area of the library. Gaps in library services to adolescents were identified and remedied with new materials, increased merchandising of collections, scheduling of programs specific to teens, and increased efforts for school/public library cooperation. An inservice presentation inspired other member libraries to try similar techniques at their buildings, even without additional funding. Seven other libraries received the assistance of both the system consultant and the project coordinator to facilitate "mini-makeovers," which focused on physical changes to the library's layout and increased merchandising to give the YA areas a new, improved look.

Continuing education for generalist library staff has traditionally been offered through system workshops, the state library association's annual conference, and regional conferences sponsored by the Youth Services section. The area of young adult services is not often emphasized at these events. The ability of this project to take free training to the geographically distant areas of the state allowed library generalists to have a high-quality continuing education experience and exposure to YA specialists from outside their own areas.

To assess the usefulness of the training and to ascertain if elements of the curriculum were incorporated into the participants' work with young adults, an evaluation instrument was sent to those participants who enrolled in the regional workshops during year one. Responses were received from 125 of the 432 generalists (29 percent return rate). Of those respondents who were responsible for acquisitions of young adult materials, 42 percent stated they had purchased some materials since the workshop that they might not have selected otherwise. Sixty-five percent "agreed" or "strongly agreed" that they felt they now understood the adolescent viewpoint better, and 67 percent indicated they were paying more attention now to the young adults who visit their libraries. Fifty-seven percent stated they had had at least one experience with a young adult in which they acted differently as a result of attending the training. Through the library staff members that serve adolescents and their new skills and knowledge, as many as ten thousand young adults (a conservative estimate) are expected to be affected by these training sessions.

During year one, the total number of staff and volunteers reached in the training sessions was 497, both generalists and specialists. In year two, 565 people attended the six regional workshops, other in-service presentations about the project, the YALSA President's Program at the Annual Conference in July 1996, and the final institute on evaluation methods on September 20, 1996. The grand total was 1,062.

As this program was primarily an initiative for staff and volunteer development, no adolescents were directly involved. However, during year two, the model sites sought the opinion of young adults through surveys and informal discussions at book talk programs. The model sites had mixed success with establishing Young Adult Advisory Councils, but several sites want to start a group in the fall (1996). One site had ten students from the local high school art club who spent three months painting a mural in the renovated young adult room. Another site involved young adults extensively in assisting with summer reading programs for children.

In the posttraining evaluation instrument, a rating scale asked the participants to indicate how their level of knowledge had improved. In combining the responses in the categories for "quite a bit" and "very much," the respondents indicated that by attending the sessions, they had improved their knowledge of adolescent development (29 percent), programming for young adults (50 percent), library reference service to young adults (36 percent), and collection development for YA materials (40 percent). They had also changed their perspective about providing library service to young adults (37 percent).

In year two, the four model sites served a total of 892 young adults through seventy-five programs. The activities ranged from homework assistance to learning to juggle. Other programs included cartooning, volunteer opportunities, craft workshops, and deposit collections of recreational reading titles at the school media centers. Several sites had double-digit increases in circulation of young adult materials and in young adult program sessions and attendance in comparison to preproject figures.

Funding

Support comprised $35,000 in year one of the grant from the New York State Library and $30,000 in year two (Title I LSCA funds). The combined expenditures included professional salaries and benefits ($16,419; Library Assistant, seven hours a week at $11.50 per hour, in year one; Young Adult Librarian, twenty-one hours a week at $13.50 per hour, in year two); purchased services, including honoraria for trainers, desktop publishing, survey design and tabulation, conference planning, and YA programs for model sites ($18,968); supplies and materials such as telephone charges, office supplies, postage, and in year two, display fixtures and YA materials for model sites ($12,309); and travel expenses for speakers, trainers, and project coordinators ($17,304).

Contact Person

Lisa C. Wemett, Webster Public Library, One Van Ingen Drive, Webster, NY 14580. (716) 872-7074 or 7075.

Youth Participation

40.
Chicago Public Library, Albany Park and Douglass Branches
Chicago, Illinois

Idea
Bus painting project

Customers
At-risk high school students

Community
Although very different in many ways, both library branches are in communities that are concerned with giving kids alternatives to illegal activities and providing them with opportunities for self-expression through art. Douglass is located in the Lawndale neighborhood of about 32,674 people, 47.3 percent of whom are twenty years old or younger. The population is almost exclusively African American. The library in Albany Park outwardly appears to be in another world, with a growing population of over 76,000: 48 percent Caucasian, being rapidly overtaken by increasing numbers of Asians, Arabs, East Indians, Bosnian refugees, and other ethnic groups. The area of Albany Park is a strong business center, as opposed to the residential setting of the Douglass branch. Although these populations do seem very different on the surface, youth in both areas are faced with the pressures of gangs, the confusion of American teenage years, a dearth of constructive things to do after school, and a strong, if unfocused, desire for self-expression.

Setting
The Albany Park branch is located in an ethnically diverse area of the North Side of Chicago. The building is thirty-three years old, 10,555 square feet, and heavily used. The collection has 65,000 books, with an annual materials circulation of 160,000. The Douglass branch, on the West Side, is sixty-seven years old and located in a predominantly (97 percent) African-American community. Douglass has a collection of 40,000 volumes, with an annual circulation of 18,000. It is used mostly by children and teens. The two libraries are very different from each other in both usage and clientele.

Douglass and Albany Park branches are both members of the "Blue Skies for Library Kids" grant project, funded by the Chicago Community Trust, through the Chicago Public Library Foundation. The grant's focus is for libraries to get involved with their communities: to find out what the community would like from its local library and to work with community resources to meet these needs.

Program Description
In order to involve high school students in an art project that would be of benefit to the library and the community as an alternative to "tagging" buildings (graffiti art done illegally on walls), two Chicago Public Library branches recruited students to paint a public transportation bus that runs on the route between the two branches. The project also involved the high schools in their areas, the Chicago Police Department, the Chicago Transit Authority, and the Chicago Public Art Group. The purpose of the finished bus, designed and executed by the young adults, is to advertise the library, stress the importance of knowledge and reading, and express the unity of the various ethnic groups represented by the libraries. This colorful bus is known as the "Knowledge Express."

Painting the bus gave the young adults a chance to collaborate with professional artists on a work of public art that would be enjoyed by a large community. It gave them a positive experience with legal art, and with paint pots and brushes rather than spray cans. Working as a group with people who do art for a living gave the teens an opportunity to reflect and talk about ways art can be a vehicle of understanding and communicating. Thinking about what they wanted to say to their neighborhoods promoted community awareness among the kids and legitimized the library in the minds of the teens, both the painters and their acquaintances. While not directly involving great numbers of teens, the bus project has provided the Youth Librarians with a take-off point for future programs serving young adults. Some of this continuing work will include the Police Department, since the bus project capitalized on good rapport between the branches and officers who work with juveniles. Seeing the bus driving down the streets has made the community more aware of reading, knowledge, and the Chicago Public Library.

Two librarians, Elizabeth Hansen and Viola Stewart, were present at planning sessions and on several weekends at the bus barn where the bus was actually painted. They helped get the teens to the barn and provided them with lunch and refreshments during the long days of painting. The student artists were actively involved in all aspects of the bus project, discussing what should be displayed, drawing the concepts themselves, and doing the actual surface painting. They were present at the "unveiling" celebration to ride the bus between the two library branches, and they received art supply gift certificates from the Chicago Public Art Group. Their work has been featured in the *Chicago Tribune* and has received a very enthusiastic reception from the community. The artists themselves and their friends became intrigued about the library and why it would offer such a program for young adults. They were genuinely interested in learning about other things that libraries do for kids, besides "making them be quiet and read books." A high school attended by some of the artists is using the bus project to advertise the library to its students and to stimulate other art projects. The artists are very proud to see their art receive positive acclaim from the community, and the city is gratified to have such a beautiful, colorful, and interesting bus for the public to ride.

Funding

The Chicago Transit Authority provided the bus, already primed, to be painted. Both library branches used $3,000 of their Blue Skies grant money to hire the Chicago Public Art Group to help design the bus, put the design outline on its surfaces, and assist in the actual painting. The bus painting should endure in good shape for six years.

Contact Person

Linda Thompson, Blue Skies for Library Kids Director, Chicago Public Library, Harold Washington Library Center, 400 S. State Street 10-S, Chicago, IL 60605. (312) 747-4784

41.
Chicago Public Library, Northtown Branch

Chicago, Illinois

Idea

Teen Study Center

Customers

Senior high school students

Community

The Northtown branch of the Chicago Public Library is located in a stable area of the city that is comprised mainly of single family homes. The population of the area, numbering about 65,374, is ethnically diverse—consisting of various Jewish groups, a growing number of Indians, Pakistanis, Koreans, and other nationalities. There are four high schools in the library's service area, and they were all represented in the first Teen Advisory Council (known also as the "T.A.C."). Among the teens who joined T.A.C., there is a wonderful gender mix, as well as representation of different cultural backgrounds: Moslems, Hindus, Christians, and others, from many countries, thus reflecting the diversity of the library's neighborhood.

Setting

The library building itself is small (10,320 square feet), a large portion of which is taken up by a meeting room that can hold 150 people. The collection is about 74,000 volumes, with an annual circulation of approximately 200,000. The surrounding community has a high percentage of professionals, and there is a strong commitment to education and reading among all groups, as is evident in the circulation figures. Rose Olszewski is the children's librarian at Northtown, and she works with youth from preschool through high school.

Program Description

In order to make the library a more welcoming place for teenagers, Chicago Public Library's Northtown branch set up a *Teen Study Center* in the meeting room. Planned and assembled by the branch's Teen Advisory Council, and set apart from the Children's Department, the *Study Center* offers a spot where high school kids can meet and study together in groups. The area is equipped with reference materials, videos, computers, and software, so that students have the information they need close at hand while they work.

In 1994 the Northtown branch became a member of the "Blue Skies for Library Kids" grant project, funded by the Chicago Community Trust through the Chicago Public Library Foundation. The focus of the grant is to get branch libraries involved with their communities: to find out what the community would like from its local library and to work with community groups and resources to meet these needs. Rose Olszewski and Michael Leonard, the Branch Head, began by doing a needs assessment of their community. Rose also assembled a Blue Skies team, comprised of Chicago Public Library's director of finance, a Park District supervisor, a local bank president, a member of the Northtown Friends group, an administrator from the Art Institute of Chicago, and a member of the Chicago Youth for Success organization.

The needs assessment found that in Northtown there are plenty of activities available for every age group except teenagers. Rose then made outreach visits into the local high schools and parks and asked teens what the Northtown branch could do to fill this void. They told her they wanted someplace to study after school, where they would not be hassled by their siblings. The Blue Skies team decided to invite teens to join in on planning ways the library could fulfill their wishes. A resulting group of thirteen students, representing four high schools, attended. These teens formed the Advisory Council, and began talking and planning.

What became clear was that the young adults did not want *programs*—they wanted a *place* to go. They also wanted this place to be stocked with materials that would help them with their homework and aid them in preparing for their futures in college or the working world. The *Teen Study Center* was the direct result of their discussions.

All the major decisions for the Center, including the curtains, furnishings, purchasing of computers and software, and rules of conduct, were made by the Teen Advisory Council. Teens painted the walls of the room with large colorful murals, expressing their thoughts and feelings. When the *Center* opened in the spring of 1995, they were in complete charge of the Grand Opening ceremony. Since then they have helped publicize the Study Center to their peers, and continue to assist in the selection of paperbacks for the library's teen leisure reading collection. Computers and software were purchased for the *Study Center*, so that the teens would be able to use databases to enhance their research or to type their papers on a word processor. Internet access is also offered free of charge in the *Study Center*, with an attempt to keep the technology as up-to-date as possible. The Teen Advisory Council continues to meet and will make any additional decisions that are needed concerning *their* study center.

The main success of the *Teen Study Center* is that it was conceived, planned, set up, and run by the Teen Advisory Council. It is also a direct, concrete result of the library responding to an actual need in the community. It gives young adults a real place of their own in the Northtown branch library. The *Study Center* is overseen by the Teen Advisory Council, which is made up of teens who volunteer their time. Rose Olszewski has a very good rapport with teens and has served as the advisor for the council as part of her work schedule. She has also volunteered her own time, kept the budget tallies, and become very involved with other community groups as an advocate for the library and for young adults.

The *Study Center* so far is enjoying growing success. During any given week, the number of teens in the *Study Center* may vary from eight to forty-eight each evening. A formal evaluation of usage and further needs will be done within the next year, after more time has elapsed and more teens find out about the existence of the center.

Funding

The *Study Center* was set up with Blue Skies funds:

Furnishings	$8,963.63
Computers	9,680.90
Supplies and publicity	1,000.00

Contact Person

Linda Thompson, Blue Skies for Library Kids Director, Chicago Public Library, Harold Washington Library Center, 400 S. State Street 10-S, Chicago, IL 60605. (312) 747-4784

42.
Chicago Public Library/Rudy Lozano Branch

Chicago, Illinois

Idea

Knight Moves Chess Club

Customers

Thirty members, chiefly boys, between the ages of twelve and eighteen are now enrolled in the *Knight Moves* Chess Club.

Community

The Lozano branch is located in Chicago's Pilsen neighborhood with a population of 45,566. It serves a clientele that is chiefly (87.9 percent) first- and second-generation Hispanic immigrants who are predominately of Mexican origin. Youth ages seventeen and under make up 41 percent of this clientele. The area has thirteen schools within its boundaries, one of which is a high school.

Setting

The Rudy Lozano branch is the largest Spanish-language library for the city of Chicago, and also draws customers from the surrounding suburbs. The branch is in Pilsen, a densely populated and poverty-stricken urban area, which serves as a port-of-entry community for Latino immigrants. The eighteen-thousand-square-foot building was dedicated in 1989. It is open long evening hours compared to many of Chicago's other library branches. The library has a large children's department as well as meeting rooms that are in constant use by community organizations.

Program Description

Knight Moves is an intergenerational and bilingual chess club at the Rudy Lozano branch of the Chicago Public Library. Especially aimed at young adults, the club is designed to give young people something recreational and educational to do with their free time that involves participation in a library program. A direct response to the problem of gang pressures, it offers an alternative after-school activity that is attractive to boys. As members of the club, players learn the game and how to improve their strategies.

Join "Knight Moves," the Rudy Lozano Branch Chess Club

Participa en "Knight Moves," el Club de Ajedrez de la Sucursal Rudy Lozano

The club was informally started a number of years ago by Branch Head Hector Hernandez, a chess enthusiast. He saw the need for a library activity that would involve adolescents who are at risk of gang recruitment, and who are not reached by traditional library programs. These young people are regularly in the library building after school and have been very enthusiastic about having something to do, in addition to their homework, at the library. The club meets Wednesday nights and is supervised by Hernandez. Hector has staged Latino Chess Championships and branch tournaments, and he has taken kids to outside tournaments as well. The club members earn T-shirts by attending six meetings of the club, and trophies are awarded at tournaments.

In 1995 the Lozano branch became a member of the "Blue Skies for Library Kids" grant project, funded by the Chicago Community Trust through the Chicago Public Library Foundation. The grant's focus is to get libraries involved with their communities: to find out what the community would like from its local branch, and to work with community groups and resources to meet these concerns. A needs assessment was done, and the Lozano Blue Skies team, comprised of librarians, members of neighborhood youth organizations, and concerned local citizens, was formed. The assessment indicated that the Pilsen neighborhood wanted more library activities for older children to keep them away from gangs and violence, and to give them something positive to do outside of school. The Blue Skies team decided to adopt and enhance the chess club as one of its projects. A chess corner was planned, brochures and flyers publicizing the club were produced, and tournaments were arranged. With the assistance of other local organizations, chess Masters were brought from Mexico to participate in Lozano's Latino Championship Tournaments and serve as Hispanic role models for the club members. The chess club is a visible sign to the community that the Lozano Branch Library has taken great steps in serving the neighborhood's need for more library activities for older children. *Knight Moves* has been featured several times in various local and city newspapers, and also on television.

In the summer of 1996, the chess corner was set up in the library foyer, directly in front of the building's large picture windows which feature, appropriately, stained glass banner-topped castles. The space was sectioned off with several portable room dividers, and existing tables and chairs were placed in this sunny area for young people to play chess. Since its creation, the chess corner is nearly always occupied by players. People going past the building can see the young people quietly and actively participating, and often stop to watch. The corner is situated directly across from the building's circulation desk, and is easily monitored from that spot. Players sign in when they arrive, but participation is not rigid. Older or more experienced youth help newer members improve their game, and parents are encouraged to play with their sons or daughters. The area requires little extra maintenance, and only a few chess pieces have had to be replaced.

Knight Moves also addresses the community's wish to have programs that will help to increase their young people's self-esteem. Through learning to play chess—a game of thought and strategic planning—young people develop a sense of accomplishment. This is reinforced as they earn T-shirts and play games in competitive, but nonthreatening, situations. The young club members feel ownership, as well, because they named their group and designed the logo for the chess club. The club also helps expand the horizons of the players, through travel outside their neighborhood to attend tournaments, and as players from other parts of the city and from Mexico have come to play at the Lozano branch. A number of the young adult club members began volunteering their time to help with the chess club and with other library tasks such as shelving. They continued donating their time and were then able to qualify as paid library pages through a Chicago Public Library incentive program.

To date, the club has been supervised almost totally by Hector Hernandez with the help of the children's librarian, Anne Ayres, during the course of their regular work schedule, plus some volunteer hours. The original group of youths that comprised the club gave it the name of *Knight Moves* and helped a local artist with the logo design, which appears on their T-shirts and all flyers and brochures advertising the club. Now that the chess corner is set up, and the 1996 annual Latino Championship has been held, the project is entering into a time of assessment and evaluation. In the future, it is planned that teen and adult volunteers will do more to assist in the club. Also, while community organizations have always helped with funding in the past, this type of support will be even more actively cultivated. Other youth organizations throughout the city and state will be contacted, to find other chess clubs with which to compete, and to find organizations that might wish to set up their own clubs with the help of *Knight Moves* members. Members of the club will be speaking to community groups, telling about what the club has meant to them, and advertising the club to their peers.

Funding

The chess corner T-shirts and trophies were purchased with Blue Skies funds. For two years, approximately $6,500 has been spent on the chess club:

Tournament fees/workshops	$2,000
Chess corner furnishings	1,000
T-shirts and trophies	1,700
Promotion/flyers	700
Other expenses	1,100

The branch was fortunate to have funds to enhance its club with the purchase of trophies, sponsorship of guest Masters and tournament fees. However, it would be very possible to have a library chess club with little funding, that would run on volunteer supervision and donations of prizes from local organizations.

Contact Person

Linda Thompson, Blue Skies for Library Kids Director, Chicago Public Library, Harold Washington Library Center, 400 S. State Street 10-S, Chicago, IL 60605. (312) 747-4784

43. Clearwater Public Library
Clearwater, Florida

Idea

Dascaloja Puppeteers

Customers

Young adults, ages ten through eighteen

Community

The population of Clearwater is 98,784 (1990 census). This does not include the many winter visitors to the area who also use the library materials. According to the U.S. Census report estimates from 1990, the population of twelve- through seventeen-year-olds for Clearwater was 5,823 or 5.9 percent of the total population. The estimates for 1995 were 6,268 or 6.3 percent.

Setting

The Clearwater Public Library System is a municipal library with a main library in downtown Clearwater and four branches serving the Clearwater area. The Clearwater Library is also part of the Pinellas Public Library Cooperative. This cooperative distributes LSCA funding as well as Pinellas County tax monies among thirteen libraries. The youth services department at the main library consists of a youth services manager, a Librarian II, and a Librarian I. There is a Librarian I at the East Library and the Countryside Library who specializes in working with youth and a Librarian II at the North Greenwood branch. Each youth librarian is responsible for a variety of programming during the school year and takes on specific programming during the summer months as specialty events take place.

Program Description

The *Dascaloja Puppeteers* program offers the opportunity for young adults to learn the art of puppeteering and performance through weekly presentations during the summer program at the library. The teens involved prepare and present a puppet show seven times a week during the summer, including plays, skits, and other live-action activities in the thirty- to forty-five-minute presentation. These programs are presented to the community and are geared toward the whole family because they take the place of regularly scheduled preschool storytimes presented throughout the year. The puppeteers work approximately six to eight weeks during the summer and, along with the regular weekly shows, present shows at summer-session and exceptional schools, recreation centers, churches, camps, and neighboring libraries. Once school begins in the fall, the puppeteers may also present a special holiday performance, depending on the availability and interest of the teens.

Begun twenty-five years ago as a way to involve teenagers in a library setting, the *Dascaloja Puppeteers* (named for the original five members) program is an opportunity for adolescents to learn the art and discipline of performance through puppetry and live theater. This series provides a free opportunity for the youth of the community to observe the theatrical art of puppetry. Over the years the puppeteers have grown in numbers and many have gone on to artistic endeavors.

Since the program replaces preschool storytimes, this allows the teens an introduction to planning, practicing, and performing puppet shows in front of a live audience. In 1996, over twenty teens participated, with ten of those working the entire eight weeks of the program, at a minimum of four hours a day, five days a week. These teens are supervised and led by one youth services librarian, whose job it is to train the teens in how to select shows, how to prepare the show through selection of puppets, taping of scripts, rehearsal, and actual presentations. The puppeteers rehearse for three hours on one day for the following week's show. The intensity of the rehearsal depends on the complexity of the presentations, as some weeks there is more than one show being presented in the thirty- to forty-five-minute program. In addition to the shows, there are also songs, skits, and other activities that the puppeteers perform with and for the audience.

Attendance ranges from fifteen to two hundred, depending on the place and time of each performance. Since this program has been established, many schools, churches, recreation centers, and neighboring libraries book a presentation at their location in advance of the summer. The only stipulation is that the program requested can not conflict with the regularly scheduled shows at libraries in Clearwater.

The average number of years that puppeteers return to participate is usually four. As they get older, other commitments conflict with the teens' priorities and they move on to other activities. To further hone their performance skills, veteran teens who continue with the puppeteers are given the opportunity to direct shows, write scripts, present original material of their own creation, or adapt skits, songs, or plays to fit the program theme. An advantage in returning each year is the ease and adaptability of these teens to rehearse faster and gain courage to perform in front of the stage instead of hiding behind it.

Two examples of how this program has affected the lives of teens include the following. One young girl, who started with the *Dascaloja* program when she was ten, had no idea that she would enjoy being part of a performance group. As she got older in the program, her vocal and theatrical skills developed to the point that she is now at a university with a full scholarship in vocal and performance arts. Another young man who joined the troupe four years ago had just moved to the United States from a European country. He was extremely shy about being in front of people and would freeze up when he had to step out from behind the stage. But with each year, he became more confident, and during the 1996 program, he was the master of ceremonies for many of the shows and was in front of the audience during most of the program, enjoying every minute and even further developing his skills as a performer.

The benefits of this program are many. The audience is treated each week to a lively program of puppets and song or skit, with teens energetically interacting with young children and their parents.

The teens themselves are able to display and develop their own talents behind and in front of the performing area. In addition, the teens who participate in the *Dascaloja* troupe come together from a wide diversity of backgrounds—"normal" family lives, broken homes, rich and poor neighbors from all across the city—and form a lasting friendship that continues throughout the year. They literally become a "family," and that closeness is evident in the shows and in behavior toward one another as well as with the librarian in charge of the program.

Prior to the start of summer, the librarian picks out the shows that the puppeteers will present to make sure that each show carries the overall summer theme and that the shows are entertaining and relatively short, no more than ten minutes each. She will visit elementary, middle, and high schools to promote the summer library program and include promotion of the *Dascaloja Puppeteers* during these talks. Applications are left at the school and are available at the library and on the library's World Wide Web homepage. Interested teens who have returned the forms are contacted the week before the summer program begins for an initial rehearsal and introduction to the rules and regulations of the troupe. During each rehearsal the overall program content is presented, with volunteers for each part of the show—songs, skits, or activity. Teens are then given the puppet script and volunteer for parts. If more than one person volunteers for a part, they must audition for the other members, and the troupe votes for the best performance. When ready, the teens audiotape the show, pick out the appropriate puppets, make any props, and rehearse. There is usually an "assistant director," a veteran puppeteer, who will lead the others in the rehearsal, offering suggestions and, if necessary, rewriting the show. Usually many suggestions of other activities that the troupe would like to do come up during rehearsal, and the librarian keeps track of these for future shows. The teens are given scheduling information with dates, times, and locations of the shows for each week. They are transported in the library van or by parents; on some days they need to carry a portable stage for performances in places that do not have a stage.

Attendance in 1996 was 3,474 for fifty-six programs; in 1995, 2,918 in attendance for forty-seven programs; and in 1994, 2,650 in attendance for forty shows. The librarian uses program statistics as the primary evaluation tool, as well as verbal and written comments from the general public and from the puppeteers themselves. In addition, letters of appreciation are received from outside agencies where the puppeteers have performed. The librarian hosts a party at the end of the summer for the puppeteers. For the past three years, a library sleepover has become the event of choice for the puppeteers and the

Dascaloja Puppeteers Saza Zdjelau, Stephen Weber, and Jonathan Day lip-synch to "Soul Man" in their portrayal of the Blues Brothers.

librarian usually includes invitations to other teen volunteers who work at the library during the summer. Certificates of appreciation, donations of food from area restaurants, and other prizes (usually donated by local businesses) are presented to the teens at the end of the summer.

Children who return year after year to watch the puppeteers perform anxiously await the time when they are eligible for the program. Many youth have grown up with this successful series and enjoy not only the pleasure of performing for others, but also making new friends and learning new performance techniques that they can use in other areas of their lives. The disciplines learned are valuable tools that the puppeteers may use as they present reports in school, perform with drama groups, school bands, or vocal choirs, or participate in other extracurricular activities in and out of school. The library is transformed into a place where they feel comfortable, not only in relating to the librarians, but also in using the facilities.

Funding

The librarian in charge of this group is part of the performance, introducing the shows and the puppeteers to the audience and overseeing the quality of each performance. She spends approximately twenty-four hours per week with these teens assisting them in show preparation, leading the rehearsal when there isn't a volunteer to do so, and transporting them to different performance locations. The puppeteer program is scheduled as part of her duties, so the approximate cost would be based on the twenty-four hours multiplied by the hourly salary rate of the librarian. Since the program began, puppets and props have been accumulated through purchase from the arts and crafts budget, using anywhere from $50 to $200 of funds annually. Other materials may include office and craft supplies. Donations of fabric, old jewelry, clothing, and other odds and ends are requested from staff and the public.

The teens volunteer their time and in 1996, 1,653 hours were volunteered by puppeteers over the summer. In 1995, 1,213 hours and in 1994, 1,015 hours were volunteered.

Contact Person

Jana R. Fine, Clearwater Public Library System, 100 North Osceola Avenue, Clearwater, FL 34615. (813) 462-6800, ext. 252

44. Farmington Community Library

Farmington Hills, Michigan

Idea

Young Adult Advisory Board

Customers

Anyone in sixth through twelfth grades within the library's service area

Community

The Farmington Community Library (FCL) serves the combined communities of Farmington and Farmington Hills, Michigan, with a combined population of approximately 85,000 and an area of thirty-six square miles. The majority of the population is Caucasian of European descent. A growing number of adolescents are from families of immigrants, particularly from Middle, Far, and Southeastern Asia, as well as Russian immigrants, and temporary residents from the United Kingdom, Germany, Japan, and Taiwan. The *YAAB* participants reflect the ethnicity of the community.

Setting

The Farmington Community Library is a suburban, two-branch, district library located twenty-two miles northwest of Detroit, with a collection size of over 190,000 items and circulation approaching three quarters of a million. FCL is part of the Metronet Consortium, an area leader in the provision of public access to the Internet, through both in-house and dial-in use. Of the American Library Association's eight service roles for public libraries, FCL has chosen the roles of Reference Library, Informal Learning Support, Popular Reading Center, and Preschoolers' Door to Learning.

Program Description

The *Young Adult Advisory Board (YAAB)* is a group of sixth through twelfth grade students from eleven public and private schools, beginning its third year. The *YAAB* provides an arena for discussion of young adult issues and concerns as these may influence YA collection development, and serves as advisors and assistants in library programming for young adults. A larger goal is to promote reading, library use, and participation in library programming to other YAs in the Farmington area. At the monthly meetings, the *YAAB* activities include: (1) assembling the *Panache Post*, a monthly newsletter; (2) planning special publications; and (3) brainstorming future programs. The newsletter includes feature articles, book reviews, and events. The print version is distributed to all middle and high schools; the Internet version is available at <http://metronet.lib.mi.us/FCL/panache.html>. The YAAB designed the Summer Reading Club in 1995 and 1996, and published "best booklists" for the past two years.

The *Young Adult Advisory Board* program provides participants with more autonomy than other area cultural institutions because the *YAAB* involves them in projects that are solely their own creation, governed and produced by them under the auspices of the library. The *Panache Post* was developed with the idea of providing young adults with access to peer reviews. The focus of the publication during the first two years was on evaluating recent young adult fiction. The electronic version promises to retain the basic premise while using the Internet environment to enlarge the scope of the newsletter. The *YAAB* encourages civic responsibility, both intra- and intergenerational, as it promotes the use of the library to

1996 Young Adult Advisory Board

a traditionally underrepresented user population and their nonparticipating peers. The activities of the group allow parents, teachers, and adults in the community to see an above-average level of participation, commitment, and input from the group. The program brings together a diverse group of students, from public to private, religious to homeschooled children, who would otherwise have no visible means of interaction.

The *YAAB* has approximately thirty students each year, with a core group that has participated from the beginning, and new participants recruited through schools, the library's community program booklet, teacher sponsorships, or the librarians' knowledge of the teen as an active library user. Participants tend to recruit like-minded friends. The monthly newsletter reaches approximately seven thousand Farmington middle and high school students in the public and private schools through distribution of the print version of the *Panache Post*. The Internet version has unlimited access. The library receives 21,000 log-ins monthly to its Internet system. Additionally, FCL librarians have posted the information of the *Panache Post* to several lists, including PUBYAC, MICHLIB, PUBLIB, and MAUD-L.

YAAB members design and write the content of the printed version of the *Panache Post*. Design changes from year to year based on the library's software desktop publishing program; suggestions are made to *YAAB* by librarians of what features can be changed. Various members of the *YAAB* write the introductory feature article for each issue. The electronic, Internet version of the *Panache* so far has been retyped by the librarians, but future versions will be created by members of the *YAAB* and loaded onto the library's homepage by the systems administrator. The new versions will include reviews of new books, the inaugural theme of the *Panache Post*, as well as reviews of websites, media such as computer games, CD-ROMs, musical compact discs and cassettes, movies, and area restaurants, and area happenings by and for middle, junior, and high school students.

The *YAAB*'s level of participation has continued to grow and extend into a variety of the library's activities. Circulation and programming statistics provide the basis of evaluation. Circulation of the young adult hardcover collection has increased over the past year by a cumulative 18 percent at both branches. The *YAAB* primarily reviews these titles in the *Panache Post*. Programming statistics also reflect the YAAB's influence and assistance at library sponsored events. Many of the middle-school age members of the *YAAB* participate in the annual "Battle of the Books," a reading-based competitive program sponsored by the library which has drawn over four hundred middle school students in each of the past two years. After the *YAAB* students reach high school level, they become monitors for the final round of the competition. Additionally, the YA Summer Reading Club was designed by the *YAAB* for the past two years. Members of the board came up with the game idea, story line, clues, and artwork. The number of YA participants in 1995 was 294, increasing to 344 in 1996. The *YAAB* also served as consultants when planning *Solve a Mystery!*, an after-hours library mystery and scavenger hunt. This event had twenty-four participants in 1995 and thirty participants in 1996, limited in size by the context of the game.

FCL provides tremendous support to adults in the community through its reference service role and to younger children and their parents through a myriad of programs. The *Young Adult Advisory Board* was conceived to fill an obvious gap in that user population. The *YAAB* allows "teenagers to take responsibility for their library and its mission of service, thus making the library a better place for everyone" as stated in *Directions for Library Services to Young Adults* (p. 20). The *YAAB* provides a centralized access point for young adults to voice their opinions, and members also serve as a conduit for information to the young adult community. The *YAAB* is an example to parents, teachers, and the community as a whole, of proactive teenagers who are involved citizens.

Funding

The program is funded by the Friends of the Farmington Library, who pay refreshment costs, any travel expenses (a trip to a local publisher is planned for the upcoming year) and printing costs. Staff time comes from the library budget. Two staff, one full-time and one part-time, plan the meetings; three volunteers (one in her seventies) and two members of the *YAAB* type the newsletter each month.

Contact Persons

Sharon Vincent and Stacy Charlesbois, 32737 W. 12 Mile Rd., Farmington Hills, MI 48334. (810) 553-0300, exts. 319, 331

45.
Hutchinson Public Library

Hutchinson, Kansas

Idea

Young adult program

Customers

Any student in sixth through twelfth grades

Community

The Hutchinson Public Library is located in a community of approximately 40,000 people. The library also serves the residents of Reno County, which represents an additional 22,000 people. The local adolescent population follows the pattern of the entire community. Hutchinson and Reno County are basically white middle-class communities. Ninety-two percent of the population is Caucasian, less than 3 percent is African-American, and 4 percent is Hispanic. Twelve percent of the teens come from families below poverty level.

Setting

Hutchinson Public Library is a single public library with over 39,000 registered borrowers. The collection now consists of over 248,000 items, including books, videos, periodicals, compact discs, and books on tape. The library is open seven days a week for a total of seventy-three hours per week. The Hutchinson Public Library is a member of the South Central Kansas Library System, which includes twelve counties and houses SCKLS headquarters. Because HPL is a member of SCKLS, any resident of those twelve counties may use the Hutchinson Public Library.

Program Description

The Hutchinson Public Library Young Adult Advisory Board has become an integral part of the library's service to young adults. The board consists of sixteen young adults who range in age from twelve to eighteen and attend either a middle or high school. At the present time there is also a student on the board who is home schooled. The students apply and go through an interview process with current Advisory Board members and two library staff. This board makes the decisions on what programs the library provides for young adults. The board also advises as to what materials should be selected and how services to young adult users might be improved.

The young adult program reaches over 300 students with a newsletter produced by the Advisory Board. Many more readers use the young adult paperback collection housed in a special area set aside for teens. There is an eight-foot-long bulletin board that the Advisory Board uses to provide pertinent information to library users, with members taking turns each month developing a theme for the bulletin board.

Students who choose to participate in the young adult program also may choose to perform volunteer duties for the library. In 1996 a new volunteer opportunity began with the development of the children's department's new technology center. Young adults attended one of two training sessions and now volunteer weekly helping younger library users learn more about the computer software available for use. Other young adults volunteer to shelve books or learn to mend books.

In 1995 the Advisory Board held a creative writing contest in March. Cash prizes were awarded and the winning stories were reprinted in their newsletter, *Youth Attractions*. In April, a special program featured Lee Look, actor, as Robert Louis Stevenson in "My Bed Is a Boat." That summer a reading program with the theme "Book a Trip around the World" was sponsored and over one hundred students participated. The readers filled out a slip for each book or two magazines read, and five names were drawn weekly for prizes. In July the reading program ended with a celebration party attended by sixty-five teens. A treasure hunt throughout the library was conducted, pizza eaten, Pictionary was played, and a grand prize package worth $75 was given away at the end of the evening. In October, a scholarship program was held to help students discover what's involved in the process of applying for scholarships. Approximately sixty students and parents attended this program.

In 1996 a beach party was held on March 17 and students were invited to "Surf the Internet!" Over sixty students were in attendance. The summer reading program was organized again with the theme, "Discover the MAGIC of Reading." One hundred twenty-four readers participated; the program ended on August 2 with another celebration party. This time a magician was hired for a magic show; Pictionary and Twister were played, pizza eaten, and a "magic" grand prize was given away.

In 1995 and 1996 the young adults sponsored a "summer clearance" book sale using leftover materials from previous book sales held by the Hutchinson Public Library Friends group. The teens hauled the books to the library garage, sorted the books by categories, and arrived at 7 a.m. the next morning to manage the book sale until 4 p.m. that afternoon.

Staffing for the young adult program is provided through regularly employed staff. The assistant director is in charge of the program and is aided by the public relations officer, the head of the adult circulation department, and a staff member from the reference department. The majority of the planning is done by the Young Adult Advisory Board. When programs are held, the Advisory Board presides at the event. Any decorating that needs to be done is carried out by them. The library staff is available to assist the students and provide supervision at programs.

The young adult program has been important in helping the adolescent population feel that they are wanted in the library and that they deserve special attention. The Advisory Board is not comprised only of students who are at the top of their class. Many are teens who like to read and have wanted an opportunity to work on their leadership skills and to volunteer in some capacity. The young adult program offers that chance for them. Running the summer clearance book sale provides the young adults an opportunity to show the community that they are willing and capable workers. People of all ages and walks of society see these teens hard at work. The older adults who manage the larger book sales are amazed at the organizational skills these teens have developed and also admire their willingness to help others.

As far as evaluation goes, the fact that sixty-five teens are willing to come to the library on a Friday night in the summer for a celebration demonstrates that the youth of our community are interested in the library programs. The scholarship program has continued to have a crowd of fifty or more for over five years. The beach party was attended by over sixty people and the attendees stayed until the library closed. Every program that has been planned has been attended by more young adult library users than projected, serving as a good reason to continue to repeat programs and develop new ones.

Circulation statistics are another gauge for the success of this program, since one goal of the program is to encourage youth to read. Before the young adult program existed, 21,000 young adult books circulated annually. In 1995, 37,000 young adult books were read. Thus far in 1996, circulation has been up 17 percent over 1995, making the projected figure over 43,000 circulations for this collection.

The program was begun to encourage youth to read and to learn leadership and organizational skills, and to help expand the library's young adult program to bring in more youth. In 1995 and 1996 the programs were planned, organized, and implemented by the Young Adult Advisory Board, and circulation of young adult materials doubled. Staff have no doubt that the program is successful and will continue to become more so.

Funding

The program has been funded by the Special Fund of the Hutchinson Public Library, and the Friends of the Hutchinson Public Library; this year it received an additional $800.00 from Multimedia Cablevision Co. T-shirts for each of the Advisory Board members were purchased for $212.00. The T-shirts have the library logo on the front and the phrase, "It's a library thing," printed across the back. The money was also used to help purchase prizes for the Summer Reading program in the amount of $200.00 and to pay for the celebration party in August. The cost of pizza for the party was $186.57 and pop was $35.00. The magician charged $80.00 and the remaining $86.43 was spent for decorations for the party.

Budget figures vary from year to year depending on the programs involved. Multimedia Cablevision Co. has adopted the program and plans to continue support. Their contribution of $800 should fund the Summer Reading program and celebration, pay for the Scholarship Fair refreshments, and fund the prizes needed for another creative writing contest. Any other expenses will be paid by the library.

Contact Person

Marcella Ratzlaff, Hutchinson Public Library, 901 North Main, Hutchinson, KS 67501, (316) 663-5441, ext. 111

46.
King County Library System, Burien Branch

Burien, Washington

Idea

ESCAPE!

Customers

Young adults, ages twelve through eighteen—specifically, the more disadvantaged who simply have nowhere else (constructive) to go on Friday nights

Community

The library serves the recently incorporated city of Burien (pop. 27,000), just south of Seattle. The region's adolescents are primarily Caucasian (approximately 86 percent), although there are increasing contingents of both Latinos and Asians among the population, too, as well as African Americans and other immigrant youth.

Setting

The Burien Library (20,000 sq. ft.) is termed a "resource library" (second largest category) in the King County Library System (now second busiest system in the nation) of Washington State. Circulation of the Burien branch was (cumulatively) 594,400 for 1996.

Program Description

Started in May 1995, *ESCAPE!* is an ongoing program for teens happening in the Burien Library's meeting room (capacity ninety-nine) every Friday night until midnight. Begun at least partially in response to the fatal shooting of a teen in the vicinity several years ago, *ESCAPE!* offers a place for teens to hang out as well as enjoy different entertainment and educational programs scheduled throughout the year. These activities range from YA author appearances, hairdresser demos (with free haircuts!), and CPR training to neo-vaudeville performers and music shows (including rock and rap music!). A personal computer with full Internet access and exciting software programs has also just been purchased for *ESCAPE!* The program has also been funded in conjunction with the running of the SWAY (South West Alliance for Youth) teen activist group run out of the local counseling center, Ruth Dykeman Youth and Family Services.

The program provides useful (and fun) activities, as well as just a positive hangout for the many teens who have nothing to do on Friday nights. Regular attendees have included teens in alternative schools, those suspended from school, school dropouts, and even homeless teens. Successes include teens known to be graffiti artists channeling their energies into an entry in a local art contest, and others who faithfully show up every Friday to help set up chairs and put up posters for the evening's activities. SWAY, a gathering of up to twenty often less-advantaged youths, has also been busy: conducting a sock drive, feeding the homeless, painting a mural for a county bus stop, simply advocating for youth interests, and more. An average of at least twenty-five teens visit *ESCAPE!* on any Friday night between seven p.m. and midnight, an ever evolving core group of ten or so regularly show up, and attendance has hit sixty and eighty for a number of the more popular programs.

One thirty-hour librarian runs the program, with assistance from one counselor from Ruth Dykeman who helps out on Friday nights. An off-duty police officer is generally in attendance, mainly to establish a presence that ensures security. Two or more teen volunteers help set up the room on Fridays, and one of the teen interns from Ruth Dykeman assists as well. (The rest of the library, fully staffed, also remains open until midnight, and this is where many teens end up spending their time.) SWAY teens plan and implement at least two *ESCAPE!* programs every six months.

Nearly all teen attendees at *ESCAPE!* are solicited for their opinions, advice, and input. Elaborate grant reports with numbers and kinds of attendees are written up every month. Once a month, attendees are asked to fill out an (anonymous) survey asking if they have used drugs or alcohol in the previous month, as well as their interest and confidence in school. It is difficult to judge success other than by negative offsets; e.g., fewer teens reported committing significant crimes since the program began; but when *ESCAPE!* hosts a program as part of a system-wide event, attendance invariably matches or exceeds those attending at any of the other libraries. *ESCAPE!* has also been receiving positive feedback from adult members of the community, including city officials and parents.

Funding

In early 1995, the City of Burien awarded a $5,000 grant to help cover costs, and the Burien Library Guild contributed $1,200 for program expenditures. In October 1995, *ESCAPE!* was awarded a three-year,

$278,000 grant by King County's Commission on Children and Families for an anti-violence campaign. The Commission cited the partnerships developed with the city of Burien, Ruth Dykeman, and SWAY for its funding decision. The grant pays the direct costs of the library program and funds a specialist position from Ruth Dykeman to provide counseling referrals. KCLS incurs the costs of general library operations and security.

Contact Person

Bruce Greeley, Burien Library, King County Library System, 14700 Sixth SW, Burien, WA 98166. (206) 243-3490

Hip-Hop, It Don't Stop!

Friday, Sept. 27 from 8-10 pm
Presented by Warrior Records & ESCAPE!

Come hear Warrior Records artists, 42 Deep and Ms. JAF, who represent the newest vibe, funk and edutainment scene. Their unique community outreach targets a diverse ethical culture of youth bringing hope through music & lyrics of vision.

This program is for teens.

Sponsored by: EsCape

Reasonable accommodation for individuals with disabilities is available; please contact the library prior to the event if you require accommodation.

Burien Library • 14700 Sixth SW • 243-3490

King County Library System *check it out!*

47.
Mesa Public Library

Mesa, Arizona

Idea

FRANK Literary Magazine

Customers

Young adults, twelve to eighteen years old or in grades seven through twelve, specifically those who enjoy creative writing and/or illustrating and want a place to display their work; those who want to belong to a group that shares common interests and goals; and those who want to read and enjoy creative writing and artwork produced by young adults. Teens are the primary audience, but many younger than twelve and older than eighteen enjoy the magazine.

Community

The Mesa Public Library serves a population of 340,000 residents, of whom approximately 10 percent are young adults. Of that 10 percent, the majority are Caucasian (80 percent), Hispanics account for 14 percent, and other minorities together make up the remaining 6 percent. The population is almost evenly divided among the twelve through eighteen-year span, but there are slightly more in the twelve through fourteen range than in the older one.

Setting

The Mesa Public Library consists of a large central library and two neighborhood branches. The library is a division of the City of Mesa Community Services. It is supported by receipts from sales tax, development fees, and utilities. The Library Board, appointed by the mayor and city council, includes a YAAC representative. The main library contains 606,114 volumes, of which 17 percent, or 35,869, are housed in the Young Adult Room. YA materials accounted for 15 percent of the total circulation (2,006,316) during the 1995–96 fiscal year. The Mesa Public Library has the only separate and identifiable young adult room in Arizona. Ongoing programs for teens include summer reading, the Young Adult Advisory Council (YAAC), a year-round volunteer staff, and a variety of educational workshops.

Program Description

FRANK Literary Magazine is an annual publication that features creative writing and artwork produced by and for young adults through the Mesa Public Library. An editorial staff of teens meets twice monthly during the school year to plan and prepare each year's edition. The staff members make all the decisions regarding the magazine. They publicize it in their schools, they solicit submissions from the community, they evaluate and select what will be published, and they help with the layout and design of the finished product. In addition, they make organizational decisions regarding their staff duties and responsibilities. A former Young Adult Advisory Council (YAAC) member serves as chief editor.

FRANK Literary Magazine

We need
Stories • Essays • Poetry • Art
and
Staff Members

For more information, call
Kellie Shoemaker, Advisor

Young Adult Room
Mesa Public Library
64 E. 1st Street
644-2734

Hear and Listen

by Dawn Garrison

Is anybody out there?
Is anybody listening to me? To us?
I didn't think so. They never do.
We are so often ignored that we're almost used to it.
Why don't they listen to us? We're people, too.
Just like everybody else, we have thoughts and opinions.
You might not like them, but it doesn't matter whether you like them or not. Just hear us out.
Remember, we are the future of the world.
And you, well, you all will be dead soon.

FRANK is distributed free of charge to area school media centers and public libraries, and extra copies sell for fifty cents to benefit the Friends of the Mesa Public Library book sale fund. *FRANK* is important for many reasons. First, it brings teens into the library, and they become aware of library services and materials. The fact that *FRANK* members are enrolled as official library volunteers further enhances their library experience by giving them a sense of ownership and control of their project. *FRANK* provides a forum for young adults to express themselves, both in written and artistic form and in creating a publication that reflects a young adult outlook and perspective. It equips the teens who produce the magazine with the skills to work together in a group and participate in the decision-making process. And, most importantly, *FRANK* enables an often misunderstood and unappreciated part of our society to demonstrate how intelligent, articulate, and accomplished they are. *FRANK* validates the adolescent experience by giving it a voice in the community. It shows everybody what teens are thinking and feeling, and in this way, others can learn what's important to young adults in their lives.

It is difficult to measure the number of young adults reached by this program. There are ten to fifteen *FRANK* staff members who serve on the editorial board each year and attend meetings twice a month during the school year. In addition, 115 people sent submissions in the first year (1994–95), with 34 accepted for publication. In the second year (1995–96), 131 submissions were received and 33 were published. These numbers reflect the young adults who were directly reached by the program, but many others may have encountered *FRANK* in other ways. Each year, copies are sent to all junior and senior high school media centers, local public libraries, and selected teachers to share with interested teens. Last year about eighty copies were sold to library patrons and about two hundred copies are to be sold this year. Proceeds from their sale are added to the Friends of the Library book sale funds, which are, in turn, used to provide additional youth programs at Mesa Public Library.

A former YAAC member, J.T. Drews, volunteers as chief editor. He runs the meetings, welcomes new members, and guides the staff in meeting deadlines. A YA librarian acts as advisor. She receives submissions and prepares them for blind review, orders publicity flyers and posters, proofreads the final edition of the magazine, and coordinates preparation for printing. In addition, a staff secretary completes the word processing for the magazine, and a graphics specialist does the layout and design.

In September, 1994, about fifteen young adults gathered to plan the first issue of a new literary magazine. The YA librarian who agreed to begin this new project had absolutely no idea how to begin, but this group didn't wait for guidance. They immediately called J.T., a former YAAC member who had graduated, waited fifteen minutes for him to show up, then elected him chief editor. In quick succession, they voted in four genre editors, a secretary, and an art director. They picked a logo and decided on submission guidelines and procedures. As their advisor watched in disbelief and admiration, they adopted rules for their meetings, arranged the whole year's dates and times to meet, drafted a rating slip they would use to judge submissions, and came up with a name: FRANK. The second hour was spent devouring three dozen chocolate chip cookies and reading the first batch of short stories and poems.

This level of youth participation has not diminished with time. The members of the FRANK staff have continued to arrange their own meeting times and review procedures. They elect a secretary every year and have persuaded J.T. to stay on as chief editor. They choose the color and type of paper for each edition, they commission a member of the staff to do the cover art, and they read and rate each submission on a scale of one to five. When the deadline arrives for each year's edition, the secretary tallies the scores and the group selects the highest rated for publication. They then organize the chosen pieces into a tentative order.

The first meeting of the year is in September, when the staff evaluates the past year and plans the next edition of FRANK. Last year they did make some changes based on their evaluation of the first year. They decided not to use genre editors and instead have three positions: editor-in-chief, secretary, and art director. They didn't think the magazine had been publicized enough so they made plans to distribute flyers and posters at schools. And they agreed to solicit writing and artwork from their friends in order to make the second edition even better than the first.

FRANK has been evaluated using a combination of observation and statistical analysis. The young adult staff has judged FRANK to be successful primarily because of the level of dedication, involvement, and enthusiasm displayed by the young adults on the editorial board. Although there were more staff members the first year, fewer actually attended meetings than the second year. During 1994–95, an average of eight teens came to each meeting as compared to 1995–96 when an average of eleven teens, virtually every member, came to each meeting. Furthermore, this second group continued to meet informally over the summer, even when there were no submissions to read. Instead, they worked to revise the FRANK brochure so that it would be ready for 1996–97.

A further indicator used to evaluate FRANK is the number of submissions received each year. Sixteen more were received the second year than the first, probably due to the editorial staff publicizing the magazine at their schools and among their friends. In addition, one hundred submissions had already been received for the forthcoming third edition of FRANK, before the first planning meeting had even taken place!

The final criteria used to evaluate FRANK is the public demand for the magazine. The first edition (eighty copies after complimentary issues were distributed) sold out in about two months and was still requested for months afterward. The printing order for the second edition was doubled to meet the expected demand.

Funding

The funds to print FRANK are provided by the Mesa Public Library's annual operating budget. The first edition's printing costs were $700 for 150 copies, and the second edition cost $1,000 for 300 copies. The library staff time to produce each edition of FRANK totals $730.22. The first edition of FRANK cost $1,430.22. The second edition cost $1,730.22.

Contact Person

Kellie Shoemaker, Mesa Public Library, 64 East First Street, Mesa, AZ 85201. (602) 644-2736

48.
New York Public Library, Belmont Regional Library/ Enrico Fermi Cultural Center

Bronx, New York

Idea

Young Men's Conference

Customers

Seventh and eighth graders from William W. Miles Middle School 118X and the Thomas C. Giordano Middle School 45 in the District 10 area of the Bronx in New York City

Community

The adolescent population in the Little Italy area of the Bronx falls into many ethnic/racial groups, mainly Italians, Mexicans, Albanians, Africans and African Americans. These groups were reflected in the classes that participated in the program.

Setting

The Belmont Regional Library/Enrico Fermi Cultural Center is located in the "Little Italy" community of the Bronx. It is one of the eighty-four branches of The New York Public Library. The library is bordered by the Bronx Zoo, the Bronx Botanical Gardens, Fordham University, and the St. Barnabas Hospital. This branch is the Italian Heritage Center for the library system, but also serves the interests of English, Albanian, Spanish, African and African-American readers due to the demographic changes in the community.

Program Description

The *Young Men's Conference* was created in response to a very successful Young Women's Conference that had been held previously. The conference provided a forum for boys in seventh and eighth grades to discuss freely their aspirations, fears, and problems and to find new ways to cope with them. Both conferences were designed to empower young teens by giving them information that would enrich their lives through presentations by speakers on relevant topics and by providing the opportunity to discuss contemporary issues with each other facilitated by young adult librarians. Award-winning YA author Walter Dean Myers addressed the *Young Men's Conference*.

The conference provided the young men with the opportunity to meet successful and professional men and to share their experiences with them. These men included librarians, an author, an AIDS activist, motivational speakers, and counselors. The program allowed the young men to meet and network with other young men from another school and share ideas with their peers in a free and unconstrained atmosphere. The morning session provided a means to discuss important moral, social, and general teenage problems and to work toward solutions. Most of the young men and the presenters used real life experiences from the local area to support their comments. This made the presentations more realistic.

On the evaluation sheets provided, some of the teens mentioned how different this program had been. Others stated that it was their first conference and others indicated that it was nice sharing ideas with boys from other schools. Most of them also liked the fact that the facilitators (YA librarians) never took over the discussion (by saying "When I was your age . . . ") but were there to keep things moving.

The success of the Young Women's Conference held in March 1995 (Women's History Month) contributed very much to the organization of the *Young Men's Conference*. The teachers and the young women who participated suggested that staging a similar conference for boys would be a great idea. After reading the evaluation sheets of their conference library staff got some ideas for organizing the *Young Men's Conference*. Additionally, during school visits young adults were asked for input regarding how to make such a program a success. The teachers were also consulted, mainly to find an appropriate date and time and to distribute permission slips to allow students to travel to the library. Teachers also acted as advisors.

Evaluation sheets were provided to the participants after the conference and the responses were very encouraging. Their comments included: "Never had this before. It was nice talking to kids from other schools. The first time no adult told us what to do or say. The pizza was good. I liked it when the man who talked about AIDS talked at our level. I enjoyed the program because it was fun. We got to find out things about other people and get to talk about ourselves." Altogether, eighty-seven young adults were reached through the work of sixteen staff members and volunteers.

Funding

The *Young Men's Conference* was made possible with funds from:

Belmont Regional Library	$ 50
S. M. Rose Bronx Council	250
Office of Young Adult Services	50

The staff of The New York Public Library were not paid overtime because the program was held within their regularly scheduled workday. Volunteers and presenters from the Bronx Health Plan participated as part of their community outreach program and did not need any financial assistance from NYPL. Walter Dean Myers received an honorarium from the funds provided by the S. M. Rose Bronx Council. The pizza lunch was paid for from the same fund, plus assistance from the NYPL Office of Young Adult Services. The funds from the Belmont Library were used to purchase name badges, art supplies, and flowers to make the day a "real" conference experience.

Contact Person

Osei Baffour, Hunt's Point Regional Library, 877 Southern Boulevard, Bronx, NY 10459. (718) 542-1881 (Mr. Baffour now works at the Connecting Libraries and Schools Project (CLASP) office of the New York Public Library.)

49. Newport Beach Public Library

Newport Beach, California

Idea

Young Adult Advisory Council

Customers

Young adults, grades seven through twelve

Community

The local adolescent population is 90.4 percent Caucasian, 5.2 percent Latino, 3.8 percent Asian and .4 percent African-American. Newport Beach is an ocean-side community with a stable population of 70,098 residents with an average household income of $61,865. Young adults between ages fourteen and twenty-four comprise 12.2 percent of the population. Over 46 percent of adults in the community have earned college degrees.

Setting

The Newport Beach City Library System was formally established in 1920. It now includes a 54,000-square-foot central library opened in 1994 and three branch libraries. The central library includes a young adult section offering young adult fiction and paperback books and magazines specifically suited to adolescents. A system collection of over 278,000 materials has a 1.3 million annual (18 per capita) circulation. The system serves over 927,000 customers each year.

Program Description

The Newport Beach Public Library's *Young Adult Advisory Council* (*YAAC*) was created to encourage use of the library by young adults, raise awareness among community youth about library resources, and enhance the library's collection for young adults. The *YAAC* is comprised of twenty teens in grades seven through twelve, recruited from six local public and private schools. All *YAAC* members are Newport Beach residents.

The first volunteer group met monthly from December 1994 to May 1996. Their primary goals were to recommend services and plan activities appealing to young adults and to aid professional staff in providing quality materials for young adults. Accomplishments included planning and hosting a series of Teen Open Houses and helping with a Young Adult Authors series which attracted hundreds of local junior and senior high school students. Four new *YAAC* members joined the council in September 1996 to replace graduating seniors.

The *YAAC* helped in stimulating the interest of local youth in library services, encouraged library use by young adults, and raised awareness of the scope and availability of library materials and online resources among local adolescents. Council members were able to serve the community by improving the library's friendliness and usefulness to their peers. In addition, they impacted the young adult collection by aiding professional staff in collection development. All council members received instruction on print reference resources, CD-ROM products on the Wide Area Network, and use of the Internet and the online computer catalog. Their expertise was passed on to local youth through events Council members helped plan, publicize, and host. These included Teen Open Houses and *YouthNet* Nights featuring scavenger hunt–style activities designed to help young adults access, understand, and make full use of library resources. *YAAC* members helped with the library's Summer Reading Program, Family Fun Day during the countywide Imagination Celebration, and other juvenile programs.

The *YAAC* also was instrumental in hosting a Young Adult Authors series featuring nationally known, award-winning authors discussing their work, the process of writing, and the world of young adult fiction. Appearances by Theodore Taylor, Neal Shusterman, Francesca Lia Block, and Michael Cart were highlights of this series.

Beyond direct participation by the twenty *YAAC* members, outreach efforts planned and implemented by the council were publicized in local media and in flyers distributed at local schools. Through these vehicles, the participation of over 4,500 local young adults in Teen Open Houses, *YouthNet* Nights, and the Young Adult Authors series was solicited. Approximately six hundred students from local elementary, intermediate, and high schools attended ten programs planned by the *YAAC* over a two-year period. Many individuals asked that both series be scheduled again next year.

The *YAAC* was overseen by the library's Youth and Branch Services Manager. In addition, two librarians and one member of the city's Management Information Services division were involved in evening *YAAC* meetings and events. At monthly meetings, *YAAC* members planned and coordinated program activities and also designed promotional flyers and posters, using library computers and art materials. Council members subsequently served as hosts,

YAAC members Megan Sutton, Mera Kriz, Librarian Sara Barnicle, Chelsea Hover, and Sydney Head meet to plan the Young Adult Author series.

photographers, and tour guides at all planned activities. They also provided input about authors solicited for the Young Adult Authors series.

All *YAAC* members submitted evaluations of each council-planned event, including suggestions for program modifications and enhancements. Each member also evaluated the *YAAC* at the conclusion of his or her two-year term. Of these evaluations, the verdict was unanimous: participation in *YAAC* was a worthwhile experience that enhanced the library and promoted its use by local youth. All members expressed a desire to continue serving on the Council. In self-assessments delivered in roundtable discussions, council members also agreed that *YAAC* participation had given them an improved understanding of the library and its resources. This will facilitate a sharing of knowledge about the library with peers, thus helping to meet the goal of using members as "magnets" for reaching young adults in the community.

While no statistics are available comparing use of the library by young adults prior to and following creation of the *YAAC*, library staff is confident that the proficiency of local junior and senior high school students in using library resources has been improved. In addition, the awareness of local youth regarding available materials, CD-ROM products, and online databases has been raised.

Funding

The *YAAC* is supported by the regular library budget. Approximately seventy-two staff hours at an average hourly cost of $22, totalling $1,584, were devoted to the project. Funding for the author series was provided through a grant from the Pacific Mutual Foundation.

Contact Person

Judy Kelley, Newport Beach Public Library, 1000 Avocado Avenue, Newport Beach, CA 92660. (714) 717-3807

50.
Stratford Library Association
Stratford, Connecticut

Idea
Youth Review Board

Customers
Students in grades seven through twelve

Community
The Stratford Library Association serves 49,500 people in this community, of whom 11 percent are young adults. Of the young adult students attending Stratford Public Schools, 24.9 percent are minorities. This can be further broken down into: 15.9 percent African-American, 6.4 percent Hispanic, 2.6 percent Asian and Native Americans. These figures are derived from the Stratford Board of Education statistics.

Setting
The Stratford Library Association is designated by the Town Council as the principal public library for the town of Stratford and receives its primary funding from the town. The library serves a population of nearly 50,000 with a budget of approximately $1.7 million (1996–97), of which 11 percent is appropriated to the young adult department. The collection of 130,000 items includes reference, fiction and nonfiction, magazines, videos, books-on-tape, CDs, and art works. A computerized online system manages circulation, PAC, acquisitions, serials, and a Community Resource File. Online and CD-ROM reference services for young adults include Grolier's Encyclopedia, SIRS Researcher, and College Choice. The library offers extensive children's, young adult, and adult programming. The young adult department staffs a busy YA homework desk, provides a separate YA area for its collection, and conducts annual seventh grade class visits.

Program Description
The Stratford Library *Youth Review Board* was established in 1987 for seventh through tenth grade students as a book review group and developed within a year into a youth participation group which includes eleventh and twelfth grade students. The *Youth Review Board* makes an important contribution to the community in that it promotes the library as a place where young adults are welcome and where their participation is valued, especially in the decision-making process. It helps young adults relate to other teens, adults, and children through its intergenerational programs, fosters reading through its monthly book discussions, encourages teen voluntarism, and aids in building self-esteem, especially for at-risk students. The *Youth Review Board* is open to all seventh through twelfth grade students, regardless of their reading levels or academic records. Therefore, members represent a good cross section of ages, interests, and abilities.

The *Youth Review Board* has reached over 175 members in its monthly meetings during the past nine years, and over 250 volunteers have participated in its Teen Volunteer Summer Program. When the volunteer program first began in the summer of 1990, twelve teens participated, and in the past four years there have been over fifty each summer. The *Youth Review Board* is overseen by the library's young adult department, which is comprised of the Assistant Director of Youth Services, one full-time young adult librarian, two part-time children/young adult librarians, and one library assistant.

Special programming in 1996 has included:

Books Build Bridges: an intergenerational reading program that brought together seniors and young adults to read to elementary school children. An orientation session was held to demonstrate storytelling techniques and to provide an opportunity for readers to select their books. On the day of the program, two sessions were held and the evaluations were positive. All participants praised the intergenerational concept. First held in 1995, this has become an annual event organized by the young adult department. An article about *Books Build Bridges* was published in *Voice of Youth Advocates*, February 1996.

The Ten Penny Tragedy: Young adults produced this play for children. They directed the play, created sets, sewed costumes, acted, designed the program, and baked refreshments to be sold at the performance. Proceeds went to purchase materials for the young adult department, based on members' recommendations for new titles, favorite series, additional paperbacks, and audiocassettes.

The Stratford Library 100th Anniversary Celebration: Young adults were involved with the two major events, Family Day and the fund-raising performance of *The Importance of Being Earnest*. Teens volunteered during Family Day by helping to host visiting author Steven Kellogg, marching down Main Street with library board members and other dignitaries, and assisting staff members throughout the day. Teens read *The Importance*

Young adults help at the library's annual book sale.

of Being Earnest prior to viewing the play. At the performance, they ushered and served refreshments. Following the performance, teens had an opportunity to discuss the play and the production with the director and actors.

Young adults also participate annually in the Teen Volunteer Summer Reading Program by helping in the children's department with story hours and arts and crafts sessions. They work with the library's board members at the annual library book sale and Stratford Community Day. Past youth participation events have included a school performance of a one-act play; *Night of 1,000 Stars*, a national library event in which young adults and other local "stars" joined in the library Read-In; the Stratford Community Fair, at which young adults distributed library card applications and program flyers; and fund-raising events such as a car wash and bake sale.

In addition, *Youth Review Board* members represent the library by serving on the Stratford Youth and Family Advisory Board. This community organization, comprised of teens and adults from town agencies, promotes support and cooperation for family and youth services. Currently, Stratford Library *Youth Review Board* members also serve on a task force to promote teen volunteerism in the community.

Central to the *Youth Review Board* are the monthly book discussion meetings. These are generally attended by students in grades seven through ten since upperclassmen often have other after-school commitments. At these meetings, members recommend titles for the annual *Gold Seal Booklist* which is used in the library to encourage reading among young adults. The booklist also serves as a guide to the Stratford middle and high schools for their recommended school summer reading lists. In June 1996, the young adults produced their ninth booklist. During the upcoming year, they are preparing to write a grant requesting funding to create a ten-year compilation *Gold Seal Booklist*. In addition to reviewing books, members also plan and evaluate all young adult library events at the monthly meetings.

The young adult staff continually seeks input from the *Youth Review Board* and other young adult patrons regarding collection development. For example, when the young adult department was updating its sports biographies, teens were asked to list some sports figures about whom they would like to read. Biographies of these people were then purchased for the department. Young adults suggested teen-oriented magazines for the department. Special collections for young adult horror, science fiction/fantasy, and mystery books were created because *Youth Review Board* members requested them. The benefits of teen input are twofold: the library's services to young adults improve because of the opportunity to give them what they want, and teens gain a sense of empowerment because they are actively participating in the decision-making process.

A notable event in the *Youth Review Board*'s history is the Teen Women's Support Group. The teens and a young adult librarian wrote a state grant for funding based on "Drugs Don't Work . . . Kids Do" and received $500 for a prevention program. The Teen Women's Support Group met at the library for eight weekly sessions, with members of the *Youth Review Board* serving as peer counselors for young women at risk. The members promoted both physical and mental health during each session by performing aerobics, serving healthy snacks, and sharing coping strategies for teen problems. An article about the Teen Women's Support Group was published in *Wilson Library Bulletin* in March 1994.

Evaluation forms are distributed annually at the June *Youth Review Board* meeting and after large programs and special fund-raisers. Teens' comments are instrumental in planning additional programs.

An important aspect of teen voluntarism is recognition by the library. A reception by the Library Board of Directors for the teenagers and their families and an annual "Make Your Own Sundae" party each summer serve to reinforce the library's appreciation of its teen volunteers.

Youth participation is a valuable component of the Stratford Library Association's young adult department. The *Youth Review Board* was fundamental in the formation of the department. It has proven to be an important asset in collection development, program planning, and fund-raising. The staff looks forward to the continued growth and success of the *Youth Review Board* as it enters its tenth anniversary year.

Funding

For the 1995–96 fiscal year, $5,500 was spent on 275 hours of youth participation programming alone. These figures were derived from the number of staff hours multiplied by the cost per staff hour. Funding came from the town budget and fund-raisers that utilized the services of teen volunteers.

Contact Person

Barbara Blosveren, Stratford Library Association, 2203 Main Street, Stratford, CT 06497. (203) 385-4167

Index

Access Ability booklist, 68
Accord, The, 3
adults
   literacy programs for, 6, 113
   sensitivity to young adults, 87–88, 89–90
advisory boards, 49–50, 100–101, 102–3
African-American booklist, 68
Afternoon of Medieval Revels, 77–78
age. *See* audience (by age)
aging awareness, 45
AIDS awareness and prevention
   quilt showings, 21–22
   Risky Times booklist, 68–69
"Airband," 80
Albany Park Branch, Chicago Public Library, 91–92
alcohol awareness, 62
Algebra Project, 3
Allen County Public Library, 47–48, 81–82
Allerton branch, New York Public Library, 25, 27
Anderson, Sheila, 39, 58
Anderson News, 60
Andrew Heiskell Library for the Blind and Physically Handicapped, 11
Angier, Naomi, 66
Arizona, Mesa Public Library, 106–8
Arlington County Public Library, 49–50
art
   bus painting project, 91–92
   Cypress Lake Center for the Arts, 8–9
   graffiti art contests, 104
Assaf, Nancy Corbin, 31, 32
at-risk youth
   AIDS awareness and prevention, 21–22, 68–69
   basketball camp for, 60–62
   bus painting project, 91–92
   peer counseling for, 114
   Summer Youth Employment Program, 23–24
   Teen Agency Program, 81–82
   Teen Parenting Course, xi, 19–20
   WINGS, 5–7
Atwell, Nancy, 4
audience (by age)
   ten to eighteen, 97–98
   eleven to eighteen, 73–74
   twelve to eighteen, 25–30, 43–44, 51–53, 71–72, 77–78, 85, 104–8
   thirteen to eighteen, 36, 40–41
   See also audience (by grade level); audience (by topic)
audience (by grade level)
   four to twelve, 45–46
   six to eight, 3–4, 8–10
   six to twelve, 47–48, 56–58, 100–101, 102–3
   seven, 21–22
   seven to eight, 109–10
   seven to ten, 83
   seven to twelve, 33–34, 42, 63–64, 111, 113–15
   middle school students, 49–50
   freshman English classes, 31–32
   junior and senior high school, 75–76
   senior high students, 53–55, 79–80, 93–94
   See also audience (by age); audience (by topic)
audience (by topic)
   at-risk youth, 5–7, 23–24, 60–62, 81–82, 91–92
   disabled youth and agencies, 11–13
   English classes (freshmen), 31–32
   incarcerated young adults, 59–60, 69–70
   librarians, 87–88, 89–90
   math students (grades seven to twelve), 33–34
   visually impaired youths, 14–15
   young men (grades seven to eight), 109–10
   See also audience (by age); audience (by grade level)
Auerbach, Barbara, 35
Ayres, Anne, 96

Baffour, Osei, 110
Baker, Michelle, 24
Baker, Stella, 82
Ball, Eileen Annie, 7
Bambenek, Jill, 72
Barnicle, Sara, 112
Bartels, Caroline, 26, 27
basketball/reading camp, 60–62
Batavia, Ohio, 45–46
Battle of the Books, 101
Beck, Agnes, 13
Bellobuono, Heather, 24
Belmont Regional Library/Enrico Fermi Cultural Center, New York Public Library, xi, 109–10
Berkeley Public Library
   Cover to Cover, 51–53
   Teen Playreaders, 53–55
   Teen Services Internet homepage, x, 36–37
blind and visually impaired
   booklists for, 68
   reading programs for, 11–13, 14–15
   Theater by the Blind, 15
Blosveren, Barbara, 115
Blue Skies for Library Kids project, 19, 20, 91, 92, 94, 95–97
Boak, Jamie, 29
Bode, Janet, 12
Book Bucks, 59
Book Buddies, 83–84
book characters, dressing as, 4
booklists, 67–69, 114
book reviews
   multilingual, 52
   Youth Review Board, 113–15
Books Are the Key, 69–70
Books for the Teen Age, 67–68
"Book Trail" programs, 74
Briccetti, Lee, 26–27
British Columbia, Richmond Public Library, 28–30
Bronx Health Plan, 110
Brooklyn Public Library, 83–84
   Main Youth Services Division, 33–35
Brown, Margaret, 50
Bundy, Candace, 41
Burien Branch, King County Library System, xi, 104–5
Burien Library Guild, 104–5
Burn, Patricia, 26
bus painting project, 91–92

California
   Berkeley Public Library, x, 36–37, 51–55
   Newport Beach Public Library, 42–43, 111–12
California State Library, 37, 43
Canada, Richmond Public Library, 28–30
Canada Post, 30
Canada Post Heritage Club, 30
Canada Safeway, 29
Canadian Chinese Radio, 29
Canandaigua, New York, 89–90
Cannon, Carol, 19–20
Carr, David, X
Carton, Debbie, 55
Celebrating the Dream II booklist, 68
Charlesbois, Stacy, 101
Chatham Square Regional Branch, New York Public Library, 14–15
Chelton, Mary K., 116
chess clubs, xi, 95–97
Chicago Community Trust, 20, 91
Chicago Police Department, 91
Chicago Public Art Group, 91, 92
Chicago Public Library
   Albany Park and Douglass Branches, 91–92
   Blue Skies for Library Kids project, xi, 19, 91, 92, 94, 96–97
   Children's Services, 85–86
   Northtown Branch, 93–94
   Rudy Lozano Branch, 95–97
   Woodson Regional Library, 19–20

Chicago Transit Authority, 91, 92
CLASP (Connecting Libraries and Schools Project), 68, 69
Clermont County Public Library, 45–46
Cliffdale Friends of the Library, 58
Clueless in the Stacks: the YA LIVE Show, 87
Coerr, Eleanor, 54
coffeehouse, 71–72
Cohen, Rebecca, 69, 70
Commission on Children and Families (King County), 104–5
Community Development Block Grant Project, 24
community involvement
    libraries and, xi
    passion for youth services and, xii–xiii
Connecticut
    Meriden Public Library, 23–24
    Stratford Library Association, 113–15
Connecting Libraries and Schools Project (CLASP), 68, 69
Crozier, Dayna, 26
Cumberland Community Foundation, 58
Cumberland County Public Library and Information Center, 38–39
    Teen Read, 56–58
Curry, Anna, ix
customer. *See* audience
Cuyahoga County Public Library, 40–41
Cypress Lake Center for the Arts, 8–9

Dade County Juvenile Detention Center, 59–60
Dade County Public Schools, 59–60
dances
    intergenerational, 46
    for visually impaired, 15
Dascaloja Puppeteers, 97–98
Day, Jonathan, 99
DeWitt Wallace—Reader's Digest/Connecting Libraries and Schools Project, 69
disabilities
    Access Ability booklists, 68
    Don't "Dis" Ability, 11–13
    physically handicapped, 11–13
    See also blind and visually impaired
Douglass Branch, Chicago Public Library, 91–92
drama
    Enchilada Players, 75–76
    produced by Youth Review Board, 113–14
    puppetry, 97–99
    Rahway Teen Roarin' Readers, 73
    Teen Playreaders, 53–55
    Theater by the Blind, 15
Drews, J.T., 107
drug awareness, 62, 104, 114
Dunbar-Pulaski Middle School, 3–4
Duval, Andrée, 30

Eastpoint, Florida, 5–7
Edwards, Margaret Alexander
    bequest of, ix
    community involvement and, xi
    and facts-versus-books dichotomy, x–xi
    skills serving young adults, xi–xii
Eldridge, Anne, 4
Ellard, Jennifer, 76
Enchilada Players, 75–76
Enter . . . the Reading Zone, 47–48
ESCAPE!, xi, 104–5
Evans, Margaret, 22
Excellence Project, ix

fantasy
    Afternoon of Medieval Revels, 77–78
    Science Fiction/Fantasy Day, 65–66
Farmington Community Library, 100–101
Fayetteville, North Carolina, 38–39, 56–58
Fine, Jana R., 99
Finney, Kay, 37
Fitzgerald, Claire, 38, 58
Florida
    Clearwater Public Library, 97–99
    Dade County Public Schools, 59–60
    Franklin County Public Library, 5–7
    Lee County Library System, 8–10
Foglesong, Marilee, 25, 69
folklore, 75–76
Fort Myers, Florida, 8–10
Fort Wayne, Indiana, 47–48, 81–82
Fort Wayne Wizards, 47
Francoeur, Marialyce, 24
Franklin County Public Library, 5–7
Franklin, Hardy, ix
FRANK literary magazine, 106–8
Fried, Betsy, 44
Friends of Richmond Archives, 29
Friends of Richmond Library, 29
Friends of the Chicago Public Library, 86
Friends of the Cumberland County Public Library and Information Center, 58
Friends of the Farmington Library, 101
Friends of the Hutchinson Public Library, 103
Friends of the Library
    Arlington County Public Library, 50
    Berkeley Public Library, 52–53
Friends of the Oak Park Library, 72
Friends of the Upper Arlington Public Library, 78
Fry, Ray, ix
funding sources
    Anderson News, 60
    Arlington County Public Library Friends of the Library, 50
    Berkeley Public Library Friends of the Library, 52–53
    Blue Skies for Library Kids grant, 20, 92, 94, 96–97
    Burien Library Guild, 104
    California State Library, 37, 43
    Canada Post, 30
    Canada Post Heritage Club, 30
    Canada Safeway, 29
    Canadian Chinese Radio, 29
    Chicago Community Trust, 20
    Chicago Public Art Group, 92
    Chicago Transit Authority, 92
    city of Burien, Washington, 104
    city of Meriden, Connecticut, 99
    Cliffdale Friends of the Library, 58
    Commission on Children and Families (King County, Washington), 104–5
    Community Development Block Grant Project, 24
    Connecting Libraries and Schools Project (CLASP), 68, 69
    Cumberland Community Foundation, 58
    DeWitt Wallace—Reader's Digest/ Connecting Libraries and Schools Project, 69
    Foellinger Foundation, 48
    Friends of Richmond Archives, 29
    Friends of Richmond Library, 29
    Friends of the Chicago Public Library, 86
    Friends of the Cumberland County Public Library and Information Center, 58
    Friends of the Farmington Library, 101
    Friends of the Hutchinson Public Library, 103
    Friends of the Oak Park Public Library, 72
    Friends of the Upper Arlington Public Library, 78
    Geneva Center of Concern, 62
    Greater Cincinnati Foundation, 46
    Hutchinson Public Library Special Fund, 103
    India Cultural Centre of Canada, 29
    J. Ben Watkins Foundation, 7
    James P. Gordon Trust, 62
    Jumpstart Scholarship Foundation, 29
    Juvenile Justice Partnership Grant, 7
    Kingstone Book Co., Ltd., 29
    Knights of Columbus, 7
    Leominster Public Library Friends of the Library, 64
    Lila Wallace—Reader's Digest Fund, 27
    LSCA grants, 10, 44, 62, 90
    McDonald's Restaurants of Canada, 29
    Merck & Co., Inc., 75
    Middle Grades Reading Network, 4
    Multimedia Cablevision Company, 103
    NAMES foundation, 22
    New York Public Library
        Office of Services for Persons with Disabilities, 68
        Offices of Special Services, 14
        Offices of Young Adult Services, 11, 13, 14, 68, 110
    New York State Library grant, 90
    Ontario County Stop DWI, 62
    Pacific Mutual Foundation, 112
    Reading Excitement and Paperbacks grant, 4
    Reading Is Fundamental grant, 4
    Richmond Auto Mall, 29
    Richmond Chinese Parents Association for Better Education, 29
    Richmond News, 29
    Rogers Community Cablevision, 29, 30
    S. M. Rose Bronx Council, 110
    Sustained Silent Reading program, 4
    United Library Services, 29
    U.S. Department of Education, 68
    United Way, 7
    Vancouver City Savings Credit Union, 29

Garman, Barbara, 62
Garrison, Dawn, 107
Gary Community School Corporation, 3–4
Geneva Center of Concern, 62
Geneva Free Library, 60–62
Gilbert, Matthew, 68
Global Beat booklist, 69
Gochnauer, Grant, 42
Gold Seal Booklist, 114
Goldsmith, Francisca, 53
Good Books booklist, 68
grade level. *See* audience (by grade level)
graffiti art contests, 104
Graham, Marilyn Long, 8, 10
Greeley, Bruce, 105

Hammond Public Library, 21–22
Hansen, Elizabeth, 92
Harvey, Sharon, 48
Head, Sydney, 112
Henderson, Susan, 30
Hernandez, Hector, 95, 96
HIV. *See* AIDS awareness and prevention
hobby development, 73
Hover, Chelsea, 112
Humphrey, Jack, 47
Hutchinson Public Library, 102–3

ideas
    Afternoon of Medieval Revels, 77–78
    AIDS awareness and prevention, 21–22
    Blue Skies for Library Kids, xi, 19
    Book Buddies, 83–84
    booklists for young adults, 67–69
    Books Are the Key, 69–70
    bus painting project, 91–92
    Clueless in the Stacks: the YA LIVE Show, 87
    Cover to Cover, 51–53
    Dascaloja Puppeteers, 97–98
    Don't "Dis" Ability, 11–13
    Earn a Buck, Buy a Book, 59–60
    Enchilada Players, 75–76
    Enter . . . the Reading Zone, 47–48
    ESCAPE!, xi
    FRANK literary magazine, 106–8
    freshman English class orientations, 31–32
    information about colleges, 38–39
    Junior Volunteers, xi, 85–86
    Knight Moves Chess Club, xi, 95–97
    librarian training, 89–90
    martial arts workshops, 15
    Math Peer Tutoring Center, xi, 33–35
    Partners in Reading, 3–4
    photo bulletin board, 79–80
    Poetry in the Branches, 25–27
    programs for visually impaired, 14–15
    Rahway Teen Roarin' Readers, 73–75
    REACT young adult book discussion group, 63–64
    Rebound and Read, 60–62
    Science and Invention Connection, 8–10
    Science Fiction/Fantasy Day, 65–66
    Sidekicks: Kids and Seniors Together, 45–46
    summer youth employment program, 23–24
    Teen Agency Program, 81–82
    Teenage Survival Guide, 40–41
    Teen Parenting Course, xi, 19–20
    Teen Services homepage, 36–37
    Teen Study Center, 93–94
    WINGS, 5–7
    Young Adult After-hours Coffeehouse, 71–72
    Young Adult Writing Contest, 28–30
    youth advisory boards, 49–50, 100–101, 102–3, 111–12
    Youth Connection, 43–44
    YouthNet, 42–43
    Youth Review Board, 113–15
Illinois
    Chicago Public Library, xi, 19–20, 85–86, 91–97
    Oak Park Public Library, 71–72
incentives. *See* prizes
India Cultural Centre of Canada, 29
Indiana
    Allen County Public Library, 47–48, 81–82
    Dunbar-Pulaski Middle School, 3–4
    Hammond Public Library, 21–22
Indiana University Northwest, 3
InfoPeople project, 37
information services
    Inform U, 38–39
    Teenage Survival Guide, 40–41
    Teen Services Internet homepage, x, 36–37
    for young adults, x–xi
    Youth Connection, 43–44
    YouthNet, 42–43
Inform U, 38–39
Internet, 36–37, 42, 100–101, 104
    See also Web sites
Ives, David, 55

James P. Gordon Trust, 62
Jones, Reggie, xii

Jumpstart Scholarship Foundation, 29
Junior Volunteers, xi, 85–86
juvenile detention centers, 59–60, 69–70, 81–82
Juvenile Justice Partnership Grant, 7

Kallsen, Peggy Nelson, 80
Kansas, Hutchinson Public Library, 102–3
Katz, Jeff, 15
Kelley, Judy, 43, 112
Kendall, Gary, 88
King County Library System, Burien Branch, 104–5
Kingstone Book Co., Ltd., 29
Klinger, Lori, 15
Knight Moves Chess Club, xi, 95–97
Knights of Columbus, 7
Knowledge Express, 91
Kriz, Mera, 112
Kwan, Nancy, 29–30

Latino Chess Championships, 95, 96
Lee County Library System, 8–10
Leita, Carole, 37
Leominster Public Library, 63–64
librarians
    skills for serving young adults, xi–xiii
    training in young adult services, 89–90
Libraries for the Future, xi
Library Services and Construction Act (LSCA) grant, 10
Lila Wallace—Reader's Digest Fund, 27
literacy programs. *See* reading programs
Literacy Wise newsletter, 3, 4
literary magazine, 106–8
live events
    Afternoon of Medieval Revels, 77–78
    "Airband," 80
    Clueless in the Stacks: the YA LIVE show, 87
    Dascaloja Puppeteers, 97–98
    Science and Invention Connection, 10
    Science Fiction/Fantasy Day, 66
Loughran, Ellen, 84
Lowry, Craig, 67
LSCA Title I grants, 44, 62, 90

Marlowe, Carol, 75
martial arts workshops, 15
Massachusetts
    Leominster Public Library, 63–64
    Massachusetts Library Association, Children's Issues Section, 87–88
mathematics
    Algebra Project, 3
    Math Peer Tutoring Program, xi, 33–35
Maynard, Judy, 60
McDonald's Restaurants of Canada, 29
mentors, 83–84
Merck & Co., Inc., 75
Meriden Public Library, 23–24
Mesa Public Library, 106–8
Meyers, Arthur S., 22
Michigan, Farmington Community Library, 100–101
Middle Grades Reading Network, 4
middle school programs, 3–4, 49–50
Moore, Anne Carroll, xi–xii
Muller, Pat, 50
multilingual resources
    book reviews in preferred language, 52
    Enchilada Players, 75–76
    Knight Moves Chess Club, xi, 95–97
    Oasis: Libros en Español Para Jovenes, 68
    for poetry, 54

Multimedia Cablevision Company, 103
Multnomah County Library, 65–66
musical performances, 104–5
Myers, Walter Dean, 109, 110

NAMES Project AIDS Memorial Foundation, 21
National Dance Institute, 15
National Helpers Network, Inc., x
neighborhood support, 3–4, 6
New Dorp Regional Branch, New York Public Library, 25
New Jersey, Rahway Public Library, 73–75
Newport, Oregon, 69–70
Newport Beach Public Library, 42–43, 111–12
Newport Public Library, 69–70
newsletters and publications
    booklists for young adults, 67–69
    FRANK literary magazine, 106–8
    Literacy Wise, 3, 4
    Panache Post, 100–101
    Y.A.P., 26
    Youth Attractions, 102
New York
    Belmont Regional Library/Enrico Fermi Cultural Center, New York Public Library, xi, 109–10
    Brooklyn Public Library, xi, 33–35, 83–84
    Chatham Square Regional Branch, New York Public Library, 14–15
    Geneva Free Library, 60–62
    New York Public Library, 25–27, 67–69
    Pioneer Library System, 89–90
    Regional Library for the Blind and Physically Handicapped, 11–13
New York Public Library, 25–27, 67–69
    Allerton Branch, 25, 27
    Belmont Regional Library/Enrico Fermi Cultural Center, 109–10
    Chatham Square Regional Branch, 14–15
    New Dorp Regional Branch, 25
    96th Street Regional Branch, 25, 27
    Regional Library for the Blind and Physically Handicapped, 11–13
    Teen Voices Web site, 25
New York State Library grant, 90
96th Street Regional Branch, New York Public Library, 25, 27
North Carolina, Cumberland County Public Library and Information Center, 38–39
Northtown Branch, Chicago Public Library, 93–94
Nowakowski, Bernadette, 86
nursing homes, 45

Oak Park Public Library, 71–72
Oasis: Libros en Español Para Jovenes, 68
Ohio
    Clermont County Public Library, 45–46
    Cuyahoga County Public Library, 40–41
    Toledo-Lucas County Public Library, 43–44
    Upper Arlington Public Library, 77–78
Olszewski, Rose, 93, 94
Ontario County Stop DWI, 62
Oregon
    Multnomah County Library, 65–66
    Newport Public Library, 69–70

Pacific Mutual Foundation, 112
Panache Post newsletter, 100–101
parenting
    self-esteem for teen parents, 14, 15, 20
    Teen Parenting Course, xi, 19–20

119

Parma, Ohio, 40–41
parties, 13, 15, 46, 51, 58, 75, 86, 102, 103, 115
Partners in Reading, 3–4
peer groups and counseling
   Teen Women's Support Group, 114
   Young Men's Conference, xi, 109–10
   Young Women's Conference, 109, 110
   See also study centers
Pendleton, Dr. Bertha, 31
Peyser, Ruth, 67
Philip Glass Buys a Loaf of Bread (Ives), 55
photographs, 79–80
physically handicapped, 11–13
Pioneer Library System, 89–90
poetry, 25–27, 54
Poetry in the Branches, 25–27
Poets House, 25
Portland, Oregon, 65–66
Printz, Mike, xiii
prisons, 59–60, 69–70, 81–82
prizes, 29, 47–48, 52, 56, 57, 58, 59, 63, 64, 102–3
   Book Bucks, 59
   for Cover to Cover participants, 52
   donations for Teen Read, 57
   for Enter . . . the Reading Zone, 47–48
   Hutchinson Public Library, 102–3
   REACTORS' Quest Award, 63, 64
   Teen Read, 56, 58
   for writing contests, 29
projects. *See* ideas
publicity
   cable tv and, 29, 30
   Knowledge Express bus painting project, 92
puppetry, 97–99

Rahway Public Library, 73–75
Rahway Teen Roarin' Readers, 73–75
REACT, 63–64
Reader's Digest
   DeWitt Wallace fund, 69
   Lila Wallace fund, 27
Read Everywhere bulletin board, 80
Reading Excitement and Paperbacks grant, 4
Reading is Fundamental grant, 4
reading programs
   adult literacy programs, 6
   Afternoon of Medieval Revels, 77, 78
   Book Buddies, 84
   Books Are the Key, 69–70
   Cover to Cover, 51
   Enter . . . the Reading Zone, 47–48
   Junior Volunteers, 85–86
   Partners in Reading, 3–4
   REACT, 63–64
   Rebound and Read, 60–62
   Teen Advisory Board, 50
   Teen Playreaders, 53–55
   Teen Read, 56–58
   Youth Review Board, 113–15
Reading Workshop, 4
Reif, Linda, 4
Richmond Auto Mall, 29
Richmond Chinese Parents Association for Better Education, 29
Richmond, Gail, 31, 32
Richmond News, 29
Richmond Public Library, 28–30
Risky Times booklist, 68–69
Rivera, Omari, 26
Rogers Community Cablevision, 29, 30

Rosokoff, Jessica, 26
Rudy Lozano Branch, Chicago Public Library, 95–97
Ruth Dykeman Youth and Family Services, 104, 105
Ruth, Jerry, 13

Sacopoulos, Eugenia, 4
Samuels, Deborah, 60
Sanabria, Diane M., 64, 87, 88
San Antonio Public Library, 75–76
San Diego Public Library, 31–32
scavenger hunts, 74, 101, 111
Schine, Joan, x
science
   Science and Invention Connection, 8–10
   Science Central, 47
Science Fiction/Fantasy Day, 65–66
Scripps Miramar Ranch Library Center, 31–32
Scripps Ranch High School, 31–32
Seeking Diversity, 4
self-esteem, 14, 15, 20
seniors
   reading programs with, 113
   teen awareness of, 45–46
service to young adults
   librarians and, xii–xiii
   WINGS, 5
Sheridan, Betty, 78
Shoemaker, Kellie, 108
Siebert, Sara, ix
Sinai Parenting Institute, 20
Society for Creative Anachronism, 65, 66
sports/reading camp, 60–62
Spyros, Marsha, 26
staff/volunteer development
   Book Buddies, 83–84
   Junior Volunteers, xi, 85–86
   Newport Beach Public Library, 111
   Pioneer Library System, 89–90
Star Trek clubs, 65
Stewart, Viola, 92
Strasser, Todd, 13
Stratford Library Association, 113–15
Streeter, Brian, 61
student pictures, 79–80
study centers, 33–35, 83–84, 94–94
Summer Reading Lists (New York Public Library), 68
summer reading programs. *See* reading programs
Sutton, Megan, 112
SWAY (South West Alliance for Youth), 104, 105

Teen Advisory Board, 49–50
Teen Agency Program (T.A.P.), 81–82
Teenage Survival Guide, 40–41
Teen Open House, 111
Teen Parenting Course, xi, 19–20
Teen Playreaders, 53–55
Teen Read, 56–58
teens. *See* young adults
Teen Services Internet homepage, x, 36–37
Teen Study Center, 93–94
Teen Voices Web site, 25, 27
Teen Women's Support Group, 114
Texas, San Antonio Public Library, 75–76
Theater by the Blind, 15
Thomas, Vinnie, 15
Thompson, Linda, 20, 92, 94, 97
Toledo-Lucas County Public Library, 43–44
tutoring. *See* study centers

United Library Services, 29
U.S. Department of Education Project for Initiating Recreational Programs for Individuals with Disabilities, 68
United Way, 7
Upper Arlington Public Library, 77–78

Vancouver City Savings Credit Union, 29
Vanover, Toni, 8, 10
Vashon High School Library, ix, 79–80
vicarious learning through books, ix, x
Vincent, Sharon, 101
Virginia, Arlington County Public Library, 49–50
visually impaired. *See* blind and visually impaired

Washington
   King County Library System, xi, 104–5
   Vashon High School Library, 79–80
Watkins, Pamela, 75
Weber, Stephen, 99
Web sites
   Allen County Public Library YA homepage, 81
   Richmond Public Library, 28, 29
   Teen Link: Good Books, 68
   Teen Services Internet homepage, x, 36–37
   Teen Voices, 25, 27
   See also Internet
Wemett, Lisa C., 90
Western Oregon Wargamers, 65
White, Ryan, 22
Williams, Luanna, xiii
WINGS, 5–7
writing contests, 28–30

YA LIVE show, 87
Y.A.P. newsletter, 26
Young Adult After-hours Coffeehouse, 71–72
Young Adult Authors Series, 111
young adults
   adult sensitivity to, 87–88, 89–90
   community engagement for, xi
   information services for, x–xi
   as library volunteers, 83–84, 85–86
   on advisory boards, 49–50, 100–101, 102–3
   participation of, ix–x
   self-image and, 14, 15, 20
   service to, xii–xiii, 5
   serving seniors, 45–46
   skills for serving, xi–xiii
   summer employment programs for, 23–24
   Teenage Survival Guide, 40–41
   Teen Parenting Course for, xi, 19–20
   vicarious learning through books, ix, x
   See also at-risk youth
Young Adult Advisory Board (Kansas), 102–3
Young Adult Advisory Board (Michigan), 100–101
Young Adult Advisory Council (California), 111–12
Young Adult Writing Contest, 28–30
Young Men's Conference, xi, 109–10
Young Women's Conference, 109, 110
youth at-risk. *See* at-risk youth
Youth Attractions newsletter, 102
Youth Connection, 43–44
YouthNet, 42–43
youth participation, ix–x
Youth Review Board, 113–15

Zdjelau, Saza, 99
Zilber, Catherine, 88

Mary K. Chelton, a cofounder of *Voice of Youth Advocates*, has been a youth services librarian, educator, writer, and advocate for more than twenty years. She has held positions in five public library systems and numerous offices within ALA and state associations. She was a consultant to both the first and second national surveys on young adult services in public libraries from the Department of Education, and she is the 1985 winner of ALA's Grolier Foundation Award for outstanding service to young people. Mary K. Chelton is an assistant professor in the School of Library and Information Management at Emporia State University.